Wrong's what I do best

Wrong's what I do best

Hard country music
and contemporary culture

Barbara Ching

To Jim,
Practice doing
wrong and you'll
be among the best, too.
Warmly,
Barbara Ching

OXFORD
UNIVERSITY PRESS

2001

OXFORD
UNIVERSITY PRESS

Oxford   New York

Athens   Auckland   Bangkok   Bogotá   Buenos Aires   Cape Town
Chennai   Dar es Salaam   Delhi   Florence   Hong Kong   Istanbul   Karachi
Kolkata   Kuala Lumpur   Madrid   Melbourne   Mexico City   Mumbai   Nairobi   Paris
São Paulo   Shanghai   Singapore   Taipei   Tokyo   Toronto   Warsaw

and associated companies in
Berlin   Ibadan

Library of Congress Cataloging-in-Publication Data
Ching, Barbara, 1958–
Wrong's what I do best : hard country music and contemporary culture /
Barbara Ching.
p.   cm.
Includes bibliographical references and index.
ISBN 0-19-510835-3
1. Country music—History and criticism.   I. Title: Hard country music and
contemporary culture.   II. Title.
ML3524 .C54   2000
781.642—dc21   99-049466

1 3 5 7 9 8 6 4 2

Printed in the United States of America
on acid-free paper

Acknowledgments

I owe thanks to so many people that I'm sure I've forgotten some, and I apologize for these omissions and any other errors that follow. The warm response my first work on this topic received at the *Arizona Quarterly* gave me the encouragement I needed to forge ahead. Among hard country artists, I owe special thanks to Merle Kilgore and Andrea Archer at Hank Williams Jr. Enterprises, to David Allan Coe, Bill and Carol Quisenberry, and to Buck Owens, Lee Ann Enns, and Jim Shaw at Buck Owens Enterprises. Among country music scholars, the staff at the Country Music Foundation, in particular Paul Kingsbury, Ronnie Pugh, Mark Medley, Kent Henderson, and Lauren Bufferd, gave me access to a wealth of material and ideas. Elsewhere, Aaron Fox, Pamela Fox, Bill Malone, Richard Peterson, David Sanjek, Jr., and Charles Wolfe have provided information, insight, and encouragement. In the music business, Terry Jenkins at Sam's Town Casino in Tunica, Mississippi, and Pat Rolfe at ASCAP in Nashville provided assistance not available within academia. At The University of Memphis, my students, especially Dorothy Bryant, and my colleagues Lesley Ferris, Allison Graham, Kevin Hagopian, and Susan Scheckel shared warmth and ideas. Chairs of the English Department while I wrote this book, William O'Donnell, Guy Bailey, Thomas Carlson, and Christina Murphy, have been particularly supportive. Without the help of Becky Argall, Biljana Belamaric, Jason Carr, Danna Greenfield, Cambria Lovelady, Rebecca May-Ricks, and

Susan Murray the end of this book would have receded into the ever-distant future. Linda Sadler's editing knowledge and talent made the final steps easy. I am grateful to the Marcus W. Orr Center for the Humanities for the invitation to present material that formed the introduction to this book. This work was supported in part by a grant from The University of Memphis Faculty Research Grant Fund. This support does not necessarily imply endorsement by the university of research conclusions. Elsewhere, Rita Barnard, Gerald Creed, Mike Hill, Bill Maxwell, Dana Phillips, and Julia Walker have provided insight, encouragement, and correction. Soo Mee Kwon, Jonathan Wiener, Maribeth Payne, and especially Maureen Buja have made working with Oxford University Press all I could hope for. The criticism and encouragement of Oxford's anonymous readers have also taught me much about what I wanted to say.

Michael Ching, the best musician and best listener I know, made writing this book as easy as it could possibly be, so I dedicate it to him.

Every reasonable effort has been made to secure permission to quote from copyrighted material; grateful acknowledgment goes to the following writers and organizations.

Music Permissions

"The American Way," by Hank Williams Jr. © Copyright 1980 Bocephus Music. Used by Permission.

"Cold, Cold Ground," by Hank Williams Jr., © Copyright 1970 Bocephus Music. Used by Permission.

"A Country Boy Can Survive," by Hank Williams Jr. © Copyright 1981 Bocephus Music. Used by Permission.

"Country State of Mind," by Hank Williams Jr. and Roger Alan Wade © Copyright 1986 Bocephus Music and Sixteen Stars Music. Used by Permission of Bocephus Music.

"Crying Time," by Buck Owens. © Copyright 1964 Sony/ATV Songs LLC, Jarest Music, Beachaven Music (Renewed). All rights on behalf of Sony/ATV Songs LLC administered by Sony/ATV Music Publishing, 8 Music Square West, Nashville, TN 37203. All Rights Reserved. Used by Permission. "The context surrounding the compositions controlled by Sony/ATV Music Publishing is purely conjecture."

"Dixie on My Mind," by Hank Williams Jr. © Copyright 1980 Bocephus Music. Used by Permission.

"White Man Sings The Blues," by Merle Haggard. © Copyright 1973 Sony/ATV Songs LLC (Renewed). All rights administered by Sony/ATV Music Publishing, 8 Music Square West, Nashville, TN 37203. All Rights Reserved. Used by Permission. "The context surrounding the compositions controlled by Sony/ATV Music Publishing is purely conjecture."

"William and Mary." Words and music by George McCorkle and Rick Williamson. © Copyright 1994. Sixteen Stars Music (BMI) / Kicking Bird Music, Inc. (BMI). International Copyright Secured. All Rights Reserved. Used by permission.

"Wrong's What I Do Best" by Michael Alan Campbell, Dickey Lee, and Freddy Weller. © Copyright 1992 Careers BMG Music Publishing (BMI) and Universal Songs of Polygram. Used by permission.

"You Never Even Called Me by My Name" written by Steve Goodman and John Prine. Turnpike Tom Music/Jurisdad Music (ASCAP). Used by permission.

Illustration Permissions

Michael Crawford cartoons courtesy of The *New Yorker* Collection 1996 Michael Crawford from cartoonbank.com. All Rights Reserved.

Freixenet advertisement courtesy of Freixenet USA.

Photographs courtesy of the Country Music Hall of Fame.

Contents

Wrong's what I do best

Introduction

This book is about hard country music for two reasons.
First, it's impossible to really understand country
music, now one of the most popular forms of
music in the United States, without recognizing
that its "country" is a disputed territory where a
mainstream-oriented pop production style reigns
over a feisty and less fashionable form—"hard
country." Second, hearing hard country music offers an important perspective on the bewildering
cultural situation, often called postmodernism, in
which we find ourselves. Conversely, once we recognize the postmodern rhetoric of cultural distinction embedded in contemporary hard country, we can hear the music as something more
significant than a stylistic variant of a harmless
breed of popular music. Although cultural critics
like Susan Sontag may well assert that contemporary culture has done away with the traditional
distinction between high and low culture,[1] you
don't find them writing an appreciative essay
on George Jones. Country music—let alone hard
country music—has not figured in any of the
now canonical discussions of postmodernity. The
difficulty of imagining it may suggest just how
remote country music is from intellectual discourse, and thus how overlooked it is in contemporary cultural politics.

"The strength of country music is its lyrics,"
says hard country star Waylon Jennings. "Your
melody goes where the words take you."[2] The
voices of the hard country stars also underscore
the importance of the words although they

scarcely have voices in the classical terms of musical accomplishment. Always expressive, often beautiful, but almost invariably untrained, they are the kind of voices that would have made music in many homes before the invention of the phonograph: intimate, personal, raised to convey the words of the song rather than to display vocal prowess. According to Peter Guralnick, Ernest Tubb "has often insisted that part of the basis for his popularity is the very modesty of his talent, encouraging the guy in the tavern who hears an Ernest Tubb record to say, 'Heck, I can sing as good as that.'"[3] The listeners' point of hearing, too, focuses most intently on the words. *Country Song Roundup*, the longest-running fan magazine, has filled the bulk of its pages since 1949 with song lyrics. Thus, learning the hard way requires going where the words take you.

I am neither an ethnomusicologist nor a musicologist. My training is in literary criticism and cultural theory, a discipline that seems particularly useful for discussing this genre of music that relies so heavily on the creation of remarkable characters and lyrics. Moreover, I was a fan of hard country long before I acquired the ability to analyze it in the language of academic discourse. Now that I know both languages, I know that both can be richer and more useful when they exchange words. This is not to say that I've ignored the music; hard country's sounds and techniques contribute to its meaning, as does its history. As popular music specialist Simon Frith puts it, "song words are only remembered in their melodic and rhythmic setting."[4] This book thus interprets hard country music by analyzing its setting, by comparing it to mainstream country music, and by placing it in a sociocultural context. I look at the stars, their songs, and their performance styles as texts. I describe the characters that hard country portrays and describe how its lyrics and characteristic sounds convey complex meanings (as opposed to clichés, commonplaces, and unvarnished "reality"). I consider how these texts address each other as well as an audience, thereby recognizing hard country music as a signifying practice that invites humanistic interpretation even as it takes place in specific historical and cultural contexts. So much writing about country music insists that it presents the life of ordinary yet exotic people: not us. At the other extreme lies a bland insistence that the music represents us all. While neither of these perspectives is completely wrong, hearing hard country isn't that easy. We can learn more, hear more, and enjoy more by listening to it otherwise.

Scholars who have broached the subject of hard country have occasionally been willing to approach it as art.[5] My focus is on the kind of art it is: self-consciously low, and self-consciously hard, a deliberate display of burlesque abjection. As Porter Wagoner put it, "I don't try to do anything for the uptown people."[6] He doesn't expect us (readers of university press books) to be receptive to his message, which is why learning the hard way requires us to listen for complexity wherever we think we hear simplicity. To keep that paradox in the forefront, I've tried to write in an essayistic style that juxtaposes academia's theoretical vision with the flamboyantly colloquial language favored by my subject(s). In other words, I've tried to talk about the music as both a scholar and a fan. But my words can't completely substitute for those of the musicians, so I urge you to listen to them sing. While some of the performances I cite are obscure, most public libraries will have a reasonable collection of records by the stars I refer to most often. Unless an endnote indicates otherwise, you can assume that the star who sang the song under discussion also wrote it. The dates listed are the first release dates of the recorded version of the song. In most cases, the date of composition is unknown, and in some cases, the copyright holder is unknown.[7]

When Richard Nixon made a presidential appearance on the *Grand Ole Opry* in 1974, he praised country music for representing "the heart of America. It talks about family. It talks about religion . . . Country music makes America a better country."[8] Likewise, in his retirement, George Bush wrote an essay for *Forbes* explaining his love for country music by comparing it to "a Norman Rockwell painting. It captures the essence of the American spirit and portrays experiences that those who work hard and play by the rules can identify with."[9] While they seem blithely unaware of a rift between country music styles, the former presidents are talking about the heart-warming qualities of mainstream country. Hard country, although it may be patriotic on occasion, unfolds in another country altogether. While sociologist Richard Peterson has recently summarized the stylistic differences between what he calls "hard-core and soft-shell" expressions, the message of "hard country" still remains uncharted territory. Nevertheless, Peterson's list of traits provides a valuable starting point. In contrast to mainstream singers' unremarkable accents, standard American English, and smooth singing style, hard-core stars tend to sing in nasalized, nonstandard English with strong "southern" or "southwestern" accents. While mainstream stars often sing about widely shared emotions and experiences, hard country stars seem to be "telling personal experiences," usually unhappy ones.[10]

What's most important about these differences is that they create *meaning*, especially once "hard country" became conscious of itself as something more than a set of stylistic traits. By the mid to late '60s, artists and other agents of the country music industry could adapt and adopt the rough edges that characterize the "hard core" in order to articulate hard country's special themes. Likewise, they could retroactively characterize artists from the recent past, such as Hank Williams, as hard country. In this light, it is entirely possible for a country artist to use hard-core traits without being "hard country." Much of the cast of the *Grand Ole Opry*, for example, might qualify as hard core by Peterson's standards even though they belong to the symbolic heart of Nashville's music business establishment. Hard country, on the other hand, is not the kind of country music that beams forth from the *Opry* every Saturday night. It does not grace mainstream magazine covers and doesn't fill the newer dance halls. Recently, it is heard *only* on small or remote radio stations and in marginal honky-tonks specifically devoted to it. Nevertheless, it rarely sings about life in the country, and it can't be isolated by a label like "Honky-Tonk Music." Its scope is far wider than barnyards and bars. It sings about the pains and pleasures of losing the American dream in a style that demands both devotion and alienation from its audience and dares the rest of the world to be disgusted. It complains in a punning, wailing, whining, twanging, thumping, grandiosely emotive style. Like hard luck, hard work, hard feelings, hard knocks, and hard times, the emotions that hard country evokes are ambivalent, a blend of anger, regret, sadness, and other dark feelings lightened sometimes by survivor's pride. Like hard words and hard science, though, hard country also conveys a certain daunting disputatiousness. Like hard rock, hard porn, and hard drugs, hard country seeks its most extreme, objectionable, and definitive form. Yet definitive does not imply unchanging; rather, because of its constitutive need to oppose the soft and easy, hard country is a position rather than a well-defined entity.

As the presidential commentaries indicate, mainstream country music is readily associated with this country's most obvious attempts to keep up appearances. While mainstream country does occasionally articulate controversial themes, more often it can be heard as a toe-tapping form of assent to the status quo. In contrast, hard country assents more begrudgingly than benignly. It certainly expresses interest in life, liberty, and the pursuit of happiness although it more often focuses on the opposite in order to amplify the resentment and resilience of those whose pursuit has been arduous. Paradoxically, this emotion-laden skepticism draws further power from the fact that while our culture seems to be undergoing rapid change, little has changed in its approach to hard country. This is not to say that hard country hasn't changed. Now almost entirely represented by a handful of aging white men, hard country sounds increasingly embattled. Its interactions with both mainstream country music and mainstream culture outside of country music remain at worst adversarial and at best invisible. This attitude dovetails with an approach to country music that is almost as common as the all-American praise cited above: condescending scorn or blithe disregard. In fact, hostile relations with mainstream culture are now essential to hard country music. Chapter 1 introduces this tendency by illustrating the way country songs often take country music or "countriness" as their theme and by contrasting several hard country approaches to this theme with mainstream country songs. This introductory chapter thus looks at how hard country talks about itself—in songs and other aspects of performance—as well as how hard country gets talked about or ignored. This chapter also explores the origins of the term "hard country" in order to explore its adversarial history.

Chapters 2–4 concentrate on the music and the musicians. In order to emphasize hard country's adversarial function both within country music and outside it, I have eschewed a strictly chronological or encyclopedic organization in favor of an exploration of key issues and stars. Through an analysis of the comically abject and unsavory characters created by George Jones, Merle Haggard, and David Allan Coe, chapter 2 explains why hard country now functions as an all-male no-man's-land. In chapters 3 and 4, I focus on the way hard country music consciously carries on musical traditions and cultural disputes as well as on its deliberate attempts to innovate in the face of its rustic reputation. Chapter 3 explores the legacy of Hank Williams Sr. While Williams's predecessors such as Ernest Tubb used the hard-core techniques outlined by Peterson, Williams drew the eyes of an unfriendly outside world into the music, hardening it in all the pejorative and self-conscious senses of the word. His son, Hank Williams Jr., needed to hoe an even harder row to consider himself a legitimate heir, and thus his struggle provides particular insight into the metaphorical range of hard country. Chapter 4 is about the Bakersfield sound, important for its freedom from Nashville's profit-maximizing, mainstreaming pressures. In particular, I focus on the exploratory missions undertaken by Buck Owens and Dwight Yoakam as they survey hard country's boundary lines. In the conclusion, I speculate about hard country's future by briefly exploring still more self-conscious creations of legacies and rebellions: the Outlaw movement of the 1970s and an ever-lengthening chain of George Jones followers.

1

"Country 'til I die"

Contemporary hard country and the incurable unease of class distinction

While Richard Peterson has convincingly argued that the history of commercial country music, beginning in 1923, can be written by following its dialectical movement between "hard-core and soft-shell" expressions (*Creating*, 229 ff.), this movement does not take place of its own accord. The dialectic works not as an automated pendulum but at least partly as a reaction to forces outside the field of country music. In fact, the term "hard country" is a relatively recent one, appearing sometime in the late 1960s and early '70s, well after Nashville's music industry had actively promoted the cross-over potential of the "countrypolitan" Nashville sound.[1] While fan magazines like *Country Song Roundup* have long been obsessed with changes and stylistic varieties in country music, they never introduced the term "hard country" with any fanfare although it gradually began to appear as a conflictual and often pejorative synonym for related terms like "hillbilly," "honky-tonk," "pure country," and "real country." (For that matter, as Ronnie Pugh has shown, the generic rubric "country" was not consistently used until around 1950.)[2] Early fan magazine rhetoric tended to take enthusiastic note of the variety of styles that fell under the rubric of "country." An article appearing in September 1955, for example, gushed over Elvis Presley as a "Folk Music Fireball."[3] Journalists breathlessly reported on Nashville's embrace of '60s counterculture music, claiming that "Nashville and her musicians would like to say . . . I love you [to Joan Baez]."[4] Glen Campbell, reveling in his pop success, expressed indifference about whether his music could be called "country" or not: "I call it really just people music myself."[5]

Yet when rock and roll came to stay, a contentious tone occasionally crept into *Country Song Roundup's* brief articles on singers. In January 1960, a controversy-stirring headline asked "Can Ricky Nelson Sing? What Do You Think?" One interviewee thought not, explaining his position by accusing Nelson of not being "country."[6] Later that year, an article on Conway Twitty, "Is He or Isn't He a Hillbilly?" took a similar approach.[7] As late as 1969, legendary producer Owen Bradley answered *Country Song Roundup's* question about "what makes a song country" with "what we mean by *real country* is that it just won't go pop," in spite of the fact that as producer of Patsy Cline and Brenda Lee, he had presided over many "country" recording sessions that had resulted in pop hits; evidently he didn't yet know the term "hard country" or assumed that *Country Song Roundup* readers wouldn't be familiar with it.[8] That same year, Ray Price, a Hank Williams protégé who made a conscious decision in the late '60s to raise himself above the honky-tonks, groped for words while justifying his shift: "[I]t got me into the homes where I've always wanted to be. . . . I don't say I want to be *pure country* cause I want to sing to the world[;] I don't want to sing to just a few people."[9] By 1970, the term "hard country" began popping up as a pejorative. Porter Wagoner noted that people malign him as "hard country," while songwriter Curly Putman ("The Green, Green Grass of Home") made a point of saying he prefers "contemporary country music" to "hard country."[10] The term is not used in songs very often, but in 1978, Moe Bandy's "Soft Lights and Hard Country Music"[11] presented a man whose drinking and cheating are aided and abetted by these things, and in 1994, Ken Mellons sang about a "Jukebox Junky" who fed his habit on "hard-core country."[12]

Just as suddenly, outsiders, too, were presumed to know what hard country was. Scholar Bill Malone did not use the term in the first edition of *Country Music USA* (1968), his magisterial history of country music, although it does appear (without fanfare) in 1985's revised edition to refer to the "older styles" of country music.[13] Among the examples he mentions is George Jones, still releasing records in 2000. In 1970, *Rolling Stone* writer John Grissim filtered his report on *Country Music: White Man's Blues* through "the Bay area Revolution." He uses the term "hard-core country" without introduction, dismissing it as "narrowly ethnic"[14] and contrasting it to the more mainstream country that was prevalent circa 1969. In his 1972 book *The Nashville Sound: Bright Lights and Country Music,* journalist Paul Hemphill, like Grissim, simply assumes his readers will recognize the term since he uses it without providing a definition. To him, hard country is where, since the death of Hank Williams, the money isn't.[15] As counterexamples, he points to the big moneymakers of the '60s like Glen Campbell and Roger Miller. He approvingly cites Miller's publisher, Jack Stapp, who praises the smooth retreat from the "damned nasal, whiny and scratchy and corny" sound that keeps hard country records from selling on the pop charts (61).

At the same time, Hemphill, like so many commentators before and since, sees hard country as popular culture's last bastion of authenticity, free from commercial values and aspirations to sophistication. "The *industry* is in great shape, yes. But you wonder about what is going to happen to the music—real Southern here's-how-it-is-down-home-folks country music," he frets (241). Nearly 15 years later, Ken Tucker, writing in the *Journal of Country Music*, wistfully offered a similarly economic distinction: "[H]ard country stands as a blunt rebuke to the watery pop-country of such best-selling acts as the Oak Ridge Boys, Alabama, and Exile."[16] While these commentators are not always particularly enamored of hard country, they often use its alleged corniness and bluntness to provide their readers with a reassuring low point. As scholar Joli Jensen points out, "something about change in country music, especially change that makes money, sparks concern" (3). Thus, commentators often hope that the "damned nasal, whiny and scratchy and corny" stuff won't disappear, not necessarily because they like it, but because it validates their own sophistication by making such a marked contrast. Christopher Wren, for example, in the pious introductory essay to *Look's* 1971 cover story on country music, demands that there "be room for both, Kris Kristofferson alongside Roy Acuff, as long as country music does not surrender its authenticity."[17] Paradoxically, this notion of "authenticity" has little grounding in any contemporary reality; rather, it provides a way of imagining that hard country music production and consumption prove that someone remains blissfully ignorant of whatever massive changes and cultural imperatives the rest of us struggle with.[18] Jensen calls this vision of country music "purity by proxy" (169); elsewhere I have described it as a self-serving desire to believe that someone, somewhere, is "acting naturally."

Even fans who attempt to praise hard country music to the unknowing public take a similar stance. Frye Gaillard admires it for clinging to its artistic vision in the face of mainstream country's "bout with success" (187). *You're So Cold I'm Turning Blue: Martha Hume's Guide to the Greatest in Country Music* lists hard country as a type, and the back cover specifically promises that this book contains "the ultimate explanation of the difference between 'hard country' and 'the Nashville Sound.'" Actually, the book contains no such "ultimate explanation" unless the note that "hard country makes no concession to fad or fashion"[19] says it all; George Jones is again cited as an example.[20] Such praise, of course, dooms its object to failure; the crossover or mainstream artist sells more records than the hard country star, and big sales require a sophisticated image and sound that pull an artist out of rustic territory. Hard country artists, ever unfashionable, languish there. The long-standing lingo for a song or artist whose appeal extends beyond country music—"crossover"—is significant in the way it conjures up the cultural boundaries that some artists can't cross.

Hume borrows her title from an obscure song ("You're So Cold I'm Turning Blue") by Davis Stewart and Harlan Howard. Although she doesn't explain her title choice, its catchiness offers slumming diversion and boundary crossing to chic and curious tourists, and the dialogue that it suggests sums up well the relationship between hard country music (turning blue) and the crossover audience (the cold ones). Lists of clever or outrageous country song titles, a perennial feature of newspaper and magazine columns, serve a similar function. Likewise, these condescending cartoons, published in the *New Yorker* in 1996, make an "in joke" that requires some familiarity with, but no deep understanding of, hard country conventions (fig. 1.1).[21] These fictional stars, much like hard country's real stars, appear as silly, self-pitying losers. When the moment came to take popular music seriously, the *New Yorker* couldn't take country in any form: its "special music issue" that year included nothing on country music although nearly every other musical genre had an in-depth article devoted to it.[22]

Hard country not only makes its meaning in this partially self-imposed and partially culturally constructed backwater; it also makes its meaning *out of it*. Recognizing this duality is essential to truly hearing the music; other approaches, no matter how sympathetic, often exercise the prerogative of the cultural elite by putting hard country in its rusticated place without exploring what that place means. *In the Country of Country* (1997), a book that vividly demonstrates this logic, tells us that country music is "about common people everywhere, for common people everywhere."[23] While author Nicholas Dawidoff doesn't use the term hard country, he does draw a distinction between the music he's talking about and country "in the best pop tradition" (14). He calls Garth Brooks, country's biggest crossover star, "a yuppie with a lariat," contrasting him to Haggard and Jones, whose lives, he assures us, "really have been hard" (15). However, he doesn't imagine that the contrast between hard and easy is in itself a source of the music's meaning. Thus, he tours the various haunts of these "common people" in an attempt to demonstrate that out in the country, common people sing in commonplaces so simple that they don't need interpretation. Likewise, the book's illustrations, a blend of archival Walker Evans-esque photos with contemporary photos taken in the same dusty docu-

CATCHIEST
SELF-PITYING
SINGLE:
"I'D BE DANCING WITH YOU IN TULSA
BUT GOD WANTS ME IN THIS WHEELCHAIR."
- PAPA DALE DUGGANS

BEST SINGLE
INADVERTENTLY
CAPTURING THE
INHERENT CLUELESS-
NESS OF MEN:
"HERE'S HOPING YOU FIND
ME WHEN YOU FIND WHAT
YOU DON'T KNOW WHAT
YOU'RE LOOKIN' FOR."
—SONNY STUBBS

BEST SINGLE CAPTURING A MAN'S NEED
TO CHEAT AND THEN LIE ABOUT IT:
"TEN YEARS I WAS FAITHFUL,
ONE NIGHT I WAS ME."
—PURVIS SHEPHERD

MOPIEST ALBUM OF 1996:
"GETTIN' TIRED OF GETTIN' FIRED."
—RANDY BLAND

CRAWFORD

Fig. 1.1: Country Music in the *New Yorker* (27 May 1996). © The New Yorker Collection 1996 Michael Crawford from cartoonbank.com. All Rights Reserved.

mentary style, reinforce this rustication. Such imagery suggests that an unchanging backwardness characterizes the lives and music of hard country stars. This book was widely heralded for its sympathetic portrayal of its subject—it received favorable reviews in both the *New York Times* and the *Washington Post*—and it has now been repackaged as a compact disc with musical selections from the stars discussed. Aimed at a mass audience, it is being advertised as a perfect introduction to country music even though *In the Country of Country* introduces few new insights. While Dawidoff conducted excellent interviews with country stars, he sanctimoniously repeats bromides that have been circulating ever since country music achieved national prominence in the World War II era.

"Almost any simple soul might write hillbilly words," asserted the unnamed journalist who covered the "Bull Market in Corn" for *Time* magazine in October 1943.[24] In 1944, Maurice Zolotov, writing in the *Saturday Evening Post*, complained that "hillbilly troupes will consistently outdraw legitimate Broadway plays, symphony concerts, sophisticated comedians and beautiful dancing girls" (Gentry, 58). Writing for *Harper's* in 1974 and singling out Merle Haggard for special opprobrium, Florence King protested that "the mind of the country music fan tends to pounce on anything that resembles a good old-fashioned reductio ad absurdum."[25] Some 20 years later, a lot of people still want to believe that country music is the polar opposite of both the complex pleasures of high culture and the relentless sophistication of everyday life, even if they try to be more polite or nostalgic about it. Dawidoff's tour guide is only one example; a trendy book about simplifying your life advises its overly complicated readers to try writing a country song. (The next tip is to get a massage.)[26] In 1996, a reporter for the *New York Times Sunday Magazine* noted the low visibility of singers like Merle Haggard in today's Nashville, then pronounced the hot stars of the '90s "as safe and clean as the neighborhood mall."[27] Other emissaries from Nashville, such as erstwhile Kennedy and Reagan chronicler Laurence Leamer, dispense with this ritual listing of absentees; Leamer's readers get only what he sees: 1996's hottest stars (Garth Brooks, etc.). Still, as the title of his book proclaims, Leamer believes that these hot new singers offer a reassuringly simple combination of *Three Chords and the Truth*.[28] Similarly, journalist Bruce Feiler admits to developing a "passion" for country music after hearing Garth Brooks, whom he describes as "no part hillbilly" yet still pure enough to offer access to "a real America, far removed from the cynicism and manipulation of New York, Los Angeles, or Capitol Hill."[29]

Contemporary cultural studies, which has made popular culture a legitimate, even fashionable, arena of interpretation, has yet to develop much scholarly interest in country music. While noted scholars such as John Fiske readily grant sophisticated powers of cultural contestation to such practices as wearing deliberately torn jeans or following the well-publicized antics of Madonna, few have turned their attention to country music. Fiske, in particular, is openly dumbfounded by it: "What is important," he claims, "is that it is there."[30] In other words, country music is elsewhere, neither a body of masterpieces nor part of the exciting here and now. Without intending to, Frith goes a long way toward explaining the lack of attention paid to country music in cultural studies: "[T]he cultural study of popular music has been, in effect, an anxiety-driven search by radical intellectuals and rootless academics for a model of consumption—for the perfect consumer, the subcultural idol, the mod, the punk, the cool commodity fetishist, the organic intellectual of the high street who *can stand in for them*."[31] By this logic, academics seeking chic should look everywhere but the "country of country." As a result, unlike those who tear their jeans, paint, sculpt, write books, and sing some other forms of popular music, hard country performers don't get to make sense for anyone outside of their quaint country. Even scholarly books devoted to placing country music in a broad cultural context, such as Cecelia Tichi's *High Lonesome: The American Culture of Country Music* and Curtis Ellison's *Country Music Culture: From Hard Times to Heaven* (Jackson: University of Mississippi Press, 1995), don't distinguish between types of country music and tend to make large claims on the basis of mainstream country music.

In short, hard country music, which isn't predominantly about rural life, occupies a bleakly rustic territory in our cultural imagination. While mainstream country can be praised for its pastoral Americanism, hard country is either invisible or an odd place to visit where you surely wouldn't want to live. Perhaps the best way to imagine it is as a field of stone, an image I borrow from "Would You Lay With Me (In a Field of Stone)," Tanya Tucker's number one hit in 1974. She was then a sultry sixteen-year-old; the song was written by David Allan Coe, a tattoo-covered ex-convict who would later become famous in his own right (see chapter 2). The song's popularity was no doubt fueled by the fact that several radio stations refused to play it because of its suggestive lyrics. It was an invitation to a sexual encounter, the protestors argued, no matter how uncomfortable and uninviting the title's question sounded. Coe, however, insisted on another meaning: he explained that he had written the song for his brother's wedding. It was a vision rather than a proposition. The song asked whether marriage vows could be stretched beyond death, whether the wedding couple could lie together in a field of (tomb)stones, whether this marriage could withstand the test of time. Of course, the lyrics do allow a suggestive interpretation; but even without Coe's counterinterpretation, the way the song is performed and produced sounds more ceremonial than erotic. It opens with a hushed a cappella chanting of the title, and ends with these same words sung as a stately round, an effect that suggests a congregation or at least some kind of gathering rather than an intimate moment.

Just as interesting as the elaboration of the field of stone as a metaphor, though, is the fact that the metaphor failed to register with those who have the power to choose what music to play. Whether the country radio station managers didn't understand Coe's metaphoric approach or whether they simply feared that their less subtle listeners wouldn't understand it is a question that can't be definitively answered; what I want to emphasize here is the cultural logic that constructs the more unsavory examples of country music as a realm of cold, hard facts, a realm where fields of stone are just that and only that. At some level it was simply assumed that the song was literally about two people having sex in a rocky field somewhere. This assumption also implies a geographic distribution of the ability to make sense and to make something of oneself: speaking and hearing imaginatively and figuratively, and making your visions register—all activities that give other cultural endeavors their prestige and interpretive scope—cannot happen in the stone "hard country" of country music.

At the same time, hard country songs often deliberately mimic the tourist's patronizing vision of the country of country. They play with the assumption that everything they say will be taken literally. Porter Wagoner poses the riddle in the last line of "The Cold Hard Facts of Life": "who taught who the cold hard facts of life?"[32] Like Sisyphus rolling his stone, hard country performers often portray themselves as poor souls condemned to endlessly state the obvious when they are in fact participating in an imaginative tradition. Sometimes they offer slices of their lives, but other times, as Ernest Tubb told an interviewer, they create hard country out of hard country. "No one, even Hank Williams, no one person can possibly live all the things that he wrote about." Williams, he claims, got a lot of ideas for songs "from lines out of my songs."[33] Once we recognize that the long-suffering, born-to-lose hard country artistic persona is a self-consciously adopted tradition, we can see it not as an example of a field of stone but as an exploration of it. That's why it's important to take this music figuratively, to grant its makers the power of figurative and complex speech that is routinely granted to artists and other people we take seriously.

Moreover, the struggle for the compelling power of figurative speech forms part of hard country's essence. In other words, it's more and more often about wresting meaning from a field of stone. Faced with self-serving misunderstanding from cultural arbiters of every stripe, hard country increasingly positions itself and its listeners as outside of contemporary American culture. In fact, the term "hard country" seems to have entered our vocabulary about the same time that the '60s counterculture held sway, and in spite of hard country's moments of hippie baiting, it, like the counterculture, is largely about refusing to follow the easy road to material success and social integration. The importance of this theme can be most easily seen by tracing the changing connotation of the word "country" in hard country music since the late 1940s. Hank Williams never sang a song about the country. He got "The Honky-Tonk Blues" by leaving his "rural route" home behind. When his contemporaries used the word, though, they were still at home there. In 1949, Little Jimmy Dickens, as stylistically "hard shell" as they come, sang a song called "Country Boy" in which he plows, milks, feeds chickens, and claims that he is better off than wealthy businessmen. In other words, he likes standing out in his field of stone and looks forward to being country even after he dies: he promises to help milk the cows in heaven.[34] Country, to Dickens's character, is a blessed state rather than an uncomfortable condition. You can still hear this kind of song on country radio today, but in 1949 you couldn't have heard threatening lyrics like Charlie Daniels's 1980 "Leave this long-haired country boy alone"—angrily addressed to an unnamed and apparently judgmental "you."[35] Unlike Dickens, the singer takes the term "country" as an insult even as he uses the term to describe himself. "Hard country" is the turning point in the signifying tradition that starts with a song like Dickens's celebratory vision of the "Country Boy" in heaven and that now needs to stress that country boys can weather the scorn here on earth. They may not see themselves as creative geniuses, yet they're not ready for the fields of stone and they want "you" to know it. The characters they create address an audience that is outside the country but looking in, the audience that they call *you*. As Buck Owens puts it in the first line of "The Streets of Bakersfield": "[Y]ou don't know me, but you don't like me."[36] This multilayered perspective, looking angrily at the successful urbanite who thinks he is looking at an unregenerate hick, is now an integral feature of hard country.

Mainstream country songs offer no such complexity. For example, Alabama, apparently the most popular country group of all time, assumes that if you love your country, you'll love their songs. Their hit single "Born Country" (1991) aims to please just about any listener. In it, you can hear how mainstream is a synonym for easy: the music is unobtrusive, the vocal harmony is pleasant, and since the lyrics associate sweet sentiments with innate patriotism, the situation that calls forth such a song isn't readily imagined. With its references to creeks, mountains, and home cooking, "Born Country" seems like an anthem along the lines of "America the Beautiful." Only a slight note of defensiveness, indicating that perhaps not everyone thinks being "Born Country" is a wonderful situation, dilutes the patriotic bliss. Nevertheless, Alabama's lyrics end by repeating the title and expressing patriotic love for "this country."[37] Ultimately, then, "country," in this song, is both a lost rural idyll and an ever-present Anywhere, USA. In this way, the song attempts to appeal to nearly everyone.

In contrast, John Anderson, a hard country star since 1980, simultaneously boasts and complains about being "Country 'til I Die" (1994). While Anderson may not be directly answering the Alabama song, he does have something to say about the nostalgic version of "country" in a culture that needs to keep someone down on the farm. As Anderson recounts his unpleasant attendance at an upscale party and subsequent visit to a doctor, almost every image of the Alabama song is replaced with a more difficult situation. Creeks and sunlit mornings become unwelcoming hostesses and condescending professionals; mama's cornbread is replaced by a nightmarish plate of sushi. More importantly, the comfort of Alabama's country birthright is replaced with Anderson's diagnosis of an impending doom and incurable unease called "country." In Anderson's song, "the country of country" has nothing to do with where he lives and everything to do with how he lives. Set in the equally privileged milieus of a high-society celebration and a doctor's office, this is a song about knowing your place. Singing about himself in an ostentatious drawl, Anderson's character learns that his "problem" with contemporary culture is tantamount to nature. His background, a purely imaginary country that is a euphemism for "class," makes social mobility impossible. His key symptom is a naive ignorance that supposedly leaves him essentially unsophisticated, incurably boorish, and permanently unable to enact the urbane rituals of the rich and powerful. Neither doctors nor powerful cocktail-partiers know how to "treat a man in [his] condition." Crucially, his unease is only communicable in their presence. The authoritative doctor claims to see "country" written all over his patient—in his looks, his speech, his gait, and even in the fact that he drives a truck. His prognosis is fatal; hence the song's title: "Country 'til I Die."[38]

In this song, then, "country" is a complex word that equates class standing with taste at the same time that it removes taste from the all-American realm of free choice. No matter what he does, this patient can't learn to make his tastes conform to those of the tastemakers. The patient senses that he should know better but those who possess the knowledge he seeks claim it can't be shared. Anderson's doctor cannot prescribe any formula that would allow his patient to cross the line that divides the powerless from the powerful and the country from the mainstream. Anderson's unease is incurable and the word "country" sums it up. Unlike other high-culture outcasts, the "country" sufferer isn't even able to tell Beethoven to roll over; he ends up simply leaving the parties and professional offices.

The analysis of taste I've used to describe hard country's incurable unease is adapted from Pierre Bourdieu's extended discussion of how cultural hierarchies legitimate class divisions in his book *Distinction: A Social Critique of the Judgment of Taste*.[39] In these terms of cultural hegemony, the long-standing distinction between the country and the city can be seen as a symbolic distinction between the sophisticated and the rustic: the possessors of cultural capital and the have-nots, the powerful and the dominated. In fact, although theorists of postmodernity have announced the end of the distinctions between high and low, the division between the country and the city still easily symbolizes such distinctions, as does the division between mainstream and hard country. In other words, although this new catholicity is conceptualized as a radically new "postmodernism," in practice it is an urban culture that remains high in comparison with the exotic and remote others that nevertheless occasionally strike its fancy.

The unheralded birth, circa 1970, of hard country in its named form suggests just that: it, too, self-consciously addresses this new form of cultural hierarchy from its quarantined, internalized, low point. Hard country notes that although traditional cultural boundaries may well be softening, the right to cross them is not universally bestowed, and the distribution of this right is in fact a particularly postmodern form of distinction between high and low cultures *and* classes. The actual places of residence are not crucial nor is an exclusively highbrow orientation. "Savoir faire," which now includes an omnivorous consumption of all the latest rages, including mainstream country,[40] is figured as urbanity while the inability to successfully negotiate with any form of urbanity signifies rusticity. Discussions of postmodern culture avoid this implicit hierarchy by simply granting the city a monopoly on cultural production and consumption.[41] But, as Peter Stallybrass and Allon White note, such cultural invisibility often masks a "psychological dependence upon precisely those others which are being rigorously opposed and excluded at the social level."[42] They could be talking about the struggling rube who now handily plays foil to the newest manifestation of "high" culture, the cyborgian master of "high" technology. This division between the "knows" and the "know-nots," as Andrew Ross has noted, is increasingly the form class division takes in postindustrial America.[43] The rube has always played the role of "know-not," but this stock character is finding work these days playing a loser stalled on the information highway. Hard country exemplifies this pattern, constructing itself and its listeners as the "low other" of American culture.[44] For example, in their truck-driving duet "Semi-Crazy," Junior Brown and Red Simpson defensively declare themselves "semi-crazy roads scholars" (1996).[45]

As traditional forms of work, and hence traditional forms of class distinction vanish, the logic of *cultural* distinction is becoming both more symbolic and significant in the postmodern era.[46] As Frith puts it, "the fact that the objects of judgment are different doesn't mean that the processes of judgment are" (*Performing Rites*, 17). In short, the codes aren't disappearing although they be may getting more difficult to parse. John Anderson's song mocks this situation; outside of hard country this situation functions as mockery. A page torn from the October 24, 1994, issue of *People* magazine illustrates this logic on both sides: on one side a picture of Buck Owens is used to exemplify the snide theme of the crossword puzzle: "in the cornfield"; on the reverse side, a picture of a repulsive hick, "aged in Oklahoma," is used to flatter readers into identifying with a readily purchasable amulet against such degradation: well-aged wine (fig. 1.2).[47] These preferences are so deeply assimilated that we tend to experience them as unconstrained expressions of personality rather than social constructions. Bourdieu calls this easy assimilation of cultural tastes a "habitus." Put simply, he means that our identities are shaped by the cultural tastes and practices that surround us and, hence, with which we feel comfortable, with which we feel "at home." *People* magazine, for example, surely intended to soothe and seduce rather than offend with this page. Indeed, those who benefit from their tastes—like John Anderson's doctor—prefer to believe that they are innate. Professionally credentialed, they nevertheless profess ignorance in the face of hard country's questions. In reality, of course, people who think Merle Haggard is a great poet become college professors, and ex-convicts like Merle Haggard get invited to sing at the White House. They may feel just like John Anderson at his party, but these exceptions, knowing that they prove the rule, can at least survey the boundary lines. Thus, hard country's stars convincingly contrast their "down-home" discomfort zone with the sophisticated trappings of the uptown and mainstream habitus. In sum, hard country music sounds out the logic of "distinction" as it operates both in the realm of country music and in postmodern American culture.

In order to put this situation in a fuller historical context, it helps to look briefly at another hard country visit to the doctor: Hank Williams's "Low-Down Blues."[48] While Anderson's unease can be described in great detail, the low down blues don't have many symptoms; feeling blue is the closest Williams comes to a description, and he never mentions any causes. In "Country 'til I Die" *country* is both the cause and the illness. The doctors in both songs, though, offer equally bleak diagnoses. William's doctor tells his patient he can recognize the disease, but, like Anderson's doctor, he can offer no remedy; his "book" says nothing about the low down blues. Evidently his training prepared him only for the maladies of the higher-placed. About the same time, Little Jimmy Dickens was (once again) more explicit about the situation. He went to the doctor and received the diagnosis of a highly contagious "Hillbilly Fever" caused by listening to country music.[49] He mentions several songs that transmitted the disease, including Hank Williams's famous "Lovesick Blues," but never indicates that he'll stop listening. Indeed, like Alabama's country native, Dickens's patient loves his "disease." In contrast, Williams's sufferer (in "Low-Down Blues"), left to his own devices, just as Anderson is, bleakly con-

Fig. 1.2: Hicks as depicted in *People* (24 October 1994).

cludes that "I'll have to get better before I can die." While Williams adapts an evocative blues vernacular to complain about the hard place he's in, Anderson, writing thirty years later, uses the word "country" to activate the simultaneously metaphorical and real codes of social distinction. He finally lists the causes and symptoms of Williams's disease.

A comparison of two chart-topping signature songs, "The Dance," sung by Garth Brooks (1990), and "He Stopped Loving Her Today," sung by George Jones (1980), summarizes the almost existential differences between hard and mainstream country. (In a 1992 survey on the best 100 country songs, *Country America*'s readers ranked "He Stopped Loving Her Today" number one and "The Dance" number three.)[50] "The Dance," although it mentions an ill-defined loss, is about looking on the bright side. Sung in the first person, the song nevertheless offers no narrative and little overt emotion. Something, perhaps death but perhaps simply some more modern desire for "personal growth," breaks up a relationship in which the singer had engaged. He sings to an absent "you" without a hint of rancor or blame. While he has suffered, he prefers having participated to the psychological safety of the sidelines. Missing the pain, he croons, would have meant missing "The Dance."[51] This philosophy is unassailable; we have all probably urged it upon friends and children. No doubt this unobjectionableness contributes to the song's popularity, all the more so since the metaphor conveys a high schooler's delight in inclusion. Brooks's delivery, with only the slightest, most gentlemanly trace of a southern accent, smoothly avoids rusticity while the instrumental accompaniment ostentatiously avoids it. While the song begins with a reassuringly countrified acoustic guitar, a New-Agey piano gradually assumes the dominant note, and a symphonic French horn adds yet another layer of calm optimism. Materials promoting the song amplified the optimistic note. Brooks introduces the video by explaining that he wants to expand the interpretation of "The Dance" so that it can be heard as more than a "love gone bad song." Instead, Brooks associates joining the dance with heroic Americanism.[52] (Unlike Coe, Brooks, evidently, can impose whatever metaphor he chooses upon his audience.) While Brooks sings the song, images of John Wayne, John F. Kennedy, Martin Luther King, rodeo champion Lane Frost, the space shuttle *Challenger* crew, and the late country star Keith Whitley flash across the screen. Perhaps the best indication of the vast embrace this song received is the coffee-table book devoted to it. Although I don't know how to verify this claim, I doubt any other country song has reached this apex of artsy display. The images, classily representational photographs capturing Norman Rockwell themes, equate just about every all-American cliché with joining in the dance. Graduations, weddings, community festivals, Little League, high school football games, and sun-drenched rural scenery are all presented as steps in the dance.[53] No wonder Bruce Feiler, with his suburban enthusiasm for mainstream country, called "The Dance" "the defining song for the entire modern era of country" (112).

In his report on Nashville's buoyant '90s, Laurence Leamer condescendingly contrasts "The Dance" to hard country themes:

> The song carried hope for what country music might do or say. There was a vein of fatalism running through the history of country music, a natural fatalism learned by poor people to whom life was something that was done to them. 'The Dance' sent the message that life was something that each person had to reach out for and grasp with all his or her might. (19)

In other words, Leamer imagines that "The Dance" could remedy the heretofore incurable unease of hard country, and he could well have cited Jones's "He Stopped Loving Her Today" as an example of such supposedly outdated fatalism.[54] While Brooks's song claims that life's ventures are best ruled by chance, Jones's character is haunted by cruel destiny. "He," in "He Stopped Loving Her Today," had a moment of romantic happiness just as Brooks's singer did, but rather than transmuting it into contentment, he fetishized his misery. According to the singing narrator, this hurt soul hasn't smiled for years. He exacerbates his pain by gazing at his beloved's picture and rereading her letters (written in 1962), underlining her words of love. While Brooks's metaphor is elastic enough to invite multiple interpretations, Jones's provides certain inescapable details. Such an approach lures listeners like Leamer into assuming Jones expects to be taken literally and that his listeners actually do so. The song, however, relies upon a gender dynamic whereby the woman represents just such a scornful but ostensibly sensible attitude.[55] (This hard country trope will be further explored in the next chapter.) So integral is this dynamic that Jones's producer Billy Sherrill insisted that songwriters Bobby Braddock and Curly Putman (the same Curly Putman who claimed to eschew hard country) add a verse about the woman before he would allow Jones to record it.[56] It begins with a version of the marriage vow, but only "he" is espousing an until-death-do-us-part commitment. The fickle woman, wanting to move on to better things, believes that time should dissolve it. The man clings all the more desperately to the vow after she breaks it. Ultimately, the narrator turns the woman's callous optimism into manslaughter. At one point, he even describes the man's obsession as *her* "prey"[ing] upon his thoughts. As the title (and the woman) promises, the narrator's friend does stop loving her one day, but that day, we realize as the song builds to its conclusion, is the day of his funeral.

While Brooks's song, especially because of the video and accompanying book, conjures up a nation of daring dancers, Jones's song describes a small circle of sympathetic onlookers who wallow in male misery. The dead man's eulogy mentions no accomplishments apart from his abject devotion to a lost cause. As proof, the woman comes to the funeral, an event the man's friends had speculated about, the singer notes in a gossipy aside, clearly condemning the woman while his wrenchingly emotive singing conveys his respect for his doggedly devoted friend. Jones's characteristic nonstandard pronunciation, with some words sung through clenched teeth while others are given an open-throated wail, makes the song audibly "country." Likewise, although the instrumentation features a pop-country string section, it also sounds hard: a muted harmonica and a steel guitar punctuate most bars with a prominent sob.

While "The Dance" appeals to its listeners' most self-congratulatory emotions, "He Stopped Loving Her Today" appeals to their ambivalence. In the interview added to the home video version of "The Dance," Brooks claims he hopes the song will be played at his funeral. Nevertheless, his promotion of the song turned it into an anthem about lasting respect whereas "He Stopped Loving Her Today"'s most positive emotion is simply last respects. "He" is an object of pity while "she," mysteriously beloved, plays a trite femme fatale with a healthy survival instinct. She, like the narrator of "The Dance," moves beyond suffering while Jones, to those unfamiliar with hard country conventions, seems to express solidarity with those who get buried by it. Yet, as ethnographer Katie Stewart puts it, "the naive schlock that this critique *sees* is the naive shlock that it *produces* in its own polemical poetics of sophisticated distance" (221).[57] Country music is no innocent bystander in this production process. Hard country dares "you" to make this mistake while Brooks and a host of cultural commentators tempt you to do it. As my description of hard country's incurable unease demonstrates, hard country is capable of creating its own critical distance through its continual elaboration of diagnostic scenarios and suffering types. Stewart goes on to note that songs of lament such as "He Stopped Loving Her Today" offer "not the voice of an 'individual' but the voice of a 'type' of person formed by a particular situation and a mode of consciousness" (222). While this song doesn't use the word "country," its place (and Jones's place) in the hard country pantheon embodies what Stewart calls a "male abjection story" (224). The unhappy ending makes this interpretation most clear: the abjectly faithful types are (hard) "country" till they die while those who escape—women and men of distinction—are not. Brooks tells the escapees that they've chosen the better path. Jones allows for no such certitude. Far from the "natural fatalism" Leamer hears in non-Brooks country, what "He Stopped Loving Her Today" and other hard country songs offer is a moment of self-conscious diagnosis. While "The Dance" voices the popular promise of pain followed by gain, "He Stopped Loving Her Today" asks a hard, permanently uneasy, question: what, exactly, is gained by a choreographed rush out of hard country?

I want to return to David Allan Coe to summarize hard country's encounter with its tourists. In "If That Ain't Country" (1977), a barroom classic too long, too sad, and too profane for commercial airwaves, Coe evokes life in one of those houses with junk cars rusting in the yard. He says they look like tombstones. The head of the family was able to buy this house thanks to the GI Bill, but he claimed it "wasn't worth all he had to kill to get it," and it appears that maintaining it further strains the family's resources. "Pa" is "covered with tattoos and scars; he got some in prison and others in bars" and still others from his work as a shade-tree mechanic. (This occupation, rather than sheer slovenliness, explains the disarray on the lawn.) The singer remembers this hardworking man as always "mean," always "tired," always "drunk." His offspring end up in prison or walking the streets. In Coe's words, this desperate emotional terrain marks the entire family's life, and it can be summed up in a term that's often synonymous with "country"—"white trash."[58] Again, this insult has nothing to do with farming or rural scenery or even a longing to regain these things. Instead, it condemns the family for ever leaving the country, for so visibly trying and failing to live the American dream. Money could mend the house's rotting roof, but the family, in Coe's words, remains "living proof" that "white trash" won't simply fade away.

Coe concludes the family saga by alluding to a series of old songs in order to suggest that his country music is for, by, and about white trash.[59] He first recorded this song two years after John Denver thanked God he was a country boy and three years after Tom T. Hall, mainstream country's most shameless sentimentalist, claimed in "Country Is" that country could be an urban address as long as you knew "your kind" or it could be simply a "state of mind."[60] In Coe's song, the indicators of country are neither blessed nor psychosomatic; instead they are a volatile mixture of hard living and hard words—and the hardest words are again aimed at the people who don't yet recognize their ideological investment in misinterpreting the country of country. These words make more sense in concert because Coe doesn't sing them; he states his premise, "If That Ain't Country," and the audience shouts the conclusion, "I'll kiss your ass," at him. (On the recorded version it sounds as if he's offering to make this submissive gesture—although the song's simultaneously angry and melancholy tone undercuts such an interpretation.)

Likewise, to those who don't know the hard country canon, the last minute

of the song sounds like nonsense lyrics. Coe is addressing both of hard country's audiences here. Out of one side of his mouth he is angrily trying to stop
"you" from clinging to your self-interested vision of country; out of the other
he is reminding his listeners who are already steeped in hard country's conventions that he is participating in a tradition of mapping the country of country. "I'm Thinking Tonight of My Blue Eyes" is a folksy love song first popu-
larized by the Carter Family in the 1920s and '30s. In the late '30s, Roy Acuff
used the melody for his religious song "The Great Speckled Bird." In 1952,
Hank Thompson used the melody to complain about a woman who preferred
the "Wild Side of Life" to settling down with him. In the first line of Thompson's sadder but wiser chorus, the singer expresses surprise that God created
"honky-tonk angels."[61] That same year, Kitty Wells used the same melody yet
again to say that "It _Wasn't_ God Who Made Honky-Tonk Angels"; men, with
their cheating and drinking, do that.[62] So Coe uses that melody and a line
from each of those songs to take his country song to the hard line, to the point
where it's about the collision between "country" and the rest of the world. The
perpetuation of the Carter Family/Acuff/Thompson/Wells song promises that
we're going to go on meeting like this whether "you" like it or not.

2

The Possum, the Hag, and the Rhinestone Cowboy

The burlesque abjection of the white male

The hard country galaxy glows with dimly christened stars. Counter to whatever logic glamour possesses, hard country singers use such pejorative stage names as Ol' Hank (Hiram "Hank" Williams, 1923–1952), the Hag (ex-convict Merle Haggard, 1937–), and the Possum (George Jones, 1931–). Alvis Edgar Owens (1929–), better known as Buck Owens, changed his first name to match that of his Okie family's mule. Johnny Cash, known as "the man in black," evokes bad guys and mourners.[1] Donald Lytle achieved stardom as Johnny Paycheck, a name borrowed "from a not-so-prize fighter who lasted less than one humiliating round with Joe Louis."[2] When they decide to preserve their given names, hard country stars stick with the fence-post plain or the downright unflattering: Ernest Tubb (1914–1984), Hank Thompson (1925–), John Anderson (1954–), or David Allan Coe (1939–)—it rhymes with John Doe. Kentucky-born Dwight Yoakam (1956–) even shares his (real) last name with the hillbillies of Al Capp's comic strip backwater, Dogpatch.[3] Waylon Jennings's (1937–) first name immediately suggests a downbeat approach (wailing). In contrast, mainstream country announces itself with reassuringly evocative monikers such as George Strait and Alabama.

Hard country stars thus strike a lowly pose from the moment their names enter our consciousness.[4] Their sad songs, whining steel guitars, and wailing fiddles set their pose to music. Their physical images, too, hardly fulfill the tall, dark, and handsome matinee ideal. While these stars can project a certain sexual magnetism, most of them could also be called pale and paunchy (see figs. 2.1 and 2.2.) These flaws, though, become more fuel for the star-making machine: George Jones and Johnny Paycheck released a duet in 1980 called "When You're Ugly Like Us,"[5] and in 1992, Waylon Jennings sang "I'm Too Dumb for New York City and Too Ugly for L.A."[6] Yet since so many people love to hear their woeful stories and their heart-wrenching voices, these stars manage to be at once rich and famous and abject failures. Cultural critics haven't been much better than hard country doctors at diagnosing this paradox,[7] but the key symptom, I think, lies in an almost forgotten term: burlesque, a comic mode that can be used to undermine any cultural ideal. Most examples of burlesque involve intentional and spectacular violations of the standards of good taste and good behavior.[8] These violations can be disgusting or hilarious depending on your attachment to the ideals in question. If your good taste justifies your social status, you may not like to see the standards of sophistication torn down too often, but if you are down so low that your only hope is some new ideal, applauding the burlesque makes good sense and good fun.

Because it so happily scorns so many cultural norms, the burlesque would seem the ideal mode for expressing and easing abjection. Yet cultural critics have yet to link the two phenomena, and country music itself has never been considered burlesque;[9] instead, many observers note its unalloyed sadness soothed by that traditional opiate: heavenly salvation. The title and comprehensive claims of Curtis Ellison's recent book on the music sum up this attitude: *Country Music Culture: From Hard Times to Heaven* (1995). On the other hand, ethnomusicologist Aaron Fox has brilliantly analyzed the "trial by irony" to which country artists often submit their themes,[10] but irony is too subtle a term for the ludicrous lapses of taste and conduct that hard country obsessively elaborates. In fact, while hard country songs often rely on irony, the modernist aesthetic that prizes irony, with its concomitant reverence for originality, is foreign to this performance style. Although many hard country stars write their own material, they also display an imitative bent typical of what poet and critic Michael André Bernstein has called "the abject hero" (22). So eagerly do hard country singers display their dependence on their forebears and peers that the compulsion to repeat the sins and songs of musical relatives has become essential to the hard country performance. Thus, rerecordings, cover versions, and duets are important components of most hard country careers. Similarly, hard country songs cultivate triteness by alluding to earlier songs and singers. For example Buck Owens's "Play 'Together Again' Again" (1979) asks a bystander to play Buck's earlier hit song "Together Again"

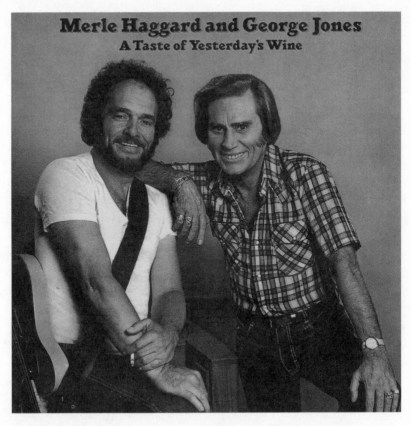

Fig. 2.1: Merle Haggard and George Jones on a 1982 album cover. Courtesy Country Music Foundation.

(1964).[11] In other words, along with creating an abject rustic persona, these singers use burlesque techniques such as repetition, imitation, allusion, and collusion to call attention to the fact that they fall short of any number of social and artistic imperatives.

Again, Bernstein, without using the term "burlesque," provides a key insight into this spectacle of failure:

> [A]bjection is a social and dialogic category, and its expression is always governed by the mapping of prior . . . cultural models. Abjection is only felt in conversation with another, with a voice, whether internal or external, whose oppressive confidence arises through its articulation of the normative values of society as a whole." (29)

Fig. 2.2: David Allan Coe, ca. 1985. Courtesy Country Music Foundation.

Celebrating their own success would poison its source, so hard country stars rarely manifest in their own right the "oppressive confidence" of which Bernstein speaks. Unlike gilded Trumps and yuppies in tasteful suits, hard country stars rise and shine due to the darkness of the background they create. Since their success lies in a formulaic articulation of failure, it can only be given plain and disdainful stage names like "the Possum" and "the Hag." In this guise, hard country stars engage in dialogue with a range of sneering and oppressively confident opponents, often called "you" or "she." Hearing this burlesque dialogue is central to understanding the unsettling emotions hard country provokes in both its fans and its detractors.

As soon as you enter into the dialogue, you have to take a joke, too. Although Bernstein recognizes that the abject hero's dialogic confrontation with "normative values" can provoke laughter, articulating the comic potential of this confrontation is not his primary purpose. Yet provoking laughter easily intensifies the shame that the abject dialogue conjures, so hard country, in its quest for the extreme, leans heavily toward the comic. Equally extreme is the fact that abjection is constantly portrayed by an absurdly unregenerate white man who jokes and suffers while women and conventionally successful men brandish the normative values that underscore abjection. Historian Peter Stearns has handily named these values "American Cool." He notes that the mores of the high-achieving white middle class have both defined the emotional norms and "seized a central place in . . . the imagination" of the twentieth century.[12] What constitutes "cool," then, is an almost purely economic success with no emotional intensity allowed, especially crying. Loren Baritz, another historian of the modern middle class, similarly speaks of its "compulsion to be reasonable, exercise control, and maintain order."[13]

Perhaps this simultaneously comic and abject destruction of "American Cool" explains why hard country now seems a virtual monopoly of white males: a truly effective *burlesque* of the American dream must be enacted by those who in theory should stoically enjoy the privileges of power. As everyone who winces at the sound of a steel guitar and a twangy nasal voice knows, hard country is most definitely uncool; its heartaches and hangovers can't even come close to the emotional restraint and impersonal cheer that wins friends and influences people. Thus, John Anderson's 1983 "Black Sheep" describes a character who is the family outcast simply because he shows little enthusiasm for the economic pursuits and conversational gambits of his brother the doctor and his sister the banker's wife. They spend their free time talking about their possessions with nary a mention of their disgraceful brother whose bragging rights center on the fact that he treats his dogs well and hopes that his wife will teach their children to pray.[14] The amusement evoked by this scenario works as a slippery slope for the shame. The joke isn't only on the singer, although due to his failure, he forfeits the prerogatives of his race and gender. Nevertheless, the listeners's laughter supports the black sheep as it rejects the predictable pleasures of white-sheep economic success.

This is not to say that white men have always monopolized hard country. Popular music scholars have often discussed the role of African Americans in country music, noting that there have *always* been black performers,[15] and many of the early stars' first lessons in their craft came from black musicians. Hank Williams, for example, credited a street singer named Tee Tot with teaching him to perform. Black harmonica player Deford Bailey was one of the first stars of the *Grand Ole Opry*, playing on the program from 1926 to 1941. Since then, however, few African Americans have achieved stardom. Ray Charles, already a prominent blues artist, released an album of country standards to great acclaim in 1962. Less spectacularly, Big Al Downing had three songs in the top 20 between 1978 and 1980.[16] The only other African American to have major success in country music far surpassed Downing's modest showing: Charley Pride enjoyed superstardom from the mid '60s to the early '80s with a series of upbeat love songs such as that paean to marital bliss, "Kiss an Angel Good Morning" (1971).[17] He often covered Hank Williams songs and claimed that "There's A Little Bit of Hank (Williams) in Me" in a 1980 album cut. While he may occasionally allude to hard country's biggest star, Pride the performer embodies an uncomplicated optimism that is antithetical to hard country.[18] Even as he chronicles bouts with manic depression in his 1994 autobiography, he insists that the condition is a controllable medical phenomenon rather than a psychological or emotional illness.[19] When he discusses his efforts at "trying to find my place in the white world of country music," he uncomplainingly characterizes them as "poignant" (156) even though he defused tension at concerts by opening with some version of this carefully crafted line: "I guess you're surprised to see me comin' out here wearin' this permanent tan and singing country music" (175).[20] By the end of his book, he asserts that there is little to hold back aspiring black country singers: "If a barrier exists now, it is most likely in their own minds and in their tastes and preferences" (287). Pride may well have suffered greatly from his hard times, but the character he presents to the world is an unquestionably successful one who suffers no incurable unease.

Two black singers with hard country leanings, Stoney Edwards and O. B. McClinton, had some limited exposure in the '70s. Edwards's 1975 single "Blackbird," with its references to "country niggers," was a sort of manifesto for a black hard country. The chorus went on to urge the Blackbird to keep singing proudly in spite of the scarecrows.[21] "Hank and Lefty Raised My Country Soul" (1973) showcased his ability to mimic these two hard country stars.[22] McClinton claimed Merle Haggard as his inspiration even as he emphasized his race in songs like "(Country Music is) American Soul."[23]

Women have obviously had great success in country music although very few recent performers could be called hard country singers. As Curtis Ellison has noted, the most popular women singers tend to sing about success (no matter how limited) (170 ff.). Tammy Wynette's image is more melodramatic than upbeat: "Stand By Your Man," her most famous song, notes that it can be "hard to be a woman."[24] Likewise, Loretta Lynn and Dolly Parton occasionally sing about hard times, but Ellison's observations seem especially accurate for the contemporary scene.[25] The biggest stars, such as Lynn, Parton, and Reba McEntire, repeatedly choose songs about women achieving independence and triumphing over adversity (170–216). Such adversity frequently takes the form of an unregenerate husband, the same type of loser who unabashedly plays and sings hard country songs. The first female stars thus staged their triumphal entry by engaging in some revisionist scolding. Kitty Wells had the first number one country hit by a woman artist with her "answer" to Hank Thompson's "The Wild Side of Life" (1951).[26] In this lament, Thompson complains about the "honky-tonk angel" who prefers prostitution to being the singer's wife. The song's first line, "I didn't know God made honky-tonk angels" is explicitly corrected in Wells's 1952 title: "It Wasn't God Who Made Honky-Tonk Angels."[27]

Wells's famous lament about women as scapegoats for masculine misdeeds could serve as women country singers' commentary on many hard country songs. Even when they aren't directly responding to masculine whining and wrongdoing, country women are often angry about such antics. Some of Loretta Lynn's most memorable songs eloquently deride these pitiful breadwinners and bedmates. In 1966, for example, she warned her man not to "Come Home a-Drinkin' (with Lovin' on Your Mind)." "The Pill" (1975), with its rustic comparison between a childbearing woman and a hen, actually celebrates the metaphor's modern inaptness: a jubilant yet exasperated woman warns her man that he can no longer "set this chicken."[28] (In "real life," Lynn credits her husband with her success simply because she had to constantly struggle against him. The words she chooses are interesting: "If [he] didn't keep telling me I was a stupid hillbilly, I never would of made it" [105].)

More recent singers have approached hard country's themes from such a detached perspective that they suggest that this material really doesn't make sense in a woman's repertoire any more. Becky Hobbs's "Jones on the Jukebox" (1988) strings together lines from Jones's songs to express a woman's heartbreak in an upbeat song that is so clever that it reveals no trace of Jones's trademark self-pity.[29] Rosie Flores's "Girl Haggard" (1993) uses Haggard titles to a similar effect although in place of failed love, Flores's character suffers from mock unrequited love: the singer claims to be a brunette stranded in a trailer park, dreaming that Merle will one day whisk her away to a better life.[30] As if to underscore the singularity of a girl Haggard, Donald Lindley, Flores's drummer and designated wisecracker, closes the song by remarking, "I really don't think I need to hear that again."

In short, women and black country singers rarely cast themselves as black sheep. Likewise, while mainstream country singers croon reassuringly about rural idylls, cloying romance, family values, and patriotism, hard country singers moan the blues of white-trash tragedy: broken homes, decrepit houses, binge drinking, dead-end jobs, and criminal records. That's why Jerry Lee Lewis's songs have always been played on country radio, and why he had such a convincing hit in 1977 with "My Life Would Make a Damn Good Country Song."[31] In tune with their names, then, the themes of hard country singers violate the standards of American dreaming. "The Night Life" (i.e., the life the singer leads) isn't "the good life," wrote Willie Nelson in one of the many hard country standards to his credit.[32] Thus, instead of striving for the good life, hard country singers unabashedly portray themselves and their listeners as the "low other" of American culture. I borrow this term from Stallybrass and White, who have argued that interlocking hierarchies of high and low are a "fundamental basis of . . . sense-making in European cultures" (3), and, as cultural historians such as Lawrence Levine have shown, American culture is not nearly so far removed from the Old Countries as we would like to think. The name of the central institution of country music, the *Grand Ole Opry* (1927–), comes from a dialogue that engages exactly this sort of "sense-making." While at first it was called *WSM Barn Dance* (1925–1927), Bill Malone explains that in 1927, George Hay's *WSM Barn Dance* played after NBC's *Musical Appreciation Hour* with Dr. Walter Damrosch. One night while introducing a number

> Damrosch remarked that "while most artists realize that there is no place in the classics for realism, I am going to break one of my rules and present a composition . . . which depicts the onrush of a locomotive . . . " When the WSM country music show came on the air, Hay announced that while there was no room for realism in the classics, the following three hours would be devoted to nothing but realism. Then Hay introduced one of the show's most popular players, Deford Bailey . . . who played a train song, "Pan American Blues," which had been inspired by the famous southern train that ran near Bailey's home. When the performance was over, Hay said, "For the past hour we have been listening to music taken largely from grand opera, but from now on we will present 'The Grand Ole Opry.'" (75)

Hard country men now repeatedly emphasize their stake in this lowland. Although Lefty Frizzell usually sang in a confessional first person, his songwriting partner Whitey Shafer claims that Lefty "wrote things from a woman's side of view, most of the time. He said, 'Always remember that.'"[33] At other times, Frizzell emphasized masculine enfeeblement; when he was 24 years old, he sang "I'm an Old, Old, Man" (1952); I "Just Can't Live That Fast

Any More," he complained four years later.[34] In at least two of his songs, Merle Haggard's complaints center on his race and gender: "I'm a White Boy" and "White Man Sings the Blues." While this emphasis on skin color presumably allows Haggard to proclaim his membership in the most powerful group in class-unconscious America, in songs like "Working Man Blues" and "A Working Man Can't Get Nowhere Today," he reminds his listeners of the hard work, hard luck, and hard times that characterize hard country lives.[35] In Haggard's vision, the working man can't "cross over" to a better life; he is permanently exiled to the "country."

Since this particular form of country music is now dominated by white males, the "low otherness" of the hard country stars can be nothing other than a painful class distinction. In fact, the theme of "White Man Sings the Blues" imagines a class solidarity that transcends race;[36] the singer, after describing a duet sung with a black bluesman, uses the chorus to comment on this harmony: he finds himself singing the blues with a black man because they're "on the same side of the railroad track where people have nothing to lose." Likewise, the "white boy" cheerfully seeks employment that doesn't require a college degree. Moreover, in Haggard's vision, the working class doesn't disappear with their traditional work. In "They're Tearing the Labor Camps Down" (1972), Haggard bemoans postwar prosperity by asking where hungry men can go. They can be pushed out of mainstream sight, but they are never out of Haggard's or other hard country minds.

Indeed, it can be argued that this desperate character underpins the most pleasant American dreams although he may now just as readily take the form of a dim-witted hacker as a reckless drifter. Hard country songs now play off and play down the "oppressive confidence" of the professional, the intellectual, and the technocrat. An early Haggard song states the situation baldly: "where I am and where I'm goin' didn't take a lot of knowin' but I take a lot of pride in what I am"; he goes on to note that when he's talking to himself, it's "man to man," which implies that the situation with other interlocutors is not so comfortably equitable ("I Take a Lot of Pride in What I Am" [1968]). More recently and more humorously, Cletus T. Judd and Buck Owens tell the story of "The First Redneck on the Internet," who thought a computer monitor was a television and the keyboard was a way to type in the name of the program he wanted to see. When he enters "WWW," he hopes to find a wrestling match but instead discovers how to empty his ex-wife's bank account and more.[37]

"High-Tech Redneck," a recent George Jones song (1993), even strips away the pride of the "know-nothing," giving the information-age ideal a typically abject spin as Jones portrays a foolish rustic's unrequited love for modern gadgets. As it turns out, the much vaunted information explosion has not scat-

tered valuable shards for just anyone to amass. This character's attempts to
join the information age only lead him deeper into redneck abjection (and perhaps debt). None of this "bumpkin"'s expensive equipment conveys knowledge and taste; without it, evidently, he would be watching rasslin' matches;
with it he can only exponentially increase the number of matches he can
watch.[38] The oxymoron that ironically yokes "high-tech" to "redneck" makes
the absence of supposedly innate taste conspicuous. Indeed, it is just that mys-
tified knowledge which renders technology unironically "high" and hence in-
compatible with rednecks. The song, then, does not mask the dynamic of class
distinction. While reveling in this technophile's burlesque lowness, the song
works by allowing Jones and his listeners to laugh at the animating lie of most
American popular culture: the equation of purchasing power with power.[39] As
Barbara Ehrenreich has claimed, the affluent have shown an increasing tendency since the 1960s to elevate their status by eschewing readily available
mass-produced items and cultural choices: "As a result, the cultural gap between the classes was beginning to take a new form: not simply more, and
more expensive, things for the more fortunate but the contrived appearance of
less" (131–132). Thus, money and the gadgets it buys isn't enough to blanch
this white man's red neck; the very abundance of his machinery worsens his
degradation. It is the lack of some mysterious acculturating knowledge, some
evidence of refined taste, that seems to permanently keep the "low other" redneck in his alienated place.

That place is often called a honky-tonk, a place where the abject male literally and figuratively hits the bottom, a degraded place where hard country
plays. Tony Scherman cites a Texas law of the '30s and '40s that defined it as a
place where "conduct . . . [is authorized that is] lewd, immoral or offensive
to public decency."[40] In fact, the name of this place bears a reminder of hard
country's archetypal character. We all know what honkies are even though I
don't think people remember that when they use the term "honky-tonk"; according to Tichi, "the very term . . . is evidently black slang meaning 'white
shack'" (7).[41] While mainstream country songs often portray the honky-tonk
as a countrified party spot,[42] whatever pleasure the hard country honky-tonk
offers is fleeting if not outright illusory. This is where men break their homes
(with some help from honky-tonk angels), waste their paychecks, fall off
barstools, and burst into tears. Dwight Yoakam's "It Won't Hurt" (1985)
wrings low comedy from drunken bragging by asserting that neither falling
off barstools nor stumbling through the street can cause pain. It is crucial to
note that the hard country honky-tonk is not even in the country; instead, it is
a space of urban desolation. Hank Williams's "Honky-Tonk Blues" (1949)
spelled out the chain of events in typically compressed style: leaving a home

on a rural route is the beginning, but the end is a bad case of the citified "honky-tonk blues."[43] The move to the city doesn't lead the man uptown. A recent song makes the class and gender configuration quite clear:

> She took off to a high-society school
> But I earned my degree from ol' Honky-Tonk U.
> She hit the highway
> I took the dirt road
> She went to William and Mary
> I went to Haggard and Jones.[44]

In this cheerfully paced chorus, the joke in the pairs of names (William and Mary versus Haggard and Jones) portrays hard country as a state of provincial ignorance and low status that can be explained by the white man's low aspirations and poor taste. Burlesque punning lets the woman rise above this squalor: at William and Mary she takes the *high* way while the male graduate of Honky-Tonk U is following Haggard and Jones down a "dirt road" to possible stardom and certain alienation.

In the meantime, his life will consist of tears and beers, staple ingredients of hard country's burlesque routines and the stepping stones to the sort of economic failure that "American Cool" is supposed to prevent. The three are in practice inseparable: "What's Made Milwaukee Famous (Has Made a Loser Out of Me)" cries Jerry Lee Lewis (1968),[45] and David Allan Coe, in a duet with George Jones, cleverly complains that he can't hold onto anything but "This Bottle in My Hand" (1980). George Jones had a huge success with "I Threw Away the Rose" (1967), a Haggard composition that gives "The Days of Wine and Roses" a hard twist: the singer claims to have entered adulthood on a path to success but then perversely chose to keep the wine and throw away the rose. Some country radio stations refused to play Webb Pierce's classic drinking song, "There Stands the Glass" (1953), since programmers took seriously the singer's ponderous alcoholic optimism: he believes that a drink can hide his tears and drown his fears; he also implies that he may have enough self-control to take only one drink.[46] However, many songs make the joke more obvious by clearly explaining that fears don't drown and tears can't be hidden. Ernest Tubb justified it in 1950 with "You Don't Have to Be a Baby to Cry"[47] and George Jones used the same metaphor in his 1990 album cut, "I Sleep Just Like a Baby," in which the singer claims to wake up crying every hour.[48] Buck Owens, too, underscored the frequency of crying jags with a song that stresses predictability as if it were introducing a weekly television show: "Crying Time" (1964). Johnny Paycheck's "The Real Mr. Heartache" plays with the game show hook of asking the title character to reveal himself by standing up and crying.[49]

In this vale of tears, the honky-tonk is the last stop. A George Jones song from 1981, "Still Doin' Time," even equates it with a life sentence: "Still doin' time in a honky-tonk prison."[50] Countless songs delusorily propose the honky-tonk as a home away from home;[51] an early Haggard hit features a hero who tries to act jubilant about his neon-lit new address, but the isolation of this character becomes clear when he begs whoever is listening to pay him a visit ("Swingin' Doors" [1966]). The only fate worse than honky-tonking is not honky-tonking. In a 1990 single, for example, George Jones portrays a humbled husband who has exhausted his homes away from home. The song begins as a beseeching telephone call to an estranged wife; the singer tells her he never should have left, then asks her to let him come home. Her solution to his dilemma, introduced by a dramatic pause, reveals that she is as mad as Kitty and Loretta would be. He's either uninformed or lying when he claims that everything has closed down leaving him no place to go. "Hell Stays Open All Night Long," she reminds him.[52]

The range of responses to such humiliation is limited, at least in the hard country lexicon. Simple acceptance is rare, although in Haggard's "Hungry Eyes" (1969), the singer sees both sides, sadly explaining that "Mama never had the luxuries she wanted but it wasn't 'cause my Daddy didn't try." This song epitomizes hard country's relationship with the outside world. Working against the singer's parents were "another class of people [who] put us some-where just below." The gender roles, too, are typical. The woman wants to have what that other class of people has but her man cannot give it to her. Haggard's character here sympathizes with his parents' plight even though he doesn't want us to pity them. After all, he is talking not about starvation but about a cultural poverty that denies his mother not necessities but the luxuries that would make her *look* different—that is, not country. Nor does he believe that this couple will eventually inherit the earth. While Garth Brooks, assuming that this is the best of all possible worlds, thanks God for "Unanswered Prayers" (1990),[53] Haggard's characters lose hope and courage as their prayers for a better way of life go unanswered. More frequent than this defensive res-ignation, though, are the songs where abjection shades into impotent rage. The opening line and title of one of the most popular songs of the '70s, Johnny Paycheck's "Take This Job and Shove It" (1977),[54] would seem to incite rebel-lion against that other class of people, but in fact the song is about the failure of such impulses.[55] While the verses describe abusive supervisors, dead-end labor, and an unhappy home, the song never goes beyond venting dissatisfac-tion. The singer's wife has left him, and the line introducing the final refrain tells us that even though his family was his only reason for holding a job, the singer can't even succeed at becoming unemployed. He will still lead a life of abject desperation: he wishes he had the nerve to actually speak the song's title to his foreman but, in fact, he's unable to take such bold action.

George Jones specializes in such feeble, fantasy-ridden mayhem. In "I'm Gonna Burn Your Playhouse Down" (ca. 1960), he explains that he's "got an achin' in my heart and arson on my mind."[56] The opening verse of his 1989 "The King Is Gone" provides an even sillier version of a story that blames women for the abject hero's failures. The song opens with the simple strumming of a desolate acoustic guitar as the singer tells his norm-enforcing, estranged spouse that he spent the previous night pouring Jim Beam out of an Elvis decanter and into an empty Flintstones jelly jar. The scene is even more carefully set when he evokes the slovenly kitchen where this binge takes place; he must clear a table even to find room for his little glass, and as he pulls up a chair, he also pulls up some of the floor. These details evoke a trailer park or a remote suburb where cars rot in front yards. Otherwise, the circumstances are deliberately ambiguous: the speaker implies that he has been unjustifiably dumped by his beloved. As his misery overtakes him, a bass and steel guitar begin to throb, and he bathetically makes his point: "I pulled the head off Elvis, filled Fred up to his pelvis, Yabba dabba doo, the King is Gone, (and So Are You)."[57] While the singer wallows in this misty self-pity, he catalogs not so much his flaws as a mate but rather his failure to live up to American standards of good taste and affluence. He sings about tacky mass merchandise and childish popular entertainments, the symbols of his lowness. He then goes on to hallucinate a dialogue with the dead and fictional characters who grace his drinking utensils. While his original addressee—his rejecting mate—evidently holds him to the standards of American Cool, his new dialogue partners validate his predilections even as they reveal his estrangement from contemporary American culture: "Elvis said find 'em young, Fred said old-fashioned girls are fun." The third (last) verse reduces to absurdity the metaphor that parallels this man's disintegration with that of Elvis: "then I broke Elvis's nose pouring the last drop from his toes; yabba dabba doo, the King is gone and so are you." Even in a spectacle of self-destruction, the hard country hero cannot outdo the bloated rock star on the bathroom floor; he must make do with broken bottles on a decaying kitchen floor.

The burlesque failure can be further heard when hard country singers articulate society's notions of what successful men are like. As George Jones sang in 1992,

> Some men look for diamonds
> Some men look for gold
> I'm just tryin' to find myself
> Before I get too old.

Different people have their ways
of measuring success.
Maybe it's not the right way
But wrong's what I do best. . . .
If they held a losers playoff,
well there'd be no contest;
cause I've had lots of practice
and Wrong's What I Do Best.[58]

Songs like this make it clear that hard country is not simply about naive blunderers and unrestrained crybabies. These types would never enter, let alone win, a "losers playoff." Indeed, elsewhere in American culture, failure is a taboo subject[59]—that's why Willy Loman, in Arthur Miller's *Death of a Salesman*, commits suicide rather than break the news of his unemployment to his family. The idealized self-made man profits from gold and diamonds, but in a burlesque universe, there are also prizes for those who pursue the prodigal pleasures of "doing wrong." This contest allows the abject male to make a spectacle of himself in a culture that defines masculine success precisely by the requirement to "mak[e] something of yourself."[60] Yet another Jones song, "The Grand Tour" (1974), uses the spectacle motif from the start: "Step right up," proclaims the inexplicably abandoned husband turned "carnival barker"[61] who invites listeners to view the painful memories on display in every room of the house.[62] His "If Drinkin' Don't Kill Me" (1981) opens with an even more ludicrous image: as the singer pulls up to his house at dawn after a night in a honky-tonk, he falls asleep over the steering wheel. This collapse sets off the horn, which announces to the whole block that he's come home drunk once again.[63] Jones sings the first line of each verse in a conversational a cappella; this technique, combined with the present-tense narration, underscores the spectacle of abjection. The chorus adds an unforgettable boast to this effect; the drunkard claims that he could use his blood to fuel a still. The title, repeated in the chorus, reminds us that the situation is supposed to be sad—"if drinkin' don't kill me, her memory will"—and the plaintive harmonica of the accompaniment evokes some semblance of sorrow. The obtrusive steel guitar, however, wobbles as if to mock the drunken stupor that the narrator falls into at the end of the last verse. Jones fans may applaud, but they must also participate in a dialogue of abjection since the whole neighborhood of abruptly awakened, upright homeowners is disgusted.

These songs seem to mirror the tabloid cocktail of comedy and failure that characterizes stories about Jones's lurid marriage to Tammy Wynette, his extravagant addictions, his arrest record, and his lavish spending sprees and bankruptcies. According to Jones's producer Billy Sherrill, in concert Jones would close "If Drinkin' Don't Kill Me" by replacing "*her* memory will" with "Tammy's memory will."[64] At the same time, Jones's drinking is reputed to be at least partly theatrical. He may have found his nickname—the Possum—thanks to his facial features, but his habit of feigning incapacitating intoxication in order to avoid unpleasant tasks allowed the name to stick.[65] The private George Jones most likely suffers greatly from unnameable demons, but the more a fan knows about Jones, the more complicated the choice between the man and the performer, and between laughter and tears, becomes. As Norro Wilson, one of Jones's chief songwriters in the '70s, says, "If people laughed at some of the things we've written, well great, 'cause we laughed, too" (Roland, 130). Jones himself mentions another possible blend of emotion—anger and hilarity—as he imagines himself in yet another abject dialogue:

> I really get mad about it when somebody calls me a hillbilly. . . .
> A lot of your so-called educated people tend to look down on other
> kinds of people, almost like they was peasants. Sure, we're from the
> country, but we went to school. I went to the seventh grade. Course
> . . . when they're talkin' like that, we're laughin' all the way to
> the bank. (Bob Allen, 180)

Jones occasionally gets some trite revenge through his last laughs and by living well, but more frequent are his public violations of masculine taboos, his breaking down and passing out. His sporadic wealth is his private pleasure, but his abjection provides burlesque pleasure whether on a disc, a stage, or a tabloid page.

"I Never Go Around Mirrors," written by Lefty Frizzell and recorded both by him (1974) and by Merle Haggard (1976), delivers another strong dose of such pleasure. Haggard's rendition begins with a plodding beat, a keening steel guitar, and what seems to be some scolding from a standard-bearer of American Cool: "I can't stand to see a good man go waste / One who never combs his hair or shaves his face / A Man who leans on wine . . . / Oh it tears me up to see a grown man cry." The chorus that follows this sole verse reveals that this song, like "Wrong's What I Do Best," actually burlesques the secrets of success. The singer explains that in order to cope with his objections to abjection, he simply arranges things so "I never go around mirrors."[66] Haggard, though, doesn't always joke about hard country abjection; in "I Can't Hold Myself in Line" (1968), for example, he forthrightly denounces the honky-tonk compulsion:

I disagree with the way that I'm living . . .
But I just can't stand myself at times
And you're better off to just leave and forget me
Cause I can't hold myself in line.
My weakness is stronger than I am
But I've always been the losin' kind
And I'm full steam ahead
Down the wrong road of life.
And I Can't Hold Myself in Line.

This song seems to hold a special place in Haggard's repertoire: he cites it in his autobiography, and the same year, he rereleased it as a duet with Johnny Paycheck (1981). In it, he seems to have internalized the middle-class mores that he usually protests in his music. He even justifies the woman who is evidently considering abandoning him.[67] Still, hard country comedy is not completely forsaken. Few other popular music forms use oxymorons like "my weakness is stronger than I am." Nevertheless, the self-hatred in this country song is plain enough; books like *The Hidden Injuries of Class* movingly describe the masculine tendency to bury the indignities of class in shamed self-recrimination and prickly pride. Haggard at his best wrenchingly uncovers this tendency, but Haggard at his worst oozes an empty self-righteousness. In a 1990 song about flag burning, for example, Haggard makes the absurd claim that only he and "Crippled Soldiers" care about the fate of the United States. (Perhaps his openly self-parodic performance in Barry Levinson's *Wag the Dog* [1997] marks the end of his superpatriot persona.)

"Okie from Muskogee" (1969) is not Haggard at his worst although it might be Haggard at his most complicated. In this song, he hits his most compellingly discordant pitch since he creates a persona who voices both sides of the dialogue of abjection. Much of what Haggard has said about this song suggests that it contains strong elements of satire. Nevertheless, those whose first (and only) exposure to Haggard is this song tend to take it as an anthem to redneck provincialism.[68] Those who have always and attentively listened to Haggard, though, recognize that the Okie is a character whose words need not be taken literally. In fact, the prettified acoustic picking and subdued brush percussion that accompany Haggard's calm delivery are far from rousing. "I didn't intend for 'Okie' to be taken as strongly from my lips as it was," Haggard says (Roland, 35). Elsewhere he notes that "it has so many different messages. It has messages that I didn't even know were there."[69] Yet in most interviews, his discussion of the song consistently underscores the autobiographical themes that have always characterized his songwriting; he mentions the family farm just 20 miles south of Muskogee.

> My father worked hard on his farm, was proud of it, and got called
> white trash once he took to the road as an Okie. . . . There were a
> lot of other Okies from around there, proud people whose farms
> and homes were foreclosed . . . and who then got treated like
> dirt. Listen to that line: 'I'm proud to be an Okie from Muskogee.'
> Nobody has ever said that before in a song. (Roland, 32)[70]

Merle was born in Bakersfield three years after his family's migration so
Merle himself is not technically an Okie from Muskogee although he has good
reason for sympathizing with the displaced and estranged men he associates
with the term "Okie."

Nevertheless, Okie pride in "livin' right" is also punctured in the song. An
Okie who had to leave Muskogee is one thing; those who stayed behind are another; they must have enjoyed more good fortune or possessed less gumption
than those who left, and the song is about life in 1960s Muskogee, not 1940s
California. In that sense, the strongly rooted Muskogeans aren't Okies at all;
they belong to the scornful "other class of people" that kept Mama down in
"Hungry Eyes." In concert, I heard Haggard introduce "Okie from Muskogee"
as a "song for mothers" in contrast to "Hungry Eyes," which he called a "song
for mamas."[71] Thus, Haggard mouths the words of his usual protagonists while
his performance twists those words into a hard country response. The description of the Okie's clothes smacks more of *Gentleman's Quarterly* than the sincere musings of an ordinary guy; only a fashion hack or an ironist would call
boots "manly footwear." Likewise, when a high school dropout who's done solitary confinement in San Quentin writes that "football's still the roughest thing
on campus, and the kids here still respect the college dean," he just might be
poking fun at the Muskogee residents who display these mild manners of the
middle class. In fact, on the record, the word "college" seems to be sung with a
bit of a sneer. The complexity of this situation becomes clear when Haggard recounts the inspirational remark that sparked the 20 minute songwriting session
that produced "Okie." He recalls that as his tour bus passed a sign that said
"Muskogee, thataway, or whatever",[72] one of his band members jokingly differ-
entiated the musical passengers from the Oklahomans; from this contrast comes
Haggard's smug first-person plural announcement in the first line that "we
don't smoke marijuana in Muskogee." Haggard himself, however, supposedly
told a reporter that Muskogee was the only place he didn't smoke it.[73] For the
smug citizens of Muskogee, the equally illegal and more forcefully mind-alter-
ing white lightning is "still the biggest thrill of all." At the end of "Okie," Haggard sings this line twice, underscoring the fact that these thrill-seeking "Okies"
don't completely hold themselves in line.[74]

The "responses" to "Okie from Muskogee" seemed to overlook Haggard's abject dialogue with the "oppressive confidence" of those straight-and-narrow-minded Oklahomans. Thus, according to Jimmie Rogers, Jerry Jeff Walker's "Up Against the Wall, Redneck" (1973) "carried the original idea [of Haggard's song] to its illogical conclusion."[75] The redneck of this song is also an Oklahoman. The chorus portrays him simply as a violent, middle-aged loser who haunts honky-tonks, torments hippies, and raises hell. The only explanation for his behavior is his upbringing; this psychopathic mama's boy bears no responsibility for his behavior; according to the song, the man's mother created this monster.[76] Lacking the tonal complexity of "Okie from Muskogee," "Up Against the Wall, Redneck," with its threatening title and third-person description of the redneck, clearly separates the singer from the subject. Similarly, Kinky Friedman's "Asshole from El Paso" (1973) presents a character so despicable that no one can seriously endorse his grotesque braggadocio.[77] While their link to "Okie from Muskogee" is clear, the "illogic" of these songs lies in the choice of epithets: although the term "redneck" certainly carries some historical and political freight, Walker's song doesn't unload it,[78] and no matter how you look at it, an asshole is just that. "Okie," however, is unmistakably a class-, race-, and history-laden name that Haggard needs in his bag of aliases. He walked away from a taping of *The Ed Sullivan Show* when he was asked to sing "Surrey with the Fringe on Top" (Hemphill, 330);[79] this refusal to mouth Rodgers's and Hammerstein's platitudes about Oklahoma indicates just how committed Haggard is to maintaining the complex stance of the hard country star.

O. B. McClinton's elaborations on this song also amplify the complexity. In 1972 he included a cover version of it on his debut album, *O. B. McClinton Country* (which clearly indicated his race). He exaggerated every aspect of the song, singing with the thickest hick accent possible, bleating the last word of each bar, and replacing Haggard's gentle acoustic accompaniment with an aggressive sawing fiddle. The contrast seemed to imply that Haggard had *not* sung a redneck anthem. Similarly, another cut on this album, "Country Music That's My Thing" pitted McClinton in a debate with his wife and friend, who question why a black man should participate in this music. His answer points to his country heroes, not only Charley Pride, but also Webb Pierce and Johnny Cash. The next year, he recorded yet another version of "Okie," this time called "Obie from Senatobie" (Senatobia, Mississippi). While professing a pride in his origins similar to Haggard's, he parades forth degrading stereotypes about southern blacks. Instead of Haggard's "we still wave old glory down at the courthouse," for example, McClinton ostensibly brags about eating watermelon down on Main Street.[80] Coming from a black man, these remarks can be easily interpreted as irony whereas Haggard's were just as readily thrown on the literal-minded fields of stone.

Finally, at least one "redneck" song preserves some of the complexity of "Okie": David Allan Coe's "Longhaired Redneck" (1975). An ex-convict like Haggard,[81] Coe claims an even closer resemblance in his chorus when he says he looks like Merle Haggard and sounds like David Allan Coe (although he mimics Haggard as he sings this line). While Haggard created an ambivalent character in "Okie from Muskogee," Coe seems to be abjectly and aggressively speaking up for himself in response to a heckler who interrupts a performance to criticize his earrings and long hair. The setting itself is significant: Coe, like his hard country compatriots, experiences unease even in a honky-tonk. The burlesque twist comes when we hear what name he wants to be called; he's upset when the heckler accuses him of not being country, and he proudly insists that his long hair doesn't cover up his red neck. He goes on to suggest that someone should inform the heckler that Coe is a tough ex-con who could resort to violence if further provoked. What is interesting about this scenario is the blurred distinction between the countercultural "hippies" that Coe rejects and the fierce redneck that he embraces. Both wear long hair and jewelry to reject middle-class masculinity (and, according to Larry King, Coe's mother claims he wore a dress until he was seven years old [73]), yet people who can't tell the difference make Coe violently angry. As in his "If That Ain't Country," the key term and distinguishing factor turns out to be "country": that's what rednecks are that hippies aren't. In other words, the differences are class markers such as education and sophistication. What the literal-minded heckler in this song wants to see is an ignorant hick, a straightforward Muskogee-esque performance featuring a simple-minded rube with an uncool brush cut and manly footwear. That's what he means when he says "country." Coe, angrily aware of the abjection such a definition both requires and conceals, refocuses the heckler's vision of "country" from an illusion of his own superiority to a threat to his safety.[82] The inappropriately ethereal "oohs" and "ahs" of the "girl singers" in the background reinforce the burlesque representation of country simplicity, but the rest of the song goes on to carefully place Coe in the lineage of hard country music; in addition to claiming a resemblance to Haggard, he claims that he can sing all of Hank Williams's songs and that Johnny Cash helped arrange his release from prison.[83] In fact, as he goes through this roll, he skillfully mimics all the hard country acts he follows even as he amplifies the angry connotations of their lexicon.

Coe in some ways is the "hardest" and thus the most burlesque performer of recent times. He bills himself as "The Mysterious Rhinestone Cowboy," an unflattering nickname that conjures up all the low-rent traumas and low tastes associated with hard country—at least until the wholesome crossover success Glen Campbell "stole" it, shortened it, and sweetened it into his own hit single (1975), autobiography title (1994), and nickname, "Rhinestone Cowboy."[84] In the meantime, Coe wrote "Would You Lay with Me (in a Field of Stone)," recorded "Stand By Your Man" in 1981, several years before Lyle Lovett and a European film director made it hip, and wrote "Take This Job and Shove It" although Johnny Paycheck had the hit record with it. Many of his own recordings are too profane for mainstream radio; "You Never Even Called Me by My Name" was his first record to receive significant airplay (1975). Written by Steve Goodman, the lyrics in many ways seem to be a series of unrelated statements. Put in the context of hard country, though, they make typically imperfect sense out of the clichés of abjection. Accompanied by an exaggeratedly twangy electric guitar and an overbearing Dobro, the solemn opening lines portray the whiny fatalism of the rustic loser: "It was all that I could do to keep from crying, sometimes it seems so useless to remain." The chorus reinforces this impression, adding a vaguely delineated woman to victimize her man.

> I'll hang around as long as you will let me
> And I never minded standing in the rain
> But you don't have to call me darlin', Darlin'
> You never even called me by my name.

In the woman's eyes, the singer is a nameless nobody, but as in "Longhaired Redneck," the mention of name-calling leads to a country-star roll call and impersonation routine; this time the singer claims that he doesn't need to be called Waylon Jennings, Charley Pride, or Merle Haggard. But whatever he is called, it is the hard country performance that gives him an identity. Coe then breaks into a recitation while the twanging and wailing continues. He tells his listeners that the songwriter claimed that this composition was "the perfect country and western song." Coe explains how he wrote Goodman a letter, arguing that a song that didn't say "anything at all about Mama, or trains, or trucks, or prison, or getting drunk" could not be considered flawless.[85] Goodman responded to the criticism by writing a new last verse; Coe then was convinced to make a record of this now perfected song:

> I was drunk the day my ma got out of prison
> And I went to pick her up in the rain
> But before I could get to the station in my pickup truck
> She got runned over by a damned ol' train.[86]

Personal disasters can't get much worse or more perverse than this, but hyperbolic hokiness is what *makes* the song perfect. It has all the elements of bur-

lesque abjection: the dialogue with a righteous and disgusted advocate of conventional manhood, the contrived comedy that pretends to endlessly restate
the obvious, and the stunning unoriginality.[87] These features make the song
part of an immediately recognizable tradition that allows the wretched white
man to emerge from the spectacle of failure with a star's name. That's entertainment, but it's also essential to the meaning of hard country. When the Possum, or the Hag, or the Mysterious Rhinestone Cowboy deliberately sink in
our estimation, they tempt us either to take up the mostly white banner of oppressive confidence or to laughingly and tearfully wave the white flag with
these winners of losers contests. They seem willing to repeat themselves until
you get their point. But when the joking is laid aside, they also remind us that
white men can and do lose that struggle, and it gets harder and harder to call it
by its name.

3

The hard act to follow

*Hank Williams
and the legacy
of hard country
stardom*

Hank Williams became
one of the greatest
American songwriters. The
keys to his greatness as a
writer were sincerity and
simplicity. Everybody
understands what a Hank
Williams song means.
    —*Roger M. Williams*

Few writers, in any
medium, have matched his
naked sincerity.
    —*Don Cusic*

He set the standard for
writing lyrics with patent
sincerity.
    —*Colin Escott*

He would tell them the
truth, and they loved him
for it.
    —*Hank Williams Jr.*

Hank Williams hardened country music in several ways.
His songs, often reminiscent of early Tin Pan
Alley or sentimental, old-fashioned ballads, form
only part of his legacy. He coupled this atavistic
aura with an exciting new drive and a dramatic voice. His lyrics dangled in an equally deli-
cate balance. Country artists sang confessional
honky-tonk songs and lost-love laments before
Williams. What he did, by writing so many of his
own songs, was turn the country singer into a
complex character. In fact, he sang as at least two
characters. Most often, he was Hank Williams, a
deathly thin yet intensely alive presence who
sang about his own agony without aestheticizing
it; if anything, he tried, and of course failed, to
anesthetize it. Nevertheless, because of his defeat,
drug and alcohol abuse are now among the defining features of hard country. In a world of
straight thinkers, Williams (and the hard acts
that followed him) sang at the extremes of high
or low, stoned or painfully sober. When he sang
as his alter ego Luke the Drifter, though, he uni-
versalized and stigmatized this wayward condition. His death at age 29—euphemistically as-
cribed to heart failure—added a compelling twist,
proof that the honky-tonk blues were as fatal as
his songs said they were. The rigors of his job
killed him, and its solaces failed him just as they
would so many in postwar urban America. More
important than this story, invariably believed to
be sad and true, is the volatile blend of anger,
irony, and burlesque abjection that Williams gen-

erated and added to hard country. He spoke with the urbane world without ever mentioning country, and his success indicated that he spoke for millions. Most importantly for hard country, his success drew the attention of millions more who would much rather not have heard his nasal plaints. His failures, described in song after song, and reflected in his drunken demise, captured the devotion of his fans. He managed to both burn out and go out in a blaze of glory. Thus, the magnitude of his stardom and his untimely death set a high performance standard of hard living and hard dying. He ranked first on *Life*'s 1994 listing of "the 100 Most Important People in the History of Country" because "he wrote the rules for what everyone since 1950 has considered true country."[1] This act is indeed hard to follow.

One reason for this difficulty is that following Williams requires an early and at least partially self-inflicted death; examining mortal wounds has thus dominated most public discussions of him while the lingering side effects have been undiagnosed. Although both his hardscrabble childhood in rural Alabama and his unprecedented stardom lend a perfect setting for a Horatio Alger–like rags-to-riches myth, it has never struck Williams's biographers as an appropriate model for telling his story. Instead, they cast his life as a sad short story; Roger M. Williams called his book *Sing a Sad Song: The Life of Hank Williams* (1970); Jay Caress subtitled his book *Country Music's Tragic King* (1979); Chet Flippo borrowed one of Williams's sadder songs to name *Your Cheatin' Heart* (1981).[2] Likewise, commentators have always noted the sadness and even despair of Williams's lyrics. Don Cusic, in his introduction to *Hank Williams: The Complete Lyrics*, culminates his list of Williams's lyrical attitudes with it: a "sense of self-mocking humor, of faith and devotion, and of deep sad loneliness."[3] Ellison counts him as a representative of country music's "tragic troubadour" tradition by arguing that he usually sang about the misery of domestic strife (72). As my epigraphs indicate, just as important as this sadness is the belief that Williams really experienced it. In short, Williams's life story and his songs interchangeably demonstrate a compelling defeat.

But intense sadness alone does not make for hard country, and focusing solely on it underestimates Williams's significance. My point here isn't to argue with other commentators; it would be impossible to deny the emotional charge that Williams conveyed. However, I do want to argue that sincere sadness, or even sadness tempered by faith and humor, isn't the only factor in Williams's charisma. What's most striking about his sadness is its cultural resonance, including *when* he sang these songs and *where* he sang them. As Richard Leppert and George Lipsitz have pointed out, to sing sad songs with such success "in an age of exuberant and uncritical progress" serves as a critique of the Happy Days myth.[4] This observation needs to be taken one step further, especially since the happy days are long behind us yet Williams still finds listeners. This durability, I think, comes from Williams's position—he was unmistakably southern, and even with success, he stayed down in the South, "moanin' the blues" on one record after another. We don't normally think of sadness, or any emotion for that matter, as a form of criticism. Emotion, almost by definition, is the opposite of the sense of rationality and irony we attribute to criticism. Indeed, critical thinking is one of the higher human skills that the poor white Southerner stereotypically lacks—hence his tendency for unrestrained emotion. Williams, despite his entrenched reputation for soul-baring sincerity, created a far more reflective and restrained character. In place of the depraved, violent, and at best ridiculous rustics projected in novels such as *Tobacco Road* and in popular '40s and '50s films such as the Ma and Pa Kettle series and still surfacing in contemporary settings such as *Pulp Fiction* and *Falling Down*, Hank Williams *ironized* the role of the violent, shiftless redneck, and he did it at a time when prosperity should have offered him middle-class propriety. He persisted in calling himself a "Long Gone Daddy" precisely because he knew he was not a father who knew best. The abjection arose because he couldn't lose sight of the notion that *someone else* knew best. As he put it in "Mind Your Own Business," this kind of censoriousness "seems to be high tone," and in this scenario, he never got to do the minding.

Publicly, however, at least in the beginning of his career, Williams worked to build up middle-class appearances. Although his relationship with Audrey, his first wife, is now portrayed as tempestuous and inspirational,[5] an early article about him in the Montgomery (Alabama) *Examiner* reports that he couldn't readily explain how his songs about troubled relationships came about since "Mr. and Mrs. Hank Williams lead a model domestic life" (cited in Escott, *Hank Williams: The Biography*, 83). A 1950 article in *National Hillbilly News* also reported on domestic harmony: "Got 'Lovesick Blues'? No sir, not Hank Williams. . . . The real Hank Williams . . . is happily married to a beautiful girl and has two fine children" (cited in Peterson, *Creating*, 182). He closed his early morning Nashville radio shows by promising his son that he would be right home although he didn't necessarily keep this promise. Even when free of the dictates of public relations, he at least occasionally envisioned family happiness; he wrote a trite poem (unpublished during his lifetime) to his son, "Little Bocephus," expressing the desire to be a model father (fig. 3.1). While he never pretended to be a churchgoer, he occasionally told reporters that his songs were divinely inspired (Williams, *Sing a Sad Song*, 112). In Au-

Fig. 3.1: Hank Williams Sr. and Jr. pose together, ca. 1951. Courtesy Country Music Foundation.

gust of 1952, his firing from the *Grand Ole Opry*, officially attributed to absenteeism, was tantamount to losing his country music imprimatur. By this point, he had in fact missed or ruined many public appearances because of drunkenness, but like any other celebrity of his day, he had nothing to gain from a public admission of addiction or recovery. As a result, this inescapably public scandal caused him more pain than any other loss, claim Waylon Jennings and Hank Jr. in "The Conversation" (written with Richie Albright). Yet two months later (about 10 weeks before his death), he sold tickets to his second marriage ceremony (to Billie Jean Jones), a tawdry spectacle that nevertheless indicates that Williams, even at the height of his shame and addictions, clung to conventional rituals of social integration.

His voice, never the high-pitched whine it has been caricatured to be, embodied this same complexity. An open-throated yet unsteady baritone, Williams learned to sing without a microphone, and afterward, he never took advantage of the intimacy it allowed (except as Luke the Drifter). Radically unlike the raw and monotonous sincerity of Roy Acuff, or the cozy crooning of Eddy Arnold, or the stolid drawl of Ernest Tubb, the three big stars he outshone when his career peaked, Williams's manner nevertheless combined the appealing features of all these styles. In two bars he could chant some words with sober smoothness while he bleated others with a crazed intensity. For example, he strangles the adjective "loveless" but follows it with a tensely crisp "mansion," in "A Mansion on the Hill." These swift shifts generated a sense of honest sorrow catalyzed by theatrical energy,[6] and to make sure that the full effect was communicated, Williams insisted that his band play as blandly as possible: "keep it vanilla" was a typical directive (Escott, *Hank Williams: The Biography*, 37). As a result, the Drifting Cowboys' limp and wallowing sound plays a lazy foil to Williams's vocal intensity. Likewise, he seldom allowed musically created emotions, such as the melancholy conveyed by a minor key, to do dramatic work for him (although the haunting "Ramblin' Man" indicates that he could do so if he chose to). In short, he sang from a self-conscious distance that in theory he couldn't achieve.

Williams's two first single releases didn't achieve it. They were traditional-sounding gospel numbers, "Calling You" and "When God Comes and Gathers His Jewels." His 1949 breakthrough hit, "The Lovesick Blues," broke that pattern even though it was neither original nor musically characteristic of country or blues. Nevertheless, this complaint gained a huge audience for Williams's uneasy irony.[7] Tin Pan Alley writers Irving Mills and Cliff Friend wrote it in 1922 for a failed musical. Yodeling blackface vaudevillian Emmett Miller recorded it twice in the '20s, and obscure honky-tonker Rex Griffin did it in 1939. Williams owned recordings of both artists' versions of this song, and it was part of his stage repertoire well before his version entered the charts in March 1949. Contemporary reports suggest that it was Williams's performance style that made this version so popular; his yodeling elongations of words like "blues" and "lonesome" and "cry" conveyed a sad state of mind even as the melody's swingy rhythm excited listeners. Nevertheless, it is important to note that Williams, even though he can't be credited with writing the song or even with adding yodels (Griffin did that), did give it an interesting mood. The last line of the last verse, "this is all I've got to say," meant no doubt to add some showbiz dazzle to the song, worked to cleverly introduce Williams's constant sorrow and conjure up an unappreciative audience critical of this one note. Similarly, the self-pitying lament "I'm nobody's sugar daddy now" announced the recurring theme of unfulfilled manhood. Crucially, Williams's delivery of the lyrics confidently spreads the incurable unease to his listeners. Initially, he seems to be describing his state for an audience unfamiliar with his plight, but one of the strangest lyrics implied that they would share his fate: "she'll do you, she'll do me," he threatens or promises. Later, a few lines ("I've grown so used to you") seem to speak directly to the woman who abandoned him unless he's making yet another promise to his audience. Griffin clarified the matter by creating intimacy with his acoustic guitar. Emmett Miller's version was even more clear: the record begins with him speaking with another man, telling him that he had the "blues" rather than the "miseries." What follows, then, is a conversation about a heartless woman.

Producer Fred Rose and the rest of Williams's entourage hated the song for just this kind of incoherence, and indeed, the straightforward appeal to the heartless woman was by far the more familiar approach. George Morgan's "Candy Kisses," for example, the number one song on the chart before Williams's song displaced it, makes a similar complaint about unrequited love, but unlike Williams's shifting lyrics, "Candy Kisses" is unequivocally addressed to the woman. Williams's more ambiguous line, however, particularly in combination with the statements he sings explicitly to the audience, establishes a bond that promises a shameful yet shared experience. As Escott notes, "for all its flaws, Hank's record was utterly compelling"; it stayed at the top of the charts for 16 weeks, longer than any song that Williams wrote for himself (*Hank Williams: The Biography*, 93). *Opry* legend has it that Williams performed six encores of it on his June 1949 debut. Long after this success, Williams was often introduced with the childish moniker "The Lovesick Blues Boy." With this song, then, he established his performance as an electrifying balance between country's routine display of distress, an experience of that emotion, and a more novel display of the display for a group of judgmental witnesses.

Over the course of his career, Williams gave himself or acquired several other names that also juggled these elements. He hated his backwoodsy, biblical given name—Hiram—and refused to let his son bear it.[8] While plain Hank or Ol' Hank seemed to be names of his own devising, he occasionally used the regular guy name Herman P. Willis to escape from the burdens of stardom although even this bland name retained his initials and a taint of self-hatred; according to the Drifting Cowboys, Herman P. Willis was their "pet name for anyone who couldn't win for losing" (Escott, *Hank Williams: The Biography*, 135). He seems not to have invented or acquired any public name evoking the stature of full-blown manhood such as Jimmie Rodgers's "Singing Brakeman." Instead, his monikers waver between callow youth and decrepitude—even "Hank," for all its country-star heritage (Hank Snow, Hank Penny, Hank Thompson, Hank Locklin), also evokes worn-out raggedness.[9]

Williams also aimed for the more down-to-earth dignity of a cowboy. His early theme song—"Happy Roving Cowboy"—was borrowed from the Sons of the Pioneers (Escott, *Hank Williams: The Biography*, 23). Later, he introduced the rhinestone-studded Nudie suit to Nashville (named for the tailor, Nudie Cohen), and he was rarely photographed and never performed in anything but fancy western wear; he was particularly careful to cover his balding head with a Stetson hat.[10] Nevertheless, his appearance sent a different message; as Little Jimmy Dickens recalled, "Hank could wear the most expensive suit and it'd look like a sack because of the way he put it on."[11] (A spinal birth defect caused him constant pain and created both the old man's stoop that most photographs capture and the initial hunger for painkillers and sedatives that posthumous legend captures.) Likewise, the name of his band, the Drifting Cowboys, was an attempt to reinforce this western image; however, as Blaser notes, cowboys, who might need to rove in order to do their jobs, weren't aimless drifters but rather "that quintessential American symbol of individualism, innocence, and optimism" (22).

No evidence indicates that Williams ever called himself "the hillbilly Shakespeare,"[12] but this title, used most frequently by MGM president Frank Walker and thus intoned in nearly all accounts of Williams's career, conveys a mixture of praise and condescension that is important to Williams's status as the king of hard country, for no matter how eccentrically Williams adapted the cowboy image, he never staked a claim to the blissful ignorance his cowboy image might have allowed him. Instead, the name "hillbilly Shakespeare" insisted upon a contrast between European high art and inbred American low life, between the sublime and the ridiculous. Williams slyly demonstrates this burlesque position in an oft-quoted interview that appeared in the *Nation's Business* shortly after his death. Ostensibly explaining his theory about success in country music, he asserts that "you got to have smelt a lot of mule manure before you can sing like a hillbilly." While nearly all who cite this remark take it literally, there's no reason to believe that Williams, growing up in the small-town boardinghouses his mother ran, had ever smelled a lot of mule manure. As an image of his experience of the social world, however, mule manure or something like it may have fit well. His summarizing comment, with its acute awareness of class conflict, suggests just that: "[T]here ain't nothing strange about our popularity these days. It's just that there are more people who are like us than there are the educated, cultured kind."[13] The attention from "the educated, cultured kind" (who, after all, would be reading and mind-ing the *Nation's Business*) exacerbated Williams's incurable unease. Neverthe-less, by encompassing an audience that included this "kind," Williams elabo-rated country music's display of emotion, transforming it into the abject dialogue discussed in the previous chapter.

The songs "Honky-Tonkin'" and "Honky-Tonk Blues" provide excellent examples of Williams's complex perspective. While they are obviously set in low places, they also evoke the voices of propriety. "Honky-Tonkin'"(1947) was one of his first successful records although he didn't become a major star until mid-1949; "Honky-Tonk Blues" was a song he recorded with it, and then rerecorded at least three other times throughout his career (Escott, *Hank Williams: The Biography*, 177). A hit version was finally released in 1952. Williams's persistence with this tune, though, indicates the hold the theme must have had on him. Earlier honky-tonk songs such as Al Dexter's 1936 "Honky-Tonk Blues" (completely different from Williams's song of the same title) or "Pistol Packin' Mama" were jolly ditties about erotic suffering. Upbeat numbers written by Hank's friend (but no relation) Curley Williams such as "Georgia Boogie" (1948) and "Fiddlin' Boogie" (1949) tell of farmers so joy-fully intoxicated that they happily sell the farm in order to spend all their time dancing or performing in town (although obviously these forgotten tunes weren't nearly as successful as Williams's laments.) Honky-tonk women, es-sential characters in earlier and later honky-tonk songs, are incidental in Williams's songs. Rather than celebrating urban amusement, his songs say that honky-tonkin' masquerades as consolation for leaving the country. While the first song implies that "honky-tonkin'" offers pleasure, it can't be gained without humiliation. The singer invites a woman to accompany him to the city; if they do go honky-tonkin' together, however, he'll be in the role of gigolo since the invitation depends on her deciding to leave her current lover (or husband) for a while. She must also be willing to finance the trip.[14] He thus reveals that stepping into a honky-tonk, the place where country music plays, actually requires masculine failure, so in both songs, Williams yodels the title words as if they were gagging him.

"Honky-Tonk Blues" elaborates on the reason the singer seeks urban diver-sion. In this song, honky-tonking becomes a compulsive repetition of failure. The singer left the country because the city promised something better, but once there he couldn't achieve it so he goes into *every* honky-tonk in town in spite of himself. The cure for these blues (he says) is going back to the farm, where, evidently, there would be no need for honky-tonk music. There the singer could mature into tranquil manhood, something the unrecorded final verse suggests hasn't happened yet. In this verse, the singer imagines himself as a boy whose parents would prohibit further visits to honky-tonks.[15] But the fantasy of going home again must have sounded so preposterous—both from Williams's personal perspective and from the easily observed course of urbanization in America—that the verse was omitted from the version intended for public release. Even the homesick verse that he does sing seems purely theatrical: for his return, he says, he'll stow his worries underneath his arm as if they were a stage prop. He's calling up an audience rather than planning the prodigal's return. With this audience, Williams portrays himself as trapped in a sophisticated social milieu that hurts him. Except for the honky-tonk, there's no place that's even remotely like home for him. Thus, Williams's happy songs, such as the nearly nonsensical "Jambalaya," evoke exotic pastoral fantasies while the addictive urban honky-tonk exerts the force of reality. This force drags him down and keeps him metaphorically down on the farm even though he has literally left it. Caught between the alienating city where he can't thrive and the disreputable honky-tonk where he's trapped, Williams achieves the complex perspective that characterizes many of his country blues songs.

Williams carried this self-conscious stance one step further with his creation of yet another name, "Luke the Drifter." Luke barely sings and never swings, specializing instead in maudlin and moralistic recitations that give him authority over both the honky-tonk crowd and the martini set. Although the characterization "the drifter" links Luke to Williams's band the Drifting Cowboys, Luke, as his biblical name implies, tends to preach rather than confess. In fact, Williams, at manager Fred Rose's urging, created this alter ego to preserve his bad reputation on the jukeboxes. At the time, jukebox operators bought more records to stock their machines than fans bought for home record players. As Escott notes, "virtually all of the operators serviced bars, and the last thing they needed was for someone to punch up a Hank Williams record and get a sermon" (*Hank Williams: The Biography*, 125). Luke's identity wasn't a secret, though, so the name wasn't so much a disguise as a way to distinguish between hell-raising and hellfire. Usually accompanied by an andante, churchy-sounding organ, Luke sanctimoniously scolds those who suffer from the honky-tonk blues, particularly those who lead astray the honky-tonk angels, in "Too Many Parties and Too Many Pals."[16] In "Everything's Okay," he describes a visit to his benighted relatives on what might as well be Tobacco Road. While they experience what seems like endless misery and deprivation, they insist they have nothing to complain about. Of course, as the middling title indicates, they have nothing to rejoice about either. Their undignified complacency confirms the worst stereotypes about ignorant hillbillies, and the squalor Luke conveys would motivate any self-respecting denizen of a rural route to brave the honky-tonk blues rather than settle for a life of mindless endurance. Luke himself has obviously renounced country life in favor of peripatetic philosophy. Likewise, against the backdrop of Hank's songs of marital woe, Luke condemns squabbling couples bound for divorce court in "Help Me Understand." In "Mind Your Own Business," a honky-tonking Hank defends himself against some apparently scandalized onlookers who are disturbed by his marital spats and late night carousing while in "Be Careful of the Stones That You Throw,"[17] Luke shows far more concern for the state of the onlookers' souls. In "Men with Broken Hearts," Luke addresses a similar crowd, but he implicitly equates them with sniveling hillbillies, first by scolding "you" for your judgmental attitude, then by asserting that even "the greatest men" never get so big that they can't cry. Williams seemed particularly proud of this composition: "Isn't that the awfullest, morbidest song you ever heard in your life," he bragged to a reporter (Williams, *Sing a Sad Song,* 128). "A Picture from Life's Other Side," which abstractly describes various people's various heartaches, simply assumes that its audience would have no knowledge of people on the losing side if Luke didn't drift between life's two sides to bring it to them. While it's hard to imagine the cosseted classes lending a sympathetic ear to Luke's sobering sermons, Blaser notes that the very fact that Williams found such a large audience "suggests that more of the nation was ready to tune in to such emotions and ideas than has usually been recognized" (22). Whether those comfortably ensconced in life's better side liked what they heard hardly matters. That they were hearing it at all, or even that Williams performed as if they were, incorporated the abject perspective into hard country music. The horrified representative of middle-class morality and good taste had to engage in an uncomfortable dialogue with the hard country star.

It's likely that many of Williams's songs were written in a similar situation. Although publicly he was known as a songwriter, and even published a book on how to write songs, he often wrote in conscious or unconscious collaboration with others. For that matter, *Hank Williams Tells How to Write Folk and Western Music to Sell* (1951) was at best a collaboration with private-school teacher and songwriter Jimmy Rule; Escott speculates that "Hank's major contributions were to put his name and face on the front, and to produce the radio spots that advertised the booklet" (*Hank Williams: The Biography,* 165). That such a book was even produced, though, indicates the importance of Williams's image as a singing songwriter. His biographers, Flippo and Escott in particular, have subjected that image to some damaging truths, detailing how Williams would occasionally buy songs from other writers, borrow extensively—even actionably—from old standards, and rework his own or others' tunes with new lyrics. For example, his "Pan American" is set to the melody of the Carter Family's "Wabash Cannonball"—although it should be noted that A. P. Carter, too, sometimes drew on public domain tunes for his compositions. According to Escott, "I Saw the Light" uses the melody (and some lyrical ideas) from Albert E. Brumley's "He Set Me Free" (*Hank Williams: The Biography*, 62). Still, to the fan in the street, Williams's songs epitomize the voice of real experience, and most of his songs were mostly his own.

One key experience, though, doesn't immediately strike the ear, especially since Williams never mentioned it when fans or interviewers wanted to hear about his craft: his collaboration with his producer Fred Rose, a recovered alcoholic, a devout Christian Scientist, a successful songwriter who delivered songs to singers as diverse as Sophie Tucker and Gene Autry, and half owner of Acuff-Rose, the only song-publishing company in town when Williams came to Nashville. Williams recorded many songs written by Rose (perhaps to reward Rose with royalties since he earned nothing as Williams's producer). It is widely believed that Rose polished many of Williams's songs,[18] and more significantly, he is listed as a coauthor on several of Williams's signature tunes: "Kaw-Liga," "I'll Never Get Out of This World Alive," and "A Mansion on the Hill." Williams's nickname for Rose—"Pappy"—says volumes about the nature of this relationship,[19] and Rose seems to have played the authority figure in many respects. He was in the studio setting the tempi and registers at every recording session. He openly disapproved of drinking songs like "My Bucket's Got a Hole in It." At the other extreme, he had little enthusiasm for Luke the Drifter's moralism. He vainly urged Williams to refine his nonstandard English pronunciation. His influence, though, was never strong enough to prevent Williams from recording what he pleased although Rose did select which recordings would be released as singles. Thus, in the songs they wrote together, the experience of constant conflict with well-heeled city slickers is well represented. "Mansion on the Hill" displays the trite sorrow of a poor man spurned by a woman who rejected his undying love in favor of another man's wealth. While "Kaw-Liga" is more upbeat, it, too, tells of a rich man's triumph—this time over a lovesick wooden Indian. "I'll Never Get Out of This World Alive" holds such a special place in Williams's repertoire that I'll return to it in the conclusion of this chapter.

Rose had much to gain from respectability, and even before his success with Williams, he bristled at sobriquets like "hillbilly." Escott cites a letter he published in the August 1946 *Billboard*: "We read all kind of books that will give us an understanding of foreign folklore, but what do we say and do about our own good ol' American folklore? We call it 'hillbilly' music and sometimes we're ashamed to call it music" (*Hank Williams: The Biography*, 46). Both profit and principle, then, drove Rose to place Williams's songs in the pop market. (More specifically, he assigned this aspect of managing Williams's career to his son, Wesley Rose.) The enormous success of this effort replicated the dialogue that Williams was already experiencing by working with Rose. His own backwoods voice couldn't crack the lucrative and (relatively) prestigious pop barrier, but his words, polished and hawked by Rose, could. In the mainstream, his voice may even have been silenced; the short announcement of his death in *Newsweek*, for example, referred to the cover versions of his songs to claim that "although he began as a performer, he was best known for his compositions."[20] Although the 1966 biopic *Your Cheatin' Heart* didn't go to this extreme, it aimed for the mass market by casting the glamorously suntanned George Hamilton as Williams and by rerecording Williams's songs with sweeter arrangements and smoother vocals supplied by Hank Williams Jr.[21] This movie, and earlier hits such as Tony Bennett's version of "Cold, Cold Heart" and "There'll Be No Teardrops Tonight," brought a different level of attention to Williams than *Opry* encores did, but it didn't necessarily take the form of warm applause. Instead, like the range of Williams's nicknames, it drew attention to the incurable unease of hard country. Escott, for example, describes Columbia Records's advertisement for Bennett's record as an insult to Williams: "Tony Bennett was caricatured in a policeman's uniform holding up traffic while a witless hillbilly leads a pig and a mule across a busy city street" (*Hank Williams: The Biography*, 145). There could be no better illustration of a country boy's humiliating encounter with the authoritative urban man.

A pair of "lonesome" songs shows just how well Williams managed to draw his appreciative audience into this state. According to Roger Williams, "I'm So Lonesome I Could Cry" is "one of the greatest country songs ever written" (105); Escott calls it "the most oft cited example of Hank Williams the hillbilly poet," yet when Williams recorded it in 1949, it was on the flip side of a silly drinking ditty, "My Bucket's Got a Hole in It." Williams's colleagues recall his concern about how the audience would interpret this sad song, originally intended as a Luke the Drifter recitation (Escott, *Hank Williams: The Biography*, 114–115). Ultimately, the song's poetic structure made it unsuitable for prosaic Luke, who didn't dramatize his emotions; on the other hand, Hank Williams usually placed his lonesome songs in immediately recognizable domestic squabbles—his 1950 hit "Long Gone Lonesome Blues," for example, complains about a cheating woman who has run off one more time. "I'm So Lonesome I Could Cry," however, wallows in a planetary depression. Time crawls, the moon and birds cry, and an autumnal death wish overtakes even the stars.[22] As the song opens, the imperative voice seems to address the audience, and the third verse asks you if you've ever seen a robin cry. Significantly, the rhetorical questions seem directed at a sympathetic rather than haughty audience. But in its penultimate line, the last verse, in a movement that is now typical of Williams's songwriting, shifts the address to an absent lover. By this point, however, the bleak imagery of the first three verses has already established an all-encompassing experience of life rather than a reaction to a love affair gone bad, and the lethargic waltzing meter promises no relief. Echoing Williams, country songwriters have chosen the word "lonesome" because its last two letters can be used to emphasize this depressive, self-loathing isolation. As Roger Miller pointed out, "The Last Word in Lonesome Is Me," and David Allan Coe amplified the observation to "There's a Whole Lot of Lonesome in Me."

The next year's "Nobody's Lonesome for Me" (1950), the flip side of "Moanin' the Blues," makes a joke about such isolation and initially places the blame on a universe of cold-hearted women—an unaffectionate mother and numberless unresponsive potential partners. The singer wants a bride— anyone will do—and complains that he hasn't been kissed since he fell out of his crib. What's most unusual about this cheery lament, however, is the way Williams casts his audience. Although ostensibly we're free from the lonesomeness that plagues him, each verse begins by ascribing unfulfilled longing to the listener as well: "everybody's lonesome for somebody else." The structure, a dull string of verses without a narrative or chorus, manages to reinforce the sense of hopelessness while the mid-tempo use of cut-time conjures a glimmer of pleasure. Although the title stresses the singer's suffering, what the song describes is actually an epidemic of the lovesick blues. As in his first big hit, the audience shares this experience, but in this song, as in "I'm So Lonesome I Could Cry," no scornful onlookers witness the pain. In this way, Williams divided hard country into two territories, the honky-tonk, where the dialogue of abjection was most often played out, and the no-man's-land of lonesome, where Williams and his peers sank even lower.

Finally, Williams performed songs in which he set himself in places so low and so lonesome that even his most adoring audience members wouldn't follow him. More remarkably, he did it without recourse to the word that his followers would find indispensable: "country." That vocabulary was certainly available to Williams: Little Jimmy Dickens had been scaling the charts with cheerily defensive songs like "Country Boy" since 1949, and Williams wrote at least one song," I Wish You Didn't Love Me So Much," for him.[23] He gave "Countrified"—his only song that dramatized rusticity—to Big Bill Lister. For himself he chose even more undignified images. Frequently, he imagines himself as a dog.[24] His first hit record, "Move It on Over" (1947), portrays a one-way conversation between the singer and a dog whose house he plans to share (since his wife won't let him in theirs). When he fantasizes about her eventual apology, he claims he won't be interested in responding since he'll be busy tending to his fleas. This pathetic metaphor, however, allows the audience to suspect that the wife has achieved good riddance, and the next year's elaboration of this theme confirms our suspicion: the singer in "I'm a Long Gone Daddy" threatens to leave his wife after languishing "in the doghouse" so long. (The melody echoes that of "Move It on Over" although the tempo is slower.) The upbeat "Howlin' at the Moon" (1951) giddily portrays the singer's doggishness—one of the band members even punctuates the verses by baying like a dog—but it's hard to believe that the object of the singer's affections would be impressed by this display. We know he won't soon be trading the doghouse for a love nest. As Escott put it (although he's talking about Williams's songs in general), "it didn't take much skill in reading between the lines to sense that when the spotlight was switched off . . . Hank was left with Hiram Williams, who was wretched company" (*Hank Williams: The Biography*, 181–182). "You're Barking Up the Wrong Tree Now," written with Fred Rose, reverses the situation: here the woman plays the dog while the singer warns her that he won't waste time fretting about her wicked ways, but in accordance with Williams's logic of abjection, he sold this song to Red Sovine rather than record it himself.

In song after song, then, Williams comes across as an unlucky dog. Although his drinking and womanizing now form part of his legend, they don't play a large role in his songs. And this silence was not completely due to country music prissiness (as it is often asserted); unflinchingly confessional songs like Roy Hogsed's 1948 "Cocaine Blues," featuring a murder under the influence, did well before Williams had his greatest success. Rather, the persona Williams created didn't see himself as a troublesome drunk; instead, he portrays himself as the victim of a loose and abusive woman. In "Lost Highway," written by Leon Payne, he does mention "a jug of wine" as a factor in his wasted life, but a deceitful woman culminates the list. (His own composition, "I Can't Escape from You," uses the very same phrase—"a jug of wine"—to describe a man's attempts to dull the pain of ill-fated love, but he gave this song, and the more upbeat "There's a Tear in My Beer," to other artists; songs about cheating men, like "The Little House We Built," were also farmed out.) Even when the singer tries not to condemn his female tormentor, as in "Cold, Cold Heart," "I Heard You Crying in Your Sleep," and "Half as Much,"[25] he finds himself shut out by her preference for other men. In "My Son Calls Another Man Daddy" a convict bemoans his (ex-)wife's preference for a respectable mate. The loss of his son, he claims, obliterates his vision of the future. (In this song, the loss of a woman hardly seems to matter.) In "Moanin' the Blues," the singer shamelessly describes to an audience several of the begging techniques he has tried to lure his woman back home. Repeating the shifting address of "Lovesick Blues" with an exaggerated, emasculating falsetto, he also offers a lecture, filled with conventional wisdom, about how to succeed with women. The last two verses, however, revert to painful display as they segue into a humiliating direct plea to the faithless one.

Whether accompanied by rage or sorrow, though, these songs of "domestic strife" often leave the singer psychically homeless, socially isolated, and almost inhuman—"like a piece of driftwood" ("May You Never Be Alone") or "drift[ing] like a wave" ("Why Should We Try Any More") or "drifting alone" ("Lost on the River"), rambling down the "Lost Highway," or mechanically walking the floor ("Your Cheatin' Heart"). Unlike Luke the Drifter, who can use his travels to make didactic claims such as "I've Been Down That Road Before" or at least to smugly defend his wanderlust ("Ramblin' Man"), heartbroken Hank's rambling leads nowhere. The title "You Win Again" glumly summarizes the constant experience of failure that Williams describes.[26] The singer tells his cheating mate that he should leave her, but he also immediately concedes that he is incapable of such decisive action. She wins because she shames him: the whole town, those ever-present, scornful onlookers that Williams brings to hard country, knows of his permanent cuckoldry. Worse, this song allows him to see himself through their eyes. In songs like "I'm a Long Gone Daddy," "I Just Don't Like This Kind of Livin'," "You're Gonna Change," or "I Won't Be Home No More," the singer threatens to leave the whimsical and unloving woman, but the lyrics also reveal the long-term humiliation that he has already suffered. Williams's mordant wit enlivens most of these songs, inviting his listeners to laugh at him, too.[27] In fact, since the singer mentions no particular place to go should he actually abandon his wife, he implicitly confirms his shame and condemns himself to still more drifting and rambling.

Worse, drifting and rambling foreshadow the ultimate failure—eternal damnation. Both "Jesus Remembered Me" and "I Saw the Light" open by equating drifting with sin. But this extreme metaphor, in Williams's imagination, also leads to redemption. In contrast to the miserable home life he so often sings about, he frequently represents heaven as the ideal home, and in spite of his sinful ways, he assumes he will go there. Thus, he looks forward to death in "I'm Going Home," "Ready to Go Home," and "A House of Gold." He also urges his listeners to plan "A Home in Heaven." He particularizes this otherwise ordinary metaphor by repeatedly imagining a heavenly reunion with his mother ("Last Night I Dreamed of Heaven," "Message to My Mother," "Mother Is Gone," "I've Just Told Mama Goodbye," "I Dreamed About Mom Last Night").[28]

While Williams's desperate love songs are readily heard as autobiography, fans have found it difficult to believe his evangelizing, and no stories about Williams's spiritual experiences circulate. Indeed, although many of the songs about heavenly homes were released as singles, and all are now available in some version or another on compact disc, none of them managed to gain a place on the charts, and the only one that is widely familiar is "I Saw the Light."[29] Nevertheless, legend takes this gospel song as an indication of blasted hopes and hard living rather than as a premonition of salvation. Minnie Pearl's anecdotes about her nihilistic conversations with Williams are often cited as evidence; questions about whatever truth they contain seem almost irrelevant given their widespread acceptance. She recounts an incident that occurred a few months before his death. While trying to keep him sober for a performance, she encouraged him to sing "I Saw the Light" with her: "suddenly he stopped and looked at me. He put his hand on mine and said, 'That's just it, Minnie. There ain't no light.'"[30] (Nevertheless, great rays of light and the first few notes of this song keep up appearances on Williams's tombstone.) Pearl also (perhaps unwittingly) undercuts Williams's mother worship by repeating one of his stories about losing a honky-tonk brawl, apparently because his mother wasn't at his side. "Hank said, 'Minnie, there ain't nobody in the world I'd rather have alongside me in a fight than my mama with a broken beer bottle in her hand'" (213). Similarly, he occasionally told acquaintances that he learned to sing by providing entertainment in whorehouses his mother ran—although there's no evidence that she did so (Escott, *Hank Williams: The Biography*, 21).

Shortly after Williams's death at least some of his acquaintances seemed persuaded that his drifting was at an end. Frank Walker wrote an open letter to Williams on the day of his death and addressed it to "songwriter's paradise." The tribute songs written immediately after his death also imagine him among the heavenly hosts—Jimmie Skinner's "Hank Williams Is a Singing Teacher in Heaven," for example. However, Fred Rose, in a letter to *Country Song Roundup* written shortly after Williams's death, suggested that the singer would always drift in his audience's ears: "I refuse to believe that Hank has migrated to a locality called Heaven, or consigned [sic] to a state of oblivion, so I intend to see, hear and enjoy the living of Hank Williams in his music."[31] Recent songs about him mirror the macho nihilism of Pearl's anecdotes and the irreligious mysticism of Rose's letter, portraying him as a lonely ghost still restlessly drifting and suffering,[32] and therefore the model of the hard country star. David Allan Coe's hit version of "The Ride" sings it most clearly. In this ghost story, the singer, hitchhiking out of Montgomery with a guitar on his back, is picked up by a gaunt and drunken Hank, who drives him all the way to Nashville then turns around and heads back to Alabama. His parting advice to the aspiring star warns that the trip isn't over; the road to stardom entails a "long *hard* ride."[33] Williams's fantasies aside, for his fans, an ascent to a comfortable home in heaven with mama would be tantamount to turning opera singer. He convinced us that his unease was incurable.

"Settin' the Woods on Fire," released as a single just three months before Williams's death, and still on the charts on the day he died, is my favorite Hank Williams song precisely because of the incurable unease it generates. He must have been delighted with his band's accompaniment for they never sounded more vanilla. A chugging bass underscores the vocal line, and although the song is theoretically another invitation to a honky-tonkin' night on the town, the solos prefigure the mourning after. The fiddle, which should generate excitement, instead limps through its solo; the steel guitar, too, knows that this is a sad song in disguise, and thus its attempts to bounce sound more like thuds (thanks again to that relentless chugging bass). Likewise, Williams must have been delighted with the personal stamp he left on a song written by Fred Rose and Ed G. Nelson in the '30s: the lyrics demand his hick diction and he obliges, emphatically singing "yeller" instead of "yellow" and enjoying many opportunities to say "far" instead of "fire." His voice fades and hoarsens as he sings the last line, a repetition of the title, so that he almost enacts a burnout as he swallows the last word. The last verse epitomizes Williams's public stance: "you clap hands and I'll start bowing," he sings, ostensibly to a woman, but possibly to his appreciative audience. "We'll do all the law's allowin,'" he promises, thereby reassuring that other audience of nervous onlookers. But after this peak experience, the last line calmly announces defeat: "tomorrow I'll be right back plowin'." In the early "Honky-Tonk Blues," that return to the rural route would have been a welcome relief but in this song it amounts to an unbroken, futile circle. He knows his place—because he can't get out of it alive. Thus, when the song ends, he seems to be taking the title literally, describing a desperate and destructive gesture rather than recreation or renewal. Those who love him may applaud, but his reassurances to those who don't, in this bleakly ironic ending, suddenly lose their potential to placate.

The honky-tonk songs may locate Williams's dilemma most precisely, the lonesome songs may bond him most tightly with his admirers, and Luke the Drifter's recitations may address the urban sophisticate most directly, but the burlesque lowness comes out most uncomfortably in the song that Williams had on the charts the day he died (1 January 1953): "I'll Never Get Out of This World Alive." Even if he hadn't died when the song was still current, the irony of the lament structures the song—another collaboration with

Rose. In it, Williams half plays the role of the dumb or vicious redneck. The other half plays with the role. The bedraggled character created in this song is conscious of scornful eyes looking down on him and he tells that audience what they're seeing: "*you're* lookin' at a man that's gettin' kind of mad," he says, simultaneously downplaying and dramatizing the rage of the stigmatized. To explain his anger, the singer provides a deadpan recitation of redneck dilemmas such as failed fishing trips, illusory inheritances, and cheating hearts. The singer admits he's a loser, but the punch line, repeated in every verse, trivializes the distinction between him and the scandalized onlooker. While the title promises that the singer will get out of propriety's line of sight, it also names a shared fate. No matter how privileged "you" are, you won't get out of this world alive, either. In the meantime, an angry man with nothing to lose wants to tell you his story, and you can hope that he's too powerless to do anything but complain. Still, he won't change, and thus he retains the potential for violent volatility; in the last verse, he announces that he doesn't intend to waste any effort on worry since "nothin's ever gonna be all right no how." The line may not have shocked Williams's earliest listeners since he had often flung it out as advice to them in his radio show patter,[34] but with this song, which shot to the top of the chart once news of Williams's death broke, he was spreading the incurable unease far and wide.[35]

Getting out of the world dead raised Hank to the peak of hard country stardom. As Ellison puts it, "the funeral . . . was a moment of collective grief for country music culture" (80), and it was handled as if it were a show. It was held in Montgomery Municipal Auditorium and the biggest stars in the *Opry*'s cast sang (no mention was made of Williams's recent firing). The promoter in charge limited the presiding minister to 10 minutes of Bible reading in order to spotlight the stars. The auditorium was filled with 2,750 mourners while an estimated 15,000 to 20,000 waited outside (Escott, *Hank Williams: The Biography*, 248). For those who couldn't attend, radio stations all over the country devoted extra time to playing his records. Frank Walker's letter said that as a result of Williams's death, the MGM record presses would work overtime to get his music to the public. As Ellison notes, 1953, the year Williams didn't live to see, was his best selling one. On this basis, *Down Beat* dubbed him "the most popular country and western performer of all time" (82). Even as the *Opry* stars were paying tribute at the funeral, Hank was begrudgingly labeled the hard act to follow. *Opry* artists services manager Jim Denny is reported to have whispered that if Hank could have spoken during the service he would have said, "I told you dumb sons of bitches I could draw more dead than you could alive" (Escott, *Hank Williams: The Biography*, 249). No wonder his son would begin his autobiography not with the details of his birth but rather with an account of his father's funeral. This morbid zenith was his starting point: "Hank alive was just a hillbilly singer—Hank dead was a myth, the Legend of Hank Williams. This is where I come in."[36]

In some ways, our picture of Hank Williams is limited by the short time he spent recording, performing, and giving interviews; unlike the stories of most of the other performers discussed in this book, Williams's struggle to create a hard persona can be briefly told. For the same reason, though, his legend has proven to be so malleable that he can be named as the father of any number of country themes. As a result, his flesh-and-blood son, Randall Hank Williams (b. 1949), usually known as Hank Williams Jr., has had to fight to stake a particular claim to them. Like other hard country stars, Hank Williams Jr. has had great difficulty filling in the blanks of country manhood with an appropriate name. Love him or loathe him, his success lies in the zeal with which he has tackled this particularly hard-country task; his name, after all, doesn't even have the shock value of novelty. Before dropping out of high school, he fronted a band called Rockin' Randall and the Rockets, and he fleetingly refers to himself by that name in scattered recordings from the late '80s on. Nevertheless, "Hank Jr.," secondary and diminutive as it may be, is the least pejorative name that Randall Hank Williams regularly calls himself. Early in his career, he also miniaturized his father's alter ego, occasionally performing as Luke the Drifter Jr. More frequently he uses "Bocephus," the name publicly bestowed on him by Hank Sr. When Hank Sr. elaborated on this name in his prolix poem "Little Bocephus," he envisioned tritely blissful scenes of sitcom fatherhood that stand in stark contrast to the life portrayed in his most popular songs. Ostensibly addressing the toddler, he professed that "a father's love" made him want "to protect you from the hands that reach out to destroy manhood and you" and "shelter you from things that make you sad."[37] The name actually reemerged in such a protective context in 1967, when Audrey objected to some rock songs that Hank Jr. insisted upon recording. Fearing that he would lose his country audience, she suggested he rock as Bocephus and continue to sing country as Hank Jr.[38] Although these early rock releases had little chart impact, in 1975, Hank Jr. released an album entitled *Bocephus*, and he henceforth used the name so ostentatiously that its meaning has been much theorized by his fans and publicists. In a letter to *Country Music* magazine, Cynthia Anderson suggested that the name is a corruption of "Bucephalus," Greek for oxheaded, and the name of Alexander the Great's favorite horse. She adds that educated Southerners often used this name for their horses.[39] Bocephus was also the name of the ventriloquist's dummy operated by *Opry* comedian Rod Brasfield, and this source was most likely Hank Sr.'s immediate inspiration.[40]

As a horse's mangled moniker or as a puppet's namesake, though, the term is hardly flattering. Nevertheless, in 1989, Warner Brothers Records created a dictionary entry as an advertisement proclaiming that the first definition of the term was "one of the most dynamic and talented musical phenomena of the last 25 years." As a verb, to "bocephize" means to "invite rowdy friends over" or to "expertly play country, rock and roll, blues, etc.; to 'do it all.'" The full-page definition concludes that "anyway you define it, Bocephus is HANK WILLIAMS JR." (fig. 3.2).

In fact, it has been defined almost any way. Definition has been the key issue in Randall Hank Williams's life. As a result, his career breaks roughly into three stages involving two aliases: first he was "Junior," a miniature Hank Williams impersonator; then he became "Bocephus," an in-your-face country rock-and-roller, and now, a bloated relic and self-imitator, he plays alternating versions of both. As a shrunken imitator of his father, he logically felt like "a novelty act, a freak, a joke" (*Living Proof*, 17). On the other hand, when he imagined forging his own career, he faced another difficulty: a countrified semblance of authenticity would require writing songs very unlike the poor-white squalor and domestic turmoil that his father articulated and that had subsequently almost defined hard country themes. Songs about hard luck and hard hearts had made his daddy rich, and him richer, thanks to Daddy's enormous posthumous popularity. As he put it, "Daddy's and my life are diametrically opposed. His life was the stuff of which country songs are made. His was up from poverty; mine is down from wealth" (58). To back "down" from these hard-luck themes would mean both betrayal and survival for Hank Jr.; it is the need to navigate this double bind that creates the protean ("do-it-all") music of Bocephus. "It's hard when you're standing in the shadows of a very famous man," the imitator whined in "Standing in the Shadows" (1966), his first successful composition, and even harder when your relation to the king of hard country only makes you the royalty-collecting prince of the hillbillies. Abdication means failure, but success requires you to meet your doom—unless you can impose a radical redefinition of what it means to be the son of Hank Williams. For this imposition, "Hank Jr." inherited an eager audience. Inevitably, the conversation expanded into questions about how a country boy can became a man, and with this issue, "Bocephus" found yet another audience.

Hank Jr.'s "dialogue of abjection" has been more complicated than that of any other hard country star. By stepping out of the shadow cast by his father, he engages both the literal and figurative voice of that abject star. That position in turn gives him a unique authority for addressing the voices his father drew into hard country, the powerful voices that put country down, whether it's "down

Bo·ce·phus (bō–sē´–fəs). *n.*

1. One of the most dynamic and talented musical phenomena of the last 25 years. 2. Academy of Country Music "Entertainer Of The Year" (1987, 1988, 1989) 3. Country Music Association "Entertainer Of The Year" (1987, 1988). 4. Winner of 15 BMI Writer's Awards. 5. *Billboard* award winner (Top Male Country Artist, Best Country Single, Top Male Artist, Top Album, Top Album Artist). 6. "Video Of The Year" honors—twice from ACM; twice from CMA. 7. Extremely popular slang expression. Origins in American South, but recognized and saluted worldwide. -*v.* 1. To invite rowdy friends over; to *bo·ce·phize.* 2. To expertly play country, rock & roll, blues, etc.; to "do it all." 3. To carry on sacred family tradition (see Hank Williams, Sr.) 4. Anyway you define it, Bocephus is HANK WILLIAMS JR.

Bocephus,
Hank Williams Jr.

Fig 3.2: A Warner Brothers advertisement for Hank Williams Jr. (1989).

from wealth" or down on the farm. "I know I'm not great, and some say I imitate," he admits in the first line of "Standing in the Shadows"; unfortunately, stepping out of those shadows as Bocephus doesn't fully solve this problem since a ventriloquist's dummy has nothing and anything to say. Repetition and complaint thus seem especially inevitable for Bocephus even as he recognizes that the wealth generated by his father's hard-luck saga leaves him with little to complain about. To generate hard country songs, then, he needs hyperbole even more blatant than the hard-core norm. His complaints are grandiosely metaphoric while his triumphs are orgiastic, and he will imitate just about anyone in order to voice them; he constantly veers between the hard place and rock, blues, jazz, gospel, and so on. As the heir of hard country's first monarch, Bocephus has made it his imperial mission to colonize most American popular music in the nearly synonymous names of hard country and the Williams family tradition. Such manic eclecticism allows Bocephus to step out of place, but it also ultimately forces him back into the role of Daddy's little puppet, endlessly mouthing other people's words. Frustrated and insatiable, Bocephus continually stages rites of passage that go wrong, drawing his fans into a spectacle in which the hard-won pleasures of hard country become mere treats while its sadness mutates into amplified anger and clumsy swagger. Bocephus is all hangovers, no heartaches. This willed jubilation is his claim to fame.

On the other hand, his early life as Hank Jr. hurt full-time. Randall was three when his father died; he publicly became Hank Jr. shortly before his ninth birthday. As he describes his first professional performance (in Swainsboro, Georgia), his tone staggers between shame and arrogance:

> I was pretty funny. I walked out on that stage with my hands stuffed into the pockets of my little black suit, with my hair all slicked back, and I sang 'Lovesick Blues' in my little eight-year-old voice. The audience *looooved* it!

His subsequent performances were no different:

> Every show was the same: I could have done anything, and the crowd would have gone wild. . . . Imagine how my voice sounded, eight years old and trying to hit those high notes, trying to break into a yodel. God, it was awful! (78, emphasis his)

Although press reports and audiences alike insisted that the child was the image of the dead man, Hank Jr., dictating his autobiography, seems compelled to deflate fantasy with painful common sense.[41] His first fans, he implies, were fools or demons to applaud such a shrunken imitation of his father. Their response, though, ensnared him. He went on to become what he was pretending to be, practicing his imitation "in front of the mirror" until he believed he could see the self-destructive, alcoholic man he had never known (80).

When he was 11, he made his *Opry* debut, dazzling the crowd with his rendition of his daddy's breakthrough song, "The Lovesick Blues"; "the next week the papers were full of how I stole the show . . . just like my daddy" (83), he recalls. His first record was that same song, released on the eleventh anniversary of his father's death, 1 January 1964. As Escott notes, "the marketing ploy devised to support the record was crassly predictable. Hank Junior was to perform that New Year's Day in Canton, Ohio. . . . 'Every Hank Williams fan will want this "first" record,' said the advertisements in the country fanzines. 'It's a keepsake to treasure forever'" (*Hank Williams, Jr.*, 4). Because the young boy was promoted as an effigy, his career as an imitator was morbidly centered on sustaining sorrow and loss, a nostalgia act that by definition had no future except as a well-publicized death wish. As a Nashville paper reported at the time, "Hank's mother said that she felt even though her son is talented in many ways, the greatest appeal is in the mannerisms, looks and treatment of a song that so greatly resembles the Hank Williams the nation loved" (Williams, *Living Proof*, 89). Accordingly, Hank Jr.'s first albums quickly capitalized on the supposed resemblance; three appeared in 1964: *Hank Williams Junior Sings the Songs of Hank Williams*, *Great Country Favorites*, *Your Cheatin' Heart Soundtrack*. His first album of 1965 was *Father and Son*. In 1966, he released the ominously belittling *Country Shadows* and the shamelessly redundant *Hank Williams/Hank Williams, Junior Again*. He made three albums of recitations as Luke the Drifter Jr. between 1969 and 1970. In 1969, he also released a collection of songs that Hank Sr. supposedly had never published, *Songs My Father Left Me*. In 1973, he released *The Legend of Hank Williams in Song and Story*; in 1974 he slightly varied the theme with *Insights into Hank Williams in Song and Story*.

At the same time that Audrey was pushing Randall down the Lost Highway, she was also encouraging him to play out in the middle of the road. His recording history through the mid '60s and early '70s reveals the same remarkable range that would later explicitly define Bocephus: Hank Jr. released cover versions of country chestnuts such as Jimmie Rodgers's "Mule Skinner Blues" and Jimmy C. Newman's 1954 hit, "Cry Cry Darling"; he rehashed pop and rhythm-and-blues hits like Jody Reynolds's "Endless Sleep" and Fats Domino's "Ain't That a Shame," and he tried out folk/rock numbers such as Bob Dylan's "I'll Be Your Baby Tonight." He released an album of western material, 1965's *Ballads of the Hills and Plains*. In 1970, he released an album of Johnny Cash songs, then showed he could be as shamelessly country-pop as Bobby Goldsboro when he scored his first number one single with the sappy "All for the Love of Sunshine," featuring clean-cut, accent-free backup singing by the righteously named Mike Curb Congregation. Throughout these years, he was also writing his own songs (as his 1966 album *My Songs* announced). Nevertheless, in live performances, he recalls, "Daddy's songs were still the backbone of my show, and it wasn't unusual for me to do a whole show of nothing but Daddy's songs, with maybe . . . just a couple of my other numbers thrown in" (*Living Proof*, 125). Just as remarkable as the scattershot variety of this body of work are the many misses and few hits it provided. In his first 11 years of recording, Hank Jr. saw two singles reach the number one spot while another 11 broke the top 10; by contrast, between 1979 and 1990, Bocephus would have eight number one records with another 21 in the top 10. In 1987 and 1988, both the Academy of Country Music and the Country Music Association voted Bocephus "Entertainer of the Year." In 1989, he won the Academy of Country Music's award for the third time.

These days Bocephus performs few songs from Hank Jr.'s repertoire, and none of them could be considered hard country classics of the era when Haggard, Jones, and Buck Owens were flourishing, and when many of Hank Jr.'s generation were listening to Jefferson Airplane and Janis Joplin. In the summer of 1968, when Haggard was peaking with "Mama Tried" and Simon and Garfunkel were toasting "Mrs. Robinson," 19-year-old Hank Jr. was languishing at the bottom of the country charts with "The Old Ryman" (written with Eddie Sovine and Buddy Lee). Like his first record, this song rushed to memorialize loss, although the *Opry*'s move from downtown Nashville's old Ryman Theater to a suburban theme park did not take place until 1974. In Hank Sr.'s voice, accompanied by the waterlogged string sound of Daddy's Drifting Cowboys (but at a dirgelike tempo they never would have used), Hank Jr. delivers this recitation reeking of folksy sanctimony. He praises the *Opry*'s stars and their songs—unobjectionable standbys like Roy Acuff's "Great Speckled Bird"—and mourns the *Opry*'s dead—Daddy, of course, but also Patsy Cline and others. A tooth-decaying female chorus intones solemn oohs and ahs at the ends of lines, suggesting that the song itself is a eulogy at country music's funeral. The contrived dialect of the last line, addressed specifically to the *Opry*'s building, also emphatically insists on a past tense: "[I]t's just a small way of saying thanks—that's why this story was wrote." Inconvenient facts, such as Daddy's firing from the *Opry*, or the *Opry*'s flourishing health, drowned in all this syrup.[42] Five months later, as Luke the Drifter Jr., the son was back with a real death and a similar recitation, mournfully describing how he "Was There the Night Red Foley Passed Away." With a chorus that quotes "There'll Be Peace in the Valley," one of Foley's innocuous signature tunes (which he sang at Hank Sr.'s funeral), the narrative verses suggest that Foley (1910–1968), an *Opry* stalwart, died a martyr to country music; in his final hours, he visits Hank Jr. in order to discuss all the problems that country singers have; worse, on that fateful night he predicts that Hank Jr., just like his father, will suffer from them.

According to his autobiography, Hank Jr. was actively courting such country martyrdom. He could not accept the adulation accorded to the spirit of his father without earning it. "It was not enough to be simply a part . . . of the legend," he explains. "That was the same thing as being a bystander. I had to *live* the legend" (*Living Proof,* 102). As long as everything came so easy, he couldn't be a hard country star. He had to go through the school of hard emotions, so with the same blend of rue and braggadocio that he uses to recount his singing debut, Hank Jr. describes the cheating, carousing, two failed marriages, and legal entanglements that characterized his late teens and early twenties. Unfortunately, the more he "live[d] the legend," the less artistic success he had. As he puts it, "my energies were all being channeled into the C&W soap opera my personal life had become, and going on stage had become almost a waste of my precious time" (150).

Moreover, "living the legend" intensified that painful experience of abjection that Lefty Frizzell called "go[ing] around mirrors." Mirror trouble was compounded by Daddy's legend, which left Hank Jr. with practically no reflection at all— "standing in the shadows," as he put it. When he finishes his account of this stage of his life, he both cites and amplifies Frizzell's song, saying that he avoided mirrors since he "didn't know who'd be looking out at me" (162). Likewise, his name became even harder to state. While he was recuperating from "exhaustion" in a Nashville hospital, a psychiatrist told him that he wrote his "name over and over and over until it became the illegible scrawl of a wild man—which is exactly what it was" (169). (Interestingly enough, he doesn't say which name.)

The most frightening thing for Hank Jr. about his career as an imitator was the ending authenticity would require. He would have to put himself in the grave before the age of 30. When he was 25, he attempted suicide, and he sang about it for several years before and after. His 1970 composition "Cold Cold Ground" explicitly links honky-tonk pleasures with a death wish; the singer boasts from his bar stool that "every fifteen minutes I can drink another bottle down and get fifteen minutes closer to that cold cold ground."[43] Although the title echoes his daddy's "Cold Cold Heart," Hank Williams Sr. rarely expressed such an explicit death wish without couching it in an ostensibly undisturbing desire for a heavenly home. Hank Jr., on the other hand, never even mentions religious salvation although he does claim to be religious: "I have my religion, my God. I'm not going to go up there on stage and try to sell it" (*Living Proof*, 214).

While Hank Jr. staggered in the shadow of Hank Sr., cheating and sad drinking songs served him as shadowy metaphors for a far less familiar trauma. In the first chapter of his autobiography, he complains about his inability to describe what he experienced as the son of a star: "[M]y life was built on the legend of Hank Williams, and I know what it's like to feel it pulling until you want to scream . . . but the right words never seem to come" (13). While Hank Jr. doesn't probe this painful inarticulation, it turns out to be a key theme in his life as a performer: he is doomed to appropriate other people's words and then doomed to be frustrated by their inappropriateness. The next line seems to be a non sequitur unless an angry speechlessness is the thread: "It's strange but my father was fascinated with guns, and that's a fascination I inherited. Maybe his fascination was rooted in the idea that even the guns couldn't destroy the demons that were tormenting him" (13). Next he describes his good aim and his philosophy of marksmanship: pulling the trigger has predictable results for which the gunman takes full responsibility. The terse and ominous last words of the chapter bring this riff back to its main theme: "It's not like life at all." Violence, in other words, doesn't provide an identity and it doesn't explain much, yet it does somehow compensate for the lack of these things. Life as Hank's son, evidently inexplicable and irresponsible, makes Hank Jr. want to reach for a gun just as it makes him "want to scream." As his desires and metaphors collide, one more metaphor suggests itself: rifle fire and screaming are actually like a melody—patterned and relatively invariable. Unfortunately, words capable of giving meaning to this damage come hard. But this difficulty, finally, is the paradox that at once places Hank Jr. in the hard country forum on abjection and also makes him unique. Angry and humiliated, like that "poor old wooden head" Kaw-Liga (and like the wooden puppet Bocephus), Hank Jr. experiences emotion at a remove yet ever on display. In fact, while his father brought this abject mode to country music, the son seems to have had no experience that has not been tangled up with performing for the conflicting demands of an adoring audience and a hostile one. Every moment seemed to encompass all the fleeting highs and destructive lows of "Settin' the Woods on Fire." Thus, like all of these wooden figures, he needs an audience if he is to have any existence at all. When he was an adolescent Hank Williams imitator, he began to lose it.

"Stoned at the Jukebox" is Hank Jr.'s final description of this particular hard spot. He claims to have written it in despair over the failure of his second marriage and a new truck: while fleeing Nashville from the one, in the other, he stopped for gas and a drink. When he couldn't start his truck again, he ended up spending the night next to the jukebox, easing his "worried mind" by killing bottles and playing his father's songs like "I Can't Help It If I'm Still in Love with You." "I love that hurtin' music, cause I am hurtin', too," the chorus concludes (163–166). While the son here seems to be claiming some right to the pain his father sang about, the first line of the chorus suggests something more complex, almost contradictory: "it's dawn and I'm still here stoned at the jukebox." The word "stoned" wasn't in Hank Williams Sr.'s lyrical vocabulary except as a primitive form of punishment; he admonished censorious types to "Be Careful of the Stones That You Throw." Consciously or not, his son is singing about this sense of the word. Watching himself, stuck playing some music machine, feeling nothing even as he seeks out pain—it's cruel and usual, another description of Junior's life as a Hank Williams imitator. But he's also getting stoned in another sense of the word: becoming like a stone, hardening—very different from the euphoria of getting high and very similar to the hard country pain of getting low. His father sang about himself as a lonely stone rolling down the "Lost Highway," but now Junior sings in his own sturdy baritone, adopting his father's quiver only for the allusion to his father's songs. "Stoned at the Jukebox" was the first song on his 1975 "concept album," *Hank Williams, Jr. and Friends*, and when listened to as part of a developing theme, it announces that the masquerade party is over even as the instrumentation unmistakably conveys hard country's recognizable rage, sadness, and wit. While the music is twangy and steely, it crisply avoids the wallowing sound of the Drifting Cowboys. While quoting his father, Hank Jr. still manages to abjectly declare his independence. Nevertheless, true to hard country tradition, he stakes his claim in the field of stone.

The last song on *Hank Williams, Jr. and Friends*, "Living Proof," reverses the cause-and-effect relationship sketched by the passive lament of "Stoned at the Jukebox." Junior now claims that "when I sing them old songs of Daddy's, seems like every one comes true," so he prays to be freed from the obligation to be "living proof." He signs off by promising himself and his audience that "I'm gonna quit singin' all these sad songs, cause I can't stand the pain." It's as if singing "Stoned at the Jukebox" in his own voice reveals that the imitator's "hurtin' music" didn't express his pain so much as it inflicted it. As he put it in his autobiography of the same title, "Living Proof" "was going to be the exclamation point at the end of the old Hank Williams Junior" (181). (In fact, by giving his 1979 autobiography the same title, he doubled the exclamation point.) In between these two autobiographical songs, Hank Jr. calls on members of the Allman Brothers Band and the Marshall Tucker Band to help him demonstrate what he will sing. In their southern-accented rock he heard music that spoke to him and in turn let him respond; the album consisted almost entirely of his own compositions and a few of theirs. The collaboration helped him "go around mirrors" without practicing his mimicry skills: reflecting on his intentions, he claims that "if I could make an album that showed the connection between country and the new rock, then I could look myself in the mirror in the morning without gagging. I'd be making *my* music, not Daddy's or Mother's or anyone else's. . . . Music for 1974 instead of 1953. A new kind of country music" (168, emphasis his).

While *Hank Williams, Jr. and Friends* was an important step for Hank Jr., he marks the true end of his 17-year mirror phase with a misstep that occurred after the recording but before the release of this album: he fell 500 feet from a Montana mountain during a 1975 hiking trip. "My life divides neatly into two parts," he explains, "with a line right down the middle from a mountain top in Montana" (189).[44] He landed on boulders that destroyed his face and left his brain exposed to the elements for hours. After several months of surgery, including the insertion of plastic plates in his forehead to protect his brain and major reconstructive work on his eyes and jaws, Hank had to learn to speak all over again. As he dictates his autobiography, he implies that the end result of this process was finding his own voice and thereby freeing himself from ventriloquism. Likewise, as he forced himself to speak, he realized that he *wanted* to perform. As he reminisces about the fall, his word choice is particularly interesting: "[I]t comes back, in slow motion, and I see a tiny, limp dummy tumbling and falling, soaring and sliding down the mountain. I feel the dummy struggle to survive and feel the hopelessness when it realizes that it can't. I see the boulders coming up like an express train. . . . I see the dummy raise his hands to his face, and I feel his shock, again" (208). Oddly enough, he takes the dummy's name to mark this new phase even though he insists that after the fall, he chose what was once forced on him and overcame obstacles where his path once was so smooth that he slid off. He *was* Hank Jr.; now, he's Bocephus. Before, he says, he was simply fulfilling a legacy: "can you really enjoy something that you were raised believing you had to do? You . . . can get a certain amount of pleasure from doing it, but it's not the same as choosing a path and sticking to it until you succeed" (87). In other words, inheritance left him no place in either the "American Cool" middle-class meritocracy or the hardscrabble hard country galaxy, while his accident made him into a worthy opponent of the one and a potential star in the other. Although the pun is cruel, it seems apt: landing on the rocks was the most extreme incident of getting stoned that Hank Jr. had ever experienced.

Just as relearning to speak epitomized Hank Jr.'s need to find his own voice, confronting his disfigurement forced him to conquer his fear of mirrors. The scarred face seems to have created a private space free from an audience (in contrast to the unscarred Hank Jr.'s earlier life that seemed almost entirely given over to enacting the life of Hank Sr.) In public, he never appears without menacing dark glasses, a low-slung hat, and extensive facial hair, all scar-covering props. This camouflage prohibits close-ups, eye contact, and most other subtleties of expression. One advantage, though, is that his demeanor, at once triumphant and forbidding, puts to rest once and for all any notion of resemblance between father and son.[45] (Moreover, Bocephus's beer-bellied profile couldn't be farther from his father's alcoholic emaciation.) Indeed, as he explains in "My Name Is Bocephus" (1986), the scars are distinguishing marks, separating

Bocephus from impostors and imitators.[46] Accordingly, in *The New South* (1977), Hank Jr. introduces his new self. As the album cover—a picture of Hank Williams Jr. holding a picture of himself that is captioned "Bocephus"—indicates, the Hank Williams imitation is not all there is. Before, according to the first cut, "Feelin' Better," he was simply putting everybody on. This intimately acoustic and andante song closes the Hank Jr. sob story and introduces the more triumphant saga of Bocephus. Recovering from the pathology of singing nothing but sad and old songs, he proposes some singing autobiography: his new music features "a little bit less of cryin' in the beer and a little of my own soul." He exposes the song that launched the careers of both Hanks as a sort of lie—at least when he sings it. Now, with the encouragement of his friends, he is writing what he feels, and he doesn't suffer from the "Lovesick Blues." (In 1980's "Whole Lotta Hank," however, he concedes that his father died from these blues. Bocephus prefers revenge. In 1995, for example, he sang "there's a big ol' smokin' crater where our house used to be, I spent all my paycheck buyin' up that TNT.")[47] As if to recognize the belligerence of Bocephus, in 1980, David Allan Coe, noting that Bocephus stood over six feet and weighed over 200 pounds, announced that he wouldn't dare call "Hank Williams Junior 'Junior.'"[48] The next line adds to the son's achievements by acknowledging the father's greatness but still refusing the diminutive "Junior."

Those feelings that Junior once masked with tunes of drunken despair he now recognizes as incurable unease, and *The New South* presents itself as antidote. In "Living Proof," the reluctant Hank Williams imitator made the odd complaint that he'd never wanted for anything "except a home." As it turns out, Nashville wasn't where he belonged; the title cut of *The New South* complains about Nashville's conformity by referring to the same old "song and dance" while "Tennessee," the penultimate cut, complains that the whole state "took the life out of me."[49] The first line of "Feelin' Better" (and hence the first line of the album) announces that in 1974 Bocephus abandoned "Music City" for a rustic Alabama home. Implicitly contrasting the songs he sings there to industry formula, Bocephus stakes his hard country claim: in Alabama, his music is homegrown—as are his other pleasures, wine and marijuana. This incantation of independence is repeated several times as the album fades out (although the album cover's table of contents does not list a reprise).

As a concept, then, *The New South* was half invitation to the Alabama house party and half ultimatum. The sole Hank Williams Sr. cover, "You're Gonna Change (Or I'm Gonna Leave)" epitomizes this message. In Hank Sr.'s version, the lyrics are strangely ambiguous: the first line of the chorus threatens that "Your daddy's mad"; the final line indicates that the singer is daddy— "you're gonna change or *I'm* gonna leave." However, the fourth verse seems to introduce a new father figure: the singer complains about his wayward woman's habit of running home to "Dad" after every disagreement. Once there, she tell[s] lies he doesn't believe. With Bocephus singing, though, the pronoun references take on yet other possibilities. Daddy's anger becomes one thing; the son/singer's leaving becomes another, and the fickle addressee's opportunistic and insincere relation to "Dad" or "Daddy" becomes the key issue. If that doesn't change, both Daddy and the singer will have grounds for ending the relationship. Performing in a percussive and solemn blues style with none of the country strings so prominent in Hank Sr.'s exasperated version, a rumbling Bocephus seems to be demanding that his audience (you) accept him in place of Daddy, and accept him on his terms. He has already left Nashville for southern rock's "Sweet Home Alabama" (as well as his father's home state), and as he sings his father's words in the style of a black bluesman, he seems to threaten to leave country music altogether.

In certain other art forms, such relentless mimicry posing as autonomy presents itself as cunningly postmodern, and this paradoxical ploy works for Bocephus even without the highbrow theoretical label. *The New South*, for all its insistence on rebirth and independence, just as insistently exhibits Hank Jr.'s old skills as a far-ranging imitator. Two more cover songs follow "You're Gonna Change." The first, Jerry Lee Lewis's "How's My Ex Treating You"[50] sounds very much like Lewis without a flashy piano. The second cover, Bill Monroe's "Uncle Pen," makes a paradoxical gesture for a singer trying to escape a legacy since in this song Monroe links his origins to the origins of bluegrass itself.[51] In a narrative about family musical traditions, Monroe casts himself as keeper of the flame ignited by his Uncle Pen; the situation, in other words, greatly resembles that of the Williams father and son. Like the Jerry Lee Lewis cover, Bocephus's version of this song features no striking stylistic innovations; the sprightly strings and plucked percussion evoke nothing but true bluegrass even though Bocephus's singing doesn't quite carry bluegrass's high vocal pitch and intensity. Nevertheless, he imagines an Oedipal happy ending by usurping Monroe's throne in the bluegrass royal family: as the closing riff fades out, he declares his version of the song "one of the best I ever heard." Waylon Jennings coproduced the album, and the last cut, "Long Way to Hollywood,"[52] is sung in his urgent vocal style. The soaring electric guitar riffs that characterized the Marshall Tucker Band punch up several songs. With this album, then, Bocephus laid claim to every form of southern popular music short of gospel (and that was yet to come).

Since as a Williams, Bocephus can make definitive statements about the meaning of country music itself, he can make it mean nearly anything he wants. He even consents to mixing Daddy's songs with his home brew, but he now insists that they're not sad songs. Such revisionism lets the good times roll and the hard times roll away, putting Bocephus in productive conflict with just about everybody who revered or reviled his father. His breakthrough song, "Family Tradition" (1979), strategically sketched the role of Bocephus Agonistes without completely alienating him from the surname that drew his audience in the first place. He speaks first of being "disowned" by the "family" of "country music singers" who disapprove of his drinking, marijuana use, and hard-country lifestyle. "I went and broke *their* family tradition," he explains (my emphasis). The next verse establishes the Williamses as a distinct clan even as Bocephus distinguishes his music from his father's. Nevertheless, he claims that drug use and singing are *his* "family tradition." The last verse re-plays Hank Sr.'s medical consultation in "Low Down Blues." Nearly done in by drinking and womanizing, Bocephus consults a doctor who asks him how he got so run down. He responds by bragging: "hey Sawbones I'm just carryin' on an old family tradition." The exultant, defiant chorus makes it clear that Bocephus enjoys this legacy; raucous backup singers, evidently under the in-fluence of the same tradition, slurrily echo the questions that Hank ostensibly refuses to entertain: "don't ask me, 'Hank why do you drink, why do you roll smokes, why must you live out the songs that you wrote'?" Just to make cer-tain that no one thinks this is a sad song, Bocephus adds an enthusiastic whoop to one of the instrumental breaks.

In concert, his fans demonstrate that they get the hedonistic message by shouting answers to the chorus's questions: Hank drinks to "get drunk"; he rolls smokes to "get stoned," and he sings to "get laid." In quieter moments, evidently, they take it as an inspiration to work hard, but to do it their way. Bocephus told an interviewer that "a lot of kids weren't thinkin' about [my] daddy in that song. They were thinkin' about Harold who used to own the plant and Harold died and now they run it this way. Or Dad used to run the gas station, but now I run it this way. I met a lot of people like that. They said, 'Man, I know what you mean'"(Nash, 512). But while Bocephus and his fans celebrate their individual triumphs in the face of priggish doctors and other critics, Hank Sr. described suffering from the "Low Down Blues" as a death-defying depression. During his medical consultation, the doctor tells him that his disease is incurable ("the trouble with you ain't in my book"), so the last verse ends in rueful despair: "All I do is sit and cry, Lord I'd have to get better before I could die." Interestingly, when Hank Jr. performs this song, the jumpy fuzz effect of the prominent lead guitar, the boogie-woogie piano, and his own voice at its most booming meld in a blues style so up-tempo that the theme of the lyrics is practically obliterated. As the last guitar riff fades, he chases off whatever angst remains with a long, calm laugh.[53]

"Family Tradition" lifted Bocephus to the top of the charts and freed him from the living proof of being stoned *at* the jukebox. Nevertheless, his postfall flaunting of his lost innocence also worked as a theme that linked him to his lost father at the same time that he insisted he had found himself. That delicately balanced tradition allowed him to enjoy a decade of being stoned *on* the jukebox. His next song, "Whiskey Bent and Hell Bound," boasts about the usual honky-tonk antics. He still loves drinking and listening to country songs, Bocephus crows, although he forbids anyone to play "I'm So Lonesome I Could Cry" or "Your Cheatin' Heart" since his father's sad songs bring him down. Instead he requests "Ramblin' Man"; he told Jimmy Guterman that "the 'Ramblin' Man' that I sing about in the song is . . . [the Allman Brothers'], not Daddy's."[54] The self-consciously created confusion reassures the many listeners who don't buy boxed sets or who don't bother to read extensive liner notes that Bocephus is still his father's son. More reassuring still is Bocephus's straightforward 1981 cover version of the song—Daddy's, not the Allman Brothers'. "Don't worry about him, and don't worry about me," he croons in the fade-out. Thus, even while singing this mournful song about perpetual alienation, Bocephus concludes that the Williamses are jolly good fellows and that nobody had better deny it. In addition to regularly cheering up Daddy's sad old songs, Bocephus albums usually featured odes to his father such as Kris Kristofferson's dimwittedly abject "If You Don't Like Hank Williams (You Can Kiss My Ass)" and Waylon Jennings's "Are You Sure Hank Done It This Way?"

Bocephus's eclectic song selection, stylistic variety, and constant reference to his father pose a riddle about the difference between a chip off the old block, a wooden ventriloquist's dummy, and the sounds of his "own soul" that Bocephus promised when he emerged in *The New South*. In fact, that title song complicates the matter further, claiming that in spite of the newly elected southern president (Carter) and other signs of southern resurgence, "the New South . . . is still the same." The pronouncements Bocephus makes in this context are at once trivial and telling. He describes the New South by cooing over Florida girls who let it be known that they aren't wearing underpants and snarling over Yankee menus featuring Danish rolls instead of ham and grits. The South is what pleases him, and his pleasures are simple matters of taste—forthright foods, exhibitionist belles, and music outside of Nashville. Only a strangely dissonant curse in this acoustic chat hints at the kind of novelty that would justify the use of the word "new": "the new South is still the same and I'm damn glad of it." This sense of angry relief indicates that he had been threatened by change even as he claims to be happy to have changed his music and his address.

That the "South" would be the contested territory, though, is hardly surprising; put another way, just because Bocephus gladly stopped impersonating the king of country music didn't mean that he was willing to toss away the keys to the kingdom. And in his mind, the "South" was the kingdom even though "the South"—like "country"—was an image that Hank Williams Sr. constantly evoked but never overtly addressed. Bocephus, nevertheless, opens his autobiography by casting his father's oeuvre as an address to the Southern soul:

> What surrounded the life . . . of my father goes beyond the whole concept of "fans" and "entertainers." He gave voice to people who had traditionally been ignored—even despised—the lower class southern white . . . the black field worker. What Hank Williams was saying was something they were hearing for the very first time—that they were important enough to have somebody write the soundtrack to their lives. (12)

What's different about the South as Bocephus sees it is his role as spokesman rather than mouthpiece. By casting himself so explicitly as an unreconstructed Southerner, Bocephus transmutes his father's humor into vindictive glee and his mournfulness into anger and threats. Refusing reconstruction, embracing (what he would probably not call) deconstruction, relentlessly contradicting himself, Bocephus utters his first fighting words when he assumes his tastes are matters of dispute. In fact, at its peak, Bocephus's music is all about disputing taste.

Bocephus often returned to this theme, and he intensified the aggression with each turn. His number one single "Dixie on My Mind" (1981) developed a more provocative contrast: the South versus New York City. The song opens with a banjo energetically broadcasting the first bars of "Dixie," and taut fiddles respond as heavy, steady percussion establishes a more moderate tempo. This unusual trio paces the whole three minutes, creating an intriguing tension that eases the acute nostalgia inherent in "Dixie" and most mainstream country songs on this theme. Utterly devoid of wistfulness, Bocephus's bellowing vocal delivery, too, conveys barely restrained anger at the cultural geography that puts the taste-making, trendsetting, politically and financially more powerful North both literally and figuratively above the South, much as heaven hovers over hell. Such logic prompts Bocephus to make a trip, but "If this is the promised land," snaps the stunned singer, "I've had all I can stand." His aversion to the clamor and crowds is typical, as is his admitted failure to fit in; the lines that resonate most distinctly, though, cut short Bocephus's identification with the traditional bewildered hick: "they don't do much huntin' and fishin' up here, you know, but I have seen a few squirrels and one porcupine." The wish-fulfilling power reversal remains unspoken but fairly obvious: he's the one who knows how to hunt and fish while the urbanites become potential prey—a fact that "Country Boy Can Survive," a later song on this theme, will make more explicit. The following year, his "If Heaven Ain't a Lot Like Dixie" cast a similar aspersion: choosing between hell and New York City, he claims, offers no choice.[55]

Although he occasionally refers to final reckonings, usually Bocephus indicates he'll always live and never die in Dixie. Instead of sinful drifting, his southern experience evokes defiant hedonism, an angry refusal to change his tune. He will, however, restate it indefinitely. For the hostile onlooker so crucial to hard country, this repetition foreshadows torture. Eleven years after "The New South," his top 10 single "If the South Woulda Won" (1988) opened with unremarkable rock guitar riffs and rhythm, but the same bars from "Dixie" that punctuated "Dixie on my Mind" resound once Bocephus sings the first two bars of every chorus. With the rock affiliation established, a brassy Dixieland style takes over. While this song again celebrated the glories of southern cuisine, it also uncomfortably amplified the political statement inherent in rebel pride: every chorus shouted that "if the South woulda won we'd a had it made," followed by Bocephus's assertion that he'd probably seek election as president of the Southern States.[56] Although he angrily denounced criticism of this song's racism, those who would have "had it made" are not a generic "we"; only a white male might *easily* imagine that he would be better off as a Confederate, especially in terms of the possible advantages that Bocephus enumerates. We'd reclaim Miami, he promises, and proposes the death dates of Lynyrd Skynyrd's Ronnie Van Zant, Elvis Presley, and Patsy Cline as national holidays. Pictures of Hank Williams (Sr.) would grace hundred-dollar bills.[57] Bocephus doesn't mention any blues musicians although he borrows from them freely. Women fare no better in this campaign platform: in a verse evidently devoted to trade and manufacturing, Bocephus begins by insisting that cars would henceforth be built in the Carolinas since imports would be banned, and he goes on to promise an upgrade in feminine deportment by mandating that all young girls be taught to speak with a southern accent.

By definition a loser, and by postbellum tradition an independent, unsophisticated, and tough creature, the Confederate male can be insultingly sketched by a number of terms that Bocephus never uses except to refuse them—"hillbilly" and "redneck," for instance. "Country Boy" is as low as Bocephus will go, and with this familiar figure, Bocephus lends a hand to those who otherwise wouldn't readily imagine themselves as Confederates. About six months after "Dixie on My Mind," Bocephus was growling that "A Country

Boy Can Survive," and this time he made a point of casting his net wider than Dixie: "we come from North California and south Alabam' and little towns all around this land."[58] Both the instrumentation and the scenario, particularly post–Oklahoma City and Unabomber, seem uncomfortably *survivalist*: simple acoustic strumming introduces the song, and only an occasional burst of fiddling ever lifts the register above an ominous rumble. The singer claims to live in the backwoods, providing his own food and building his own weapons. The contrast with New York City is sharpened as he tells the story of a businessman "friend" there who "never called me by my name, just hillbilly." Nevertheless, the slicker wasn't as street-smart as he imagined; for a small sum of money, he died at the hands of a robber with a switchblade. The hunter "hillbilly," on the other hand, imagines that in the same situation he would "spit some beechnut" in the attacker's eyes, then "shoot him with my ol' 45." While Luke the Drifter could mock his backward kin in "Everything's Okay," Hank Sr. never imagined that he was more powerful than his uptown tormentors. Living poorly was as close as he came. "You're lookin' at a *man* who's gettin' kinda mad," Hank Sr. sang. He goes on to catalog his hard luck, wryly concluding that "no matter how I struggle and strive, I'll never get out of this world alive." The country *boy*, way more than "kinda mad," concludes otherwise. In Hank Sr.'s song, "you"—the scandalized, better-off onlooker—triumph since the hard-luck eyesore appeasingly promises to fade away. In Bocephus's version, "you" lose—either by dying in New York City or by eventually enraging "country folks" who have no plans for getting out of this world dead or alive, and no intention of conforming to your desires: "if you ain't into that, we don't give a damn." More frightening still is the strain of uninhibited pleasure that fuels the song's violence; the bare necessities of country life include homegrown drugs and alcohol. The meter of the title emphasizes the word "can," and the final bars confirm the triumph of hedonistic survivalism; rather than a fade-out, Bocephus prolongs the final "survive" into a seven-syllable yell, and a drum roll closes it off.

In his early '80s songs about "country" and the "South," Bocephus—I could even say Randall—actually sounds like *somebody*, not somebody else. In the nearly interchangeable "South" or "country," he had found his defining metaphor; it had little to do with economic hard luck but everything to do with the troubling relationship between manhood and success. In his mind, those who achieved these things were urban and northern, and they not only paid too high a price for them, they bought them at the expense of Southerners and other country boys. Although Hank Sr. had hoped to protect his son from the forces that would undermine his "manhood," Bocephus ultimately chose to remain a country boy, unharmed, perhaps, but armed and dangerous. "The

American Dream" (1982) overtly states the case against American manhood: it's too much pain and too little gain. Who really wants it or needs it? he asks his listeners. With "Hail to the Chief" playing in the background, he similarly questions the efficacy of Reaganomics.[59] His answer to all these questions is a simplistic fear that the American dream is making us crazy, but in another song he offers his alternative: the "Country State of Mind."

In those glitzy years, Manhattan, the most obvious symbol of American cultural capital, acquired some new rivals on prime time, and Bocephus quickly distinguished them from his New South: "This ain't *Dallas*, this ain't *Dynasty*," he sings in my favorite Bocephus song, "this is makin' a livin' down in Tennessee" ("This Ain't *Dallas*," 1985). The skewed geography makes sense symbolically as sites of success are juxtaposed to states of struggle. However, the "Country State of Mind" (1986) provides shelter from both; there, time *isn't* money, work doesn't get done, and boys have no reason to become men. There, all of country's hardship is cast off except for that dangerous, intoxicated mixture of pleasure and anger: the singer portrays himself fishing in the shade, sipping the ever-present homemade wine, and refusing to race with rats. "I don't got a lot but I think I got it made," concludes the first verse. Whereas Hank Sr. had the honky-tonk blues precisely because he couldn't return to his "daddy's farm" and submit to straight and narrow parental discipline, Bocephus portrays a family relationship that reinforces his country triumph; while in some sense he is still a "country boy," he nevertheless imagines his sway over "the old man" who is relegated to the kitchen, calling request lines in hopes of hearing "my"(not his) "kind of music." The last verse even sketches some sympathy for "the rednecks and the preppies"; lacking the liberating wisdom that comes from the country state of mind, they seek momentary release in citified "discos and honky-tonks." Although Bocephus claims to understand how they feel, the sound of the song—its ominous tempo, its druggy rumble, and its slurred vocal delivery—indicates that his patience for other states of mind may be limited.

Although they are mapped as countercultural capitals, the New South and the Country State of Mind never fully escape the logic of domination, especially the losing part. In the chorus of the homophobic "Dinosaur," for example, Bocephus whimpers that he should have died a long time ago; in the verses he casts himself as an unevolved geezer surrounded by gender-bending disco musicians. He adopts a collective "we" as he leads his fellow dinosaurs out of a honky-tonk-turned-disco. For the most part, he leads them to a world without real women as well. Neither the cruel partners nor idealized mothers who loomed so large in his father's songs, women serve Bocephus at best as playthings. His paeans to blissful irresponsibility frequently hit the top 10. In 1980 his "Women I've Never Had" proclaimed his preference for happiness over sadness (as well as his desire for frequent new partners); "I'm for love; I'm for happiness," he crooned five years later ("I'm for Love"), and in 1990, he summed up the meaning of life as "Good Friends, Good Whiskey, and Good Lovin'." Thanks to this insistent hedonism, he has become known to most of America as the grinning host of rowdy Monday Night Football parties. Thus, whether the cause is personal or political, Bocephus foments rebellion only to lead his fossilized country boys to a brave new world or never-never land, leaving real men and real power in place.

Nevertheless, Bocephus's pop optimism is never completely shameless, and thus he has never become a pop star. His rustication is his most symbolic failure and thus a persistent fount of pessimism: he's ever a boy and always down on the farm, no matter how big it is. His 1980 album *Habits Old and New* illustrates this dilemma in both its song selection and cover design. A picture of Hank Sr. hangs on the wall behind Bocephus, who mimics his pose while leaning against the car in which his father died. Bocephus, it is implied, has survived to enjoy success, hanging on to both his own life and the Cadillac—that ultimate symbol of nouveau success and disputable taste. "Dinosaur" premiered on this album, but two songs, "The Blues Man" and "All in Alabama," celebrate the fact that Bocephus, 31 years old in 1980, escaped the curse of his father's early death. His rockabillied version of Daddy's "Move It on Over" even seems to gloat about this Oedipalesque triumph. It sounds as if Daddy, rather than a dog, is being asked to give way although in many ways the conquered territory is still a doghouse. Thus "The American Way" angrily describes the (relative) lack of prestige hard superstardom brings Bocephus, and goes on to associate his situation with the South and with "the folks without the dollars and without white collars." Accompanied by tense and typical country picking, he begins by complaining that flights to Boston take off on time while those to Birmingham linger at the last gate. The most striking encounter he describes is with "some high society lady" who sees no status in his expensive Nudie boots so instead scornfully asks him if he's parked his horse nearby. "No Ma'am it's between my legs and you're too fat to ride," he snarls. The metaphor doesn't quite work since the woman never presumed to be a rider, but this scenario, in which an uppity woman embodies an unattainable sense of "American Cool," is so familiar that its sense is already made. In his encounter with this woman, he might as well be wearing overalls or a service uniform since the symbols of his success mean so little to her. In other words, outside of hard country, "Bocephus" means failure—yet his imperial mission requires him to constantly leave the country to prove it. While women and whiskey can't bring Bocephus down, the hard country he was born into ultimately has some impenetrable borders—particularly when you don't set your sights on heaven.

His adaptation of Muddy Waters's "Mannish Boy," recorded sometime in the late '80s, likewise addresses the ambition and frustration inherent in hard country. This song choice speaks volumes through its title alone, and as Bocephus told Jimmy Guterman, "if you listen to the words of that song, you learn the story of Bocephus. That story, that's what I'm all about" (unpaginated).[60] The angry white male is not color-blind; he simply prefers this association to his rustication. Wrapping up his conversation with Guterman, he explains: "[P]eople are mistaken: Daddy wasn't a hillbilly. He was a bluesman. He was a rock and roller. And I'm in the same family tradition." Nevertheless, he opens his autobiography by commenting on his father's reaction to the word "hillbilly": "[H]e hated that word when it came from a Yankee, 'cause it wasn't meant any different than 'nigger'" (10). Ultimately, Bocephus equates his rustication with a racial slur. He thus feels compelled to rewrite black music much as he must ring changes on his father's legacy. Whereas Haggard uses the "white man singing the blues" theme to balance sympathy with separateness, Bocephus asserts his superiority by assuming that black music is about him. In his version of "Mannish Boy," he adapts the first verse by describing the familiar story of his childish days spent standing in a grown man's shadow; later verses play with the notion of the mannish boy by parading only the most legalistic and hedonistic definitions of male adulthood: "I'm a man way past twenty-one. I drinks Jim Beam and I has my fun" and "I got something in my pocket every one of you little girls wanna see." While Muddy Waters also bragged about his sexual magnetism, none of these words is his. Whereas Waters sang out the letters in the song title, Bocephus instead letters one of his names; oddly enough, spelling it out only allows more ambiguities to creep in: "H, A (child), N Capital K. That spell Hank, and that doubles as man." Beginning by imitating his father, now doubling as a man, still calling himself a child, still imitating his father and many others, Bocephus constantly needs new territory to hide from shame and self-loathing. No wonder his appropriation of this blues song ends with his calling himself a "big ol' ugly man."

The man in the mirror, then, ultimately announces his own abjection and invites his audience to confirm it. Early in his post-imitator years, Bocephus recognized this hateful reflection as the very source of hard country creativity: "I hate to, but I got to get back to gettin' stoned, 'cause I just ain't been able to write no songs" ("I Just Ain't Been Able," 1979). Thinking straight and escaping punishment lead to invisibility; as Daddy, the Possum, the Hag, and the Rhinestone Cowboy demonstrate repeatedly, in hard country, public acclaim requires public humiliation. The chorus of "Leave Them Boys Alone" wonders about who will "cast the first stone" (1983, written with Dean Dillon, Gary Stewart, and Tanya Tucker, who must have learned something about getting stoned from "Would You Lay with Me," and featuring solos by Ernest Tubb and Waylon Jennings). This song, backed by a drunken chorus, issues strangely contradictory orders: initially addressed to the supposedly stifling Nashville music industry, it ends by suggesting that the audience, too, should "Leave Them Boys Alone." In the last verse, Jennings recalls attending a concert at which Hank Sr. "didn't show." Although the assembled fans were angry, Jennings asserts the justice of the situation; Hank Sr. should have been allowed to sing alone. Then, of course, he really wouldn't show. Ultimately, the chorus rectifies this illogical conclusion: some member of the hostile audience will need to cast the first stone, and probably countless others, if the hard country show is to go on. Getting stoned, after all, is its vitalizing abjection.

No wonder, then, that after swearing off "crying in [his] beer," Bocephus had to swear it back on. In 1989, he became Hank Jr. again, releasing "There's a Tear in My Beer," a technologically contrived duet with his father. Supposedly written for "Big" Bill Lister, a little-known colleague of Hank Sr., this song turned up on a demo tape years later when Lister cleaned out his attic. Lister turned the treasure over to Hank Jr., who then recorded his own voice over the track. In a similar feat, the song's video splices shots of Junior over some rare live footage of Hank Sr. (Guterman). Such mechanical yoking of father and son was the sort of "living proof" Hank Jr. had fought to disprove 15 years earlier (although he was at least introducing an unknown song in this case). The lyrics, showing Hank Sr. at his most baldly anesthetic, also cast their shadow back over the "stoned at the jukebox" torture that the emerging Bocephus had endured and abandoned. This song promises that the lovelorn singer will in fact be stoned at the jukebox: he promises to drink until he's "petrified." In Bocephus's case, the reverse also happened: he unwittingly revealed that nothing he said about himself was set in stone.

Ultimately, if there is any difference between Junior the imitator and Bocephus the new man, it is that Bocephus makes a great show out of fabricating differences whereas Junior specialized in spitting up images. So slight is this distinction that only vociferous insistence allowed it to be noticeable at all. Eventually, however, Bocephus had protested too much. His fifty-eighth album, *Lone Wolf* (1990), served as his last howl, particularly in contrast to his first rebel yell, *Hank Williams Jr. and Friends* (1976). His breakthrough album emphasized integration into a new pack while his breakdown album was about isolation. Although in his liner notes, Bocephus linked the title cut to "Country Boy Can Survive," that song, like "Dinosaur," ultimately evoked a disgruntled counterculture of country folk. Unsurprisingly, the lyrics to "Lone Wolf" portray an untamed and solitary beast; the acidulated metal guitars and growly vocal reinforce this rabid image. The cover photo also strengthened this impression with its blend of survivalism and nostalgia: framed in tooled leather, it depicts a heavily armed, fur-wrapped Bocephus in a desolate wilderness. As a nostalgic reliquary, *Lone Wolf* displayed Bocephus's mimicry to the fullest even though it lacked the customary Hank Sr. cover. Instead, "Man to Man" (cowritten with Tommy Barnes) ostensibly declares Bocephus's adulthood and equality vis-à-vis his shadow-casting father. He now sees himself as a different breed of canine altogether, far removed from the domestic doghouse that his father so uneasily inhabited. The song brags about his renunciation of his youthful attempt to fill his father's shoes. Imagining a phone call to heaven, in the chorus he asks to speak "Man to Man" with his father. Nevertheless, he addresses the verses to his audience. In the final one, he announces that he now wants to name himself and leave the puppet's nickname behind; he goes on to speculate about how Hank Sr. might react to the fact that he was once called Bocephus but he's now Rockin' Randall Hank. The allusive quality of both the words and music, though, indicates that the declaration of independence fails. In his liner notes, Bocephus described this tune as "a rockabilly gospel song," a bizarre amalgam, particularly since there's nothing prayerful about the song in spite of its heavenly setting.

But more imitative and undercutting than "Man to Man"'s frantic musical eclecticism is the source of the title: in Hank Sr.'s "Little Bocephus," the father tells his son that "you're my buddy, man to man." The country boy or mannish boy isn't quite claiming full adulthood after all; he's still just mimicking something he's heard. Moreover, this song is just one cut of an album that is characterized by stylistic strain. "Rockin' Randall Hank" also includes Jimmy C. Newman's cajun "Big Mamou" (written by Link Davis), with Jimmy singing along in French, a reverent repetition of the jazz standard "Ain't Nobody's Business,"[61] and a roaring cover of David Houston's classic "Almost Persuaded"[62] which the liner notes characterize as "a rock version of a country standard with yodeling. Pretty different." Although the drummer fails to beat on a kitchen sink, the song does feature Van Halen's Sammy Hagar on lead guitar, as well as a horn section. The obnoxious "Hot to Trot" uses Dixieland jazz to accompany yet another equine sexual metaphor. "I Mean I Love You" witlessly quotes Richard Nixon ("let me make this perfectly clear"). An accelerated and amplified "Stoned at the Jukebox" takes Bocephus back where he started, although the liner notes make no mention of the fact that he had recorded this song 15 years earlier for *Hank Williams Jr. and Friends*. Even *Lone Wolf*'s packaging failed to observe "Man to Man"'s message; while Bocephus was putatively casting off that nickname, his liner notes introduce the first cut, the kitschy country "Good Friends, Good Whiskey, Good Lovin'," as a "Bocephus anthem."

The Bocephus anthem was his last song to break the top 10. (Since 1992, he has failed to appear even in the top 40.) Every other release from *Lone Wolf*, especially "Man to Man," fared poorly. His next album, *Pure Hank* (1991), openly attempted to relaunch the falling star. Billed in the *Bocephus News* as a "return to PURE HANK MUSIC" (emphasis theirs), the album featured songs in only two styles: the rowdy southern rock championed by the mid-'70s Bocephus and the weepy country stuff that was one of Hank Jr.'s specialties. Bocephus is clearly represented by a cover of Lynyrd Skynyrd's "Simple Man,"[63] a song about fathers and sons that, according to the liner notes, Bocephus's own son (later known as Hank III) particularly likes. On the other hand, he rerecorded "(I've Got My) Future on Ice,"[64] a "crying-in-his-beer" number that Hank Jr. recorded in 1970. In spite of the desire for Hank purity, the album packaging reinforced this sense of split identity. A marketing questionnaire asking listeners to rank the songs, name their favorite beer, and so on, was prefaced by "a note from Hank Junior" signed "Bocephus." A poster-like photograph was schizophrenically captioned in each corner: "Bocephus," "Hank Williams Junior," "Rockin' Randall," and "Pure Hank." The 1996 album *A.K.A. Wham Bam Sam* proposed yet another pseudonym (the song "Wham Bam Sam" is about a drummer in a seedy strip joint!). Whereas in his 1979 autobiography, Hank Jr. saw his life split into two parts, it now seems as if any album release could amount to yet another identity. Evidently, Bocephus is now reliving the mirror dread that had plagued Hank Jr.: whose face looks out?

He's also rewriting history even as it repeats itself. As late as 1990's "Man to Man," Bocephus was blaming his mother for forcing him to imitate Hank Sr. and congratulating himself for breaking away. However, his "Hand Me Down," released on September 17, 1996 (Hank Sr.'s 73rd birthday), significantly recasts the family tradition. Although the lyrics startlingly resemble Freddie Hart's 1965 "Hank Williams's Guitar,"[65] Hank Jr. roots his composition in "real" Williams life, describing in the liner notes how he found a note addressed to him in his father's guitar case.[66] He cries as he reads the instructions to take the guitar and "make it ring and talk in our good old family way." Accompanied by emphatic twanging and a country beat, the chorus elaborates on this legacy, explaining how Hank Sr. advised his son to pass the guitar on once he became tired of the business: "Hand me down, my son, to your son, teach him all your songs and how his granddaddy moaned and tell that boy to carry on."

In fact, that is exactly what Bocephus has done; although he sings this song alone, it appears on an album entitled *Three Hanks: Men with Broken Hearts*. The third "Hank" is Hank Jr.'s son by his second wife. Born in 1972, and originally named Shelton, Hank III bears an eerie resemblance to his gaunt grandfather. Like Hank Jr., he had very little actual contact with his father and little support for his musical efforts before this project. He claims to have played in "real hard, heavy" metal/thrash bands. "I did that for as long as I could. Played shows for $10. You know, I starved; creatively starved tryin' to do my kind of music. I never got any help from anybody up top, like Dad or nothing."[67] Even as Hank III, he admits that he didn't actually work on *Three Hanks* with his father although the album features many "beyond the grave" singalongs with Hank Sr. Each living Hank recorded his part separately, a fact that the photographs in the album would seem to deny: there are several shots of Hank Jr. and Hank III listening to playbacks and leaning into microphones together. That Hank III willingly reveals these unfamilial facts suggests that he may suffer from an anger similar to his father's pre-Bocephus rage. In fact, his one solo number, "'Neath a Cold Gray Tomb of Stone," imagines a stoning worse than his father's jukebox torture: the solace of an early grave.[68]

Yet it is the memory of his father's rage that makes this pseudocollaboration and new legacy seem so morbidly crass and nonsensical; after all, in "Living Proof," the imitator's farewell song, Hank Jr. begged God to keep his son from playing the guitar and singing the blues. In his autobiography, he names the fear that the tradition would continue as one of the factors leading to his suicide attempt: "I'd imagine my son being forced into the music business, just like I was, and I'd feel so sick inside" (176). Equally ironic is this album's inclusion of yet another version of "Move It on Over," one of the songs Bocephus adapted to declare his independence. Nevertheless, in "Hand Me Down," Hank Jr. recognizes no such painful complications. Although it can easily be heard as his farewell to public life, especially since he imagines his enshrinement in the Country Music Hall of Fame, he also makes the tantalizing offer of more music, bragging that he still has songs by Hank Sr. that no one has heard. What Hank Jr. had to find was his own identity; what Bocephus discovered is that the search is never-ending. He has had to constantly find new sources of distinction, yet he's never achieved the singularity that would soothe the incurable unease of hard country. It's a losing battle, and now we see Hank Jr. losing it. He's called in another Hank to carry on, yet in order to do that he's had to eat and dispute the taste of some of his best words.

4

Drawing hard lines

Buck Owens,
Dwight Yoakam,
and the Bakersfield
Sound

Buck Owens, like Bocephus, made it his mission to expand
hard country's borders. Any other approach, he
would argue, is only "assembly-line music." Not
that his music isn't assembly-line; he willingly
admits that many of his songs sound alike, and
he repeatedly refers to that sound as a kind of
machine, a "freight train" or a "hydromatic." But
his music isn't *only* assembly-line music; at the
same time that he openly discusses his standard
formula, Owens also proudly notes the many
lines he crossed.[1] What separated him from his
Nashville competitors is that he copied, even
parodied, *himself* with wondrously successful
machines of his own devising. As he puts it, "I
found a sound that people really liked, that radio
liked . . . I found this basic concept and all I did
was change the lyrics and the melody a little bit
. . . I just left it the same and sold it to them
over and over again."[2] In the mid-1960s, at the
peak of his career, Owens produced his own recordings with his own band, and he wrote most
of his own material. In contrast, many Nashville
stars of that era were guided by a handful of
Nashville producers, singing what they were told
to sing, accompanied by the same musicians who
played for the last singer to rent the studio and
who would stay for the next one. Owens crossed
this Nashville assembly line and many others in
order to stay "country" in the volatile 1960s. He
professed little interest in moving to Nashville or
joining the *Grand Ole Opry*, explaining to *Coun-*
try Song Roundup in 1966 that "I'm a loner."[3] In

a 1969 article for his fan club publication, he claimed that southern country music was traditional "while the progressive continues to center on the West Coast."[4] He thus based his operations in Bakersfield, California, an agricultural and industrial center at the southern tip of the San Joaquin Valley and home to many dust-bowl migrants. Rather than structuring his touring schedule around weekly *Opry* appearances, he specialized in pleasing crowds at all sorts of unlikely cosmopolitan venues: Carnegie Hall in 1966; Kosei Nenkin Hall in Tokyo in 1967; the Johnson White House and San Francisco's rock-oriented Fillmore in 1968; the London Palladium in 1969; and the Sydney (Australia) Opera House. In order to advertise his international appeal, he often released live albums from these locations. His song sources were equally varied. His "mutual admiration" society with the Beatles was widely commented on when the rock group covered "Act Naturally" in 1965 (Fenster, "Under," 27). In 1965, he released an album featuring Chuck Berry's "Memphis"; three years earlier, he had covered the Drifters' "Save the Last Dance for Me"; in 1969, he took Berry's "Johnny B. Goode" to the top of the charts (although an Atlanta country station burned all his records in protest),[5] and in 1971, he had a top 10 single with Simon and Garfunkel's "Bridge Over Troubled Water."

Nevertheless, in 1965, Owens placed a full-page advertisement in Nashville's *Music City News* (and other trade publications) in order to announce his "pledge" to sing "no song that is not a country song." In 1997, Owens still insisted that his song selections fulfilled this self-imposed pledge. Without ever crossing out of hard country, he distinguished himself by drawing and crossing several boundary lines. While his arrangements featured classically country fiddle and steel guitar, they sounded nothing like those coming out of Nashville. Owens's revved-up percussion, the solid-body steel Telecaster electric guitars, the manic tempi, and volume stole Music City's thunder in its mellow mid-'60s string-section, backup singer phase. As *Bakersfield Californian* journalist Robert Price explains, while Nashville faced the rock and roll challenge "by moving away from the rockabilly influences that had always loitered on its fringes, Bakersfield embraced the sound of electric guitars and drums."[6] According to Malone, the Fender Telecaster electric bass guitar, in particular, modernized not only the sound but also the look of country bands since it replaced the bulky stand-up bass (*Country Music USA*, 203–204).

When "Act Naturally" climbed to the top of the country charts in mid-1963, the two chart-topping songs preceding it were Bill Anderson's saccharine "Still" and Hawkshaw Hawkins's "Lonesome 7-7203," riding a morbid crest of popularity due to the singer's death (with Patsy Cline) in an airplane crash a few months earlier. Just as interesting, though, is the contrast with the rock hits of the day. "Act Naturally"'s twang and electric guitar riffs exploded amidst the smooth "wall of sound" girl-group craze and other adolescent approaches to lyrics; The Crystals' "Da Doo Ron Ron," the Chiffons' "He's So Fine," and Lesley Gore's "It's My Party" were all in the pop top 10 when "Act Naturally" scored, as was The Beach Boys' first top 10 single, "Surfin' USA," and Peter, Paul, and Mary's "Puff the Magic Dragon." As country musician Herb Pedersen put it, "in the early 1960s, rock 'n' roll was getting kind of sappy. We'd grown up with Jerry Lee Lewis, Little Richard and the Everly Brothers. Then came Frankie Avalon and the Italian crooners. Sappy stuff. People started switching over [to country]. I switched over" (Price, "Bakersfield," A6). The spaces between Nashville's sweet sadness and pop's adolescent mood swinging became Owens country. He put "in" whatever was "out," not only the country elements cited by Malone, but also the rougher edges of early rock, including the zing of Dick Dale's surf guitar and the masculine passion of Elvis Presley pre-1960. In fact, he combined his own split impulses; before he signed with Capitol in 1957, he recorded on Bakersfield's Pep label using two names. Buck Owens recorded standard country fare, while Corky Jones released a few rockabilly numbers. But on his Capitol recordings, he claims, he was ready for incongruity and integrity: "I knew what I wanted my music to sound like. Critics at the time, they thought my guitars were . . . a little too bright, and the drums was too loud."[7] Elsewhere, he describes his sound as "a locomotive comin' right through the front room" (Kienzle, 24).

In 1956, however, when Owens began recording, his music did not sound like a locomotive coming through the front room. These early recordings, with their subdued percussion, unobtrusive guitar work, and languid steel guitar playing, sound like typical 1950s country. The themes, too, are typical. "House Down the Block" describes a man mourning the family home that he can no longer enter due to his infidelity. Overcome with remorse, he wishes he were dead. In "Please Don't Take Her," the singer begs another man not to steal his girl. The upbeat love song "You're fer Me" (remade in 1961 as "You're for Me") mundanely imagines living happily ever after with a wife and children. In contrast, "Leavin' Dirty Tracks" makes a misogynistic attack on a country girl who ran off to the honky-tonks only to learn that "country feet were never made for city streets" (hence the accusation made in the title). As punishment, the angry country boy left behind tells her that he'll never take her back since she has "crossed the line."

Owens quickly learned that country boys can step out of line even if they can't completely cross over. In fact, country songs, in Owens's mind, seem to work best when they step out of line, when they create a scandal, when they redefine country: "I would aggravate people a bit if I had the notion. All those people that all knew that they had the description of what country was and how you didn't step over that line. . . . I never talk to those kind of people, and they would say, 'how can he do that? He just walks off and leaves me,' and my manager would say, 'that's Buck Owens.'"[8] Since the *Music City News* can be seen as the official organ of "those kind of people," Owens was certainly telling them something by placing his pledge there, even if he did walk off and leave them.[9] Nearly 10 years later, in 1974, he seemed compelled to tell them again, this time in a parody song based on a 1973 hit by Doctor Hook and the Medicine Show called "The Cover of the *Rolling Stone*" (written by Shel Silverstein). Both versions contrast popular success with the critical cachet of being pictured on the cover of a respected industry magazine. In spite of getting richer, he couldn't get his picture on the cover of the *Music City News*, Owens sang. This complaint, no matter how jocular, indicates how far from the country music establishment Owens felt and how little it hurt him. In the same song, he bragged about his numerous Nudie suits and the high fees that he earned: 10 thousand dollars for one show's worth of picking and grinning.[10] Drawing the line around Nashville, staying out of that city, kept Owens spectacularly country. Accusing Nashville of keeping him down and out only added drama to his abject rags-to-riches story. At the same time, the very notion of drawing an easily discernible line provokes Owens to derisive laughter as he recounts a story from his early days in the music business:

> Reminds me of Fuzzy Owen . . . he used to put these people on, they'd come up and say "well how do you get started" (imitates a whining voice). Fuzzy would say, well you go to the starting line. The guy'd say, "where's the starting line" (whining again). He'd say, "well it's up near Porterville up there. Just go over and ask somebody where the starting line is"(laughs). I'd say to Fuzzy, "somebody's gonna come back down and cut your legs off." I really believe that some people believed that and might have went up there looking for the starting line.[11]

Jokes like this one, whether sung or recounted, draw boundary lines around Owens's country even as they entertain his audience. In other words, Owens's line cannot be where anyone else can approach it; instead, it must constantly shift so that he can stay rustically out of touch with the latest trends and coolly set them at the same time.

In 1966, Owens hoped to set such a trend with an announcement that he promised would "make the Atomic bomb seem like a firecracker": he claimed he would "hereafter . . . call my music American music (country)." Although he insisted that he was "proud to be a country entertainer," he also argued that widespread literal-mindedness about what that label meant brought him to this decision: "I find that so many people are laboring under the mis-apprehension of what country music is. It makes them think of outhouses . . . overalls . . . tiny towns. They're uneducated as to what country music really is."[12] Three years later, in his fan club magazine, by then called the *All-American*, he developed his attack on ignorance into an almost scholarly treatise; this time, rather than rejecting the icons of rustic white-trashdom, he gave a brief history of country music and emphasized its international success, concluding that "the important thing now that it has attained success is to get it into the proper perspective. It is music born of this country . . . American Music . . . and should be treated as such."[13] Just as he did in "The Cover of the *Music City News*," Owens stressed the riches and sewed rhinestones over the rags. In his liner notes to *Bridge Over Troubled Water*, a 1970 album featuring three Simon and Garfunkel songs as well as one by Donovan and one by Bob Dylan, Owens gives country an even more ambitious scope, claiming that "any song that has the right ingredients of simple everydayness can be a Country song—even classical things."[14] Unlike Hank Jr., who angrily asserts his rights over American music, Owens happily assumes a successful reign: "I never heard anybody call it American music before I did," he told me, after noting that "the *Grand Ole Opry* has got a sign up on the freeway there since about 1974 when they moved out there and they said 'The Home of American Music.'" Although the signs point away from Bakersfield, he doesn't want to declare his unease incurable.

Blithely drawing these kinds of hard yet shifting lines is what Owens's music is all about. His distinctive sound has been well analyzed by others; how this sound created distinctive meanings, though, has seldom been discussed. In addition to the infectious excitement generated by rock techniques, Owens's songs usually work by both evoking and altering country's codes: the steely sound, whether generated by the electric guitar or the traditional pedal steel, chirpily mimics steel's resilience rather than its countrified weepiness. Similarly, Owens's piercing tenor exhilarates rather than wails; he typically opens a song with a capella pickup notes (rather than the more traditional instrumental introduction), a technique that immediately creates a sense of pleasant suspense. His visual image reinforces that sense. On many album covers, he and his band, clad in glittering Nudie suits, greet the fans with broad grins.

Unlike fellow dust-bowl migrants Merle Haggard and Woody Guthrie, Owens shows little interest in commemorating hard times. His family left Texas when he was seven; they settled in Mesa, Arizona, and Owens finished the westward trek in 1951 when he moved to Bakersfield to work in the honky-tonks. As he told Dawidoff, "those were terrible times. I don't remember 'em very good, and I'm glad I don't" (236). In more expansive moments, he views the Okies' struggle as a necessary obstacle: "We're not the only people that ever felt intolerance. I think everybody that's ever amounted to anything has felt it. If they haven't, they've missed something."[15] He did not sing about the experience of intolerance until 1976, and even then, he chose an upbeat acoustical number. "California Oakie" [sic] broadly traces the ascent of three generations: the Oakie's parents were displaced by the dust bowl while his children are destined to live a better life thanks to the opportunities found in the San Joaquin Valley.[16] Likewise, Owens's fan club materials freely document the good life he enjoys—playing golf and dressing his mother in mink. An autobiographical mural he commissioned for his performing hall in Bakersfield illustrates a similar rags-to-riches trajectory: an Okie jalopy with a mattress strapped to the top first catches the eye in the left-hand corner; familiar figures from the Bakersfield music community follow; as the eye travels upward and to the right, Owens and the Buckaroos tower over the Bakersfield crowd; the mural culminates in scenes of global glory such as the Sydney Opera House.

In spite of his pledge, Owens rarely took "country" as a theme to sing about, particularly in the '60s. Likewise, he avoided typically hard country themes. His four marriages would indicate that he may have experienced at least as much domestic strife as the most hardened honky-tonk habitué, and in fact, his career required years of barroom dues-paying. Nevertheless, masculine cheating, drinking, and hell-raising don't even get lip service from him. Whereas fellow Bakersfield star Merle Haggard presents himself as a harddrinking working man singing to working men, and nearly every country singer before and after him aspires to at least the patina of sincerity, Owens draws lines between himself and his fans. His "Country Singer's Prayer" thanks God for getting him out of the cotton fields.[17] He views the years he spent playing in honky-tonks as attendance at trade school rather than at a school of hard knocks. He makes a great point of telling interviewers that he never drank or smoked, and he doesn't seem to have much sympathy for those who do. "Damn fools. I saw people get drunk, get out of control, and spend their week's pay in one night. . . . I saw people's lives break apart, wives go crazy, men go nuts. . . . I always looked at it that it's better if they do it where I'm playing than down the street where somebody else was singing" (Dawidoff, 240). He worded this sentiment a little more charitably in a "tribute" to his fans in 1967: "It Takes People Like You to Make People Like Me."[18] Although his 1967 song "Sam's Place" (written with Red Simpson) celebrates a real honky-tonk in Richmond, California, it doesn't use the word "honky-tonk," and it says nothing about alcohol.[19] Instead, it praises (and no doubt exemplifies) Sam's loud, good-time country band and offers nonsensical lyrics naming Sam's patrons—such as "shimmy-shakin' Tina" from Pasadena.

Whereas most hard country stars mine their own hard times for material, Owens makes a point of playacting. When I asked about the sincerity of his songs, in particular about a 1969 Capitol Records advertisement that proclaimed that "Buck Owens Lives Every Word," he responded: "There's no way, no way I could have lived everything I talked about. . . . There's a great deal of acting in the entire thing." Likewise, his songwriting, he says, was rarely inspired by personal experience or observation or even careful crafting. "I was listening for a catchy phrase. I would write it and make it fit," he explains.[20] The story of "Tiger by the Tail"'s composition is a good example: Owens recalls that on a trip through Texas with Harlan Howard, gasoline ads urging you to "put a tiger in your tank" were everywhere, so he suggested that they come up with a song called "Tiger by the Tail." He was so pleased with the lyrics Howard scrawled that he set them to music instantly (Kienzle, 58).[21]

Although Owens had a distinctive sound in the context of the Nashville-dominated 1960s, in California, he was participating in a thriving musical culture that was already quite distinct from Nashville. Nevertheless, he also managed to create his own lyrical themes from his immediate musical influences. Most influential were the Maddox Brothers and Rose, billing themselves "The Most Colorful Hillbilly Band in America" thanks to their gaudy matching suits, loud music, and goofy stage antics. This Modesto-based family had been performing since 1937 and recording since 1947. "Oh, folks! Were they hot! And not only were they hot, they were fun," said Owens to Rose Maddox's biographer Jonny Whiteside,[22] adding that their success lured him into the music business (96). They were Alabama-born "Okies" who brought an even more manic sense to depressing country themes than Owens would and played even harder with Nashville's conventions. Maddox band member Jimmy Winkle even suggests that "the Maddoxes' brand of corn is certainly a partial basis for the development of Owens's "Hee Haw" television series" (160).[23] Several early recordings exemplify that corn. On a 1947 cover of Hank Williams's "Honky-Tonkin'," band members whistle, laugh, and chatter nearly nonstop as Rose invites some lovelorn fellow to mend his heart in a honky-tonk with her. A slap bass and happy fiddle seem to demonstrate just how good honky-tonking could feel, and to confirm that, the song ends with Rose giggling wildly. Their 1947 version of Woody Guthrie's "Philadelphia Lawyer," a social justice ballad about a cowboy who shoots a city-slicker lawyer who tries to steal his wife, starts out as a typically acoustic folk number sung calmly by Rose. After the first verse, however, a few snickers and giggles are audible, and as the story unfolds, the laughter gets ghoulish. At the climax, a startling pistol shot shifts the performance into unalloyed comedy. The last line, which informs listeners that the number of Philadelphia lawyers has gone down by one, comes across as a punch line. "Hooray for alimony," giggled Rose in another song that takes domestic discord as its ostensible theme ("Alimony," 1951). Their 1949 cover of Hank Thompson's "Whoa Sailor" works as a duet between Fred and Rose, a pairing that strips the naivete from this tale of a serviceman's encounter with a prostitute. "Quit yer beefin'," Fred knowingly interjects, as the woman, who has not yet seen his bankroll, indignantly rebuffs his first advances. Their version of "Brown Eyes," a Carter family–style song about burying a lover, burlesques this lugubrious conceit with a crescendo of background blubbering. With their country, protorockabilly, gospel, folk, western swing, hillbilly string-band flair for the send-up, the Maddoxes sported a wild eclecticism that foreshadowed Owens's interesting line-drawing practices. As Whiteside put it, "their kaleidoscopic juxtaposition of song styles . . . was something new and different. They tackled everything and made it their own. . . . From such wildly diverse songs the Maddoxes compiled a catalogue that many other performers would never dream of integrating into a cohesive set" (121–122). Owens did dream of it—he even released a pair of duets with Rose in 1961, and he combined this high-spirited borrowing with some newer influences to achieve the commercial success that eluded the Maddoxes.

Owens had more direct exposure to Tommy Collins than he had to the Maddoxes: he played lead guitar on Collins's early singles when Collins seemed destined for stardom. Born Leonard Sipes in 1930, Collins came to Bakersfield from Oklahoma to pursue his career in the early '50s. "For some reason," Collins told Dawidoff, "Bakersfield had the truest form of hard country music" (237). Once there, he took his stage name, Tommy Collins, from the cocktail and became one of Bakersfield's first national stars.[24] According to Whiteside, Collins took inspiration for his early material from Fred Maddox's "cheery, leering style" (160) although Collins's favorite theme, a country boy's sexual awakening, maintained an air of innocence that the Maddoxes never had. For example, on a 1950 recording of "Sally Let Your Bangs Hang Down,"[25] Fred Maddox snickered about voyeurism. The singer claims to know the secret of the woman's sex appeal since he spied her in a "perfect pose" as she was undressing. In contrast, Collins would naively address songs to an aggressive, experienced woman. The title of his first single tells her "You Better Not Do That" although by the time the song ends, he's changed his mind (1954). His follow-up release eagerly asks "Whatcha Gonna Do Now?" Another early song, "You Got to Have a License," continues this theme. "I Always Get a Souvenir" ingenuously confesses to fetishism. As Collins's career burned out, Owens recorded a whole album of Collins's material including "I

Always Get a Souvenir" (*Buck Owens Sings Tommy Collins*, 1963). Significantly, Owens never released any singles written by Collins.

On his own hit records, Owens transformed Collins's boyish sexuality into more abject adult begging for a woman's attentions while slyly blending Collins's air of ignorant bliss with the sexually charged imagery favored by the Maddoxes. The remake of "You're fer Me" provides an excellent example of Owens's balancing act. In 1961, he softened the rustic diction; on the 1956 record he sings "yer fer me" while in the later version, his pronunciation of the first two words is basically standard English. He also dropped the original closing verse, which promised the snug happiness of a home and family, replacing it with the vaguely suggestive desire to "hook" the good-looking woman that the song addresses. According to Kienzle, "this record marks the first appearance of the famous Owens 'freight train' sound" (56), an observation that a comparison with the original bears out.[26] The second time around, Owens uses a faster tempo, a happier fiddle, and pronounced guitar fills, all creating a sense of exciting potential that replaces the contentment conjured by the 1956 version.

In fact, in the second version of the song, we're never told whether the singer and the woman live happily ever after although the music may prompt a positive interpretation. But as Owens developed his own musical style and message, listeners could also hear a thrilling form of denial. While his characters optimistically dodge rustic contamination, they rarely catch the women of their dreams. The case of "Tiger by the Tail" is again interesting in this respect: a risqué metaphor first hits the ear, but as the song unfolds, an emasculating danger replaces the power promised by high-octane fuel or a captive female companion. "There ain't no way to slow you down," the singer complains, concluding that the tiger's enthusiasm "takes the wind from my sails." This rollicking song, with its hints at impending impotence thanks to feminine insatiability, is an extreme version of Owens's favorite subject: men as gentle stokers of the home fire, suffering patiently and powerlessly at the hands of the kind of heartless, honky-tonkin' women Rose Maddox portrayed. Most other hard country stars link romantic disasters to their own abject failures at work, in barrooms, and in the big city, but the men that Owens portrays fail simply because they're vulnerable to feminine charms. Haggard occasionally dramatizes such abandonment with more detail and a note of righteous self-pity: both "The Farmer's Daughter" (1971) and "Holding Things Together" (1974) are sung by proudly struggling single fathers, but Owens's men are encumbered with nothing but longing.

Owens's earliest audience recognized his theme immediately. Joe Maphis claims that hearing a then-unknown Owens sing in a Bakersfield honky-tonk in 1952 inspired him to write "Dim Lights, Thick Smoke (and Loud, Loud, Music)",[27] a song complaining about a woman who prefers honky-tonking to homemaking (Horstman, 226). Owens's first song to hit the Top 40, "Second Fiddle" (1959), cast the man in this long-suffering role; he followed that up with a similar complaint: "Under Your Spell Again." In 1961, "Foolin' Around" begged a promiscuous woman to come home to fool around with her abandoned mate.[28] "Fool Me Again" makes a similar request.[29] In his next single, "Under the Influence of Love" (written with Harlan Howard), he confesses to being a fool and a failure incapable of even leaving a memory behind. Even then, he hopes the woman who left him will deign to break his heart again. On album cuts made that year, he pines to be "The One You Slip Around With" and tells a wayward woman that the "Key's in the Mailbox" whenever she's ready to head home.[30] In 1962, he admits to being "Nobody's Fool but Yours."

Musical analysts note a distinctive style change with the prominence of electric guitars from 1963 onward, but this "new" sound did little to alter Owens's familiar themes save turn up the volume. "Act Naturally"(1963),[31] his breakthrough song, glorified erotic suffering and explicitly linked it to show business success. The singer claimed to be playing the part of a sad and lonely man, a role he believed would lead to stardom. A 1964 album cut claims that the wandering sweetheart might return if someone would just "Close Up the Honky-Tonks."[32] In 1966, he compared this abjection to poverty as he seeks to be reunited with a woman who rejected him. He claims to be hungry for her love, and thus, "Waitin' in [her] Welfare Line."[33] He released "In the Palm of Your Hand," a slower-paced song, twice; in 1966, and again as the title cut of a 1973 album. Then, the cover featured a comical drawing of Owens smilingly perched in a woman's oversized, highly manicured hand. "Who's Gonna Mow Your Grass," a number one hit in 1969, featured a fuzz-tone guitar without the usual rock-macho posturing that accompanies it; instead, a discarded lover hopes to regain favor with a fickle sweetheart by reminding her about all the menial chores he willingly performs (including acting as her puppy dog and serving her breakfast in bed). In 1972 Owens made a Nixonian promise with "You Ain't Gonna Have Ol' Buck to Kick Around No More": "the last time was the last time, but this time it's for sure," he blusters. That same year, he covered one of the few country standards about impotence when he recorded "Too Old to Cut the Mustard" with his son Buddy Alan.[34] "Arms Full of Empty," a 1973 single, happily complains about a woman who stole the car and emptied the bank account before she ran off, yet concludes with the singer promising not to hold a grudge should she return. As Owens's recording career sputtered out in the late '70s, he was still lamenting and abetting masculine failure in "Hangin' In and Hangin' On."

In spite of the pathetic states they describe, these songs, nearly all recorded in jumpy cut time, fill dance floors. And Owens sings happier songs still. For example, "Love's Gonna Live Here" (1963) gaily asserts (on the basis of no particular evidence) that the singer's lonely home will someday be happy. The title doesn't use the word "again," but the chorus ends with that word, slightly hinting that although bright spots lie ahead, forever may be too much to expect. "Gonna Have Love" (1965, written with Red Simpson) sketches a similar emotional terrain: a man waiting passively for love that he believes he will have since he just received hopeful news from a woman who left him. Once she returns, he shamelessly promises to cling to her like a vine. Don Rich's surfing guitar riffs make the whole ordeal seem painless, although again the optimistic title does not fill the last bar in either the verse or chorus; instead the less hopeful words "one more time" fill that emphatic slot, again modifying the promise of happiness into something less than ever after. "Open Up Your Heart" (1966) hopes for "blue skies again" although the use of that favorite word indicates that this heart had slammed shut at least once before. "Hello Trouble," an "integral part of Buck's live repertoire" (Kienzle, 57), stages a slightly more concrete version of this drama: the singer, alone in a house, seems to associate his suffering with domestic routine. In the first verse, he wakes up to see the woman who abandoned him (evidently more than once) heading up the front walk; he greets her with the words of the chorus: "Hello, Trouble, welcome home." In the second verse, he invites her to tell him lies over coffee as he admits that he endures deception in order to have the pleasure "a little bit of trouble" occasionally brings him.[35] The Wilburn Brothers' 1962 hit "Trouble's Back in Town" contrasts sharply with Owens's suggestive glee; in this song, female backup singers warn "Uh-oh" while the male duo dreads the upheaval sure to follow from this fickle woman's return.[36]

Owens's own songs only occasionally acknowledge the trauma of such instability. "Over and Over Again," a 1963 album cut, sorrowfully describes an on-again, off-again romance. In "No Fool Like an Old Fool," a comfortably sad shuffle, the singer reproaches himself for repeatedly swallowing "the same old lines." Both "Together Again" (1964) and "Crying Time" (1964), the best-known of Owens's slow-dancing ballads, shift the accent to misery. In the first one, the singer claims that the turbulent relationship the song portrays is the only thing that matters to him, although the title, as usual, doesn't promise that the reunion is permanent. "Play 'Together Again' Again" (written with Charles Stewart and Jerry Abbott), a duet he recorded with Emmylou Harris in 1979, confirms the suspicion that the song is about an endless cycle of happy reunions and heartbreaks. Likewise, "Crying Time" rolls around with gloomy regularity: "it's crying time *again*" mourns the opening bar, and as the song proceeds, the singer displays a long-standing familiarity with all its portents.

When I asked him about his many songs in which men suffer in women's hands, Owens seemed unwilling to comment at much length although he did indicate that madness, even, anger, may be buried somewhere in the method. "I think that's the way I felt, subconsciously," he said, noting that Don Rich, his favorite band member, "always thought I hated [women]." As if to confirm this insight, he added that Rich "was such a smart guy for his age."[37] (He was 12 years younger than Owens.) Rich's comment is as startling as it is intriguing: the happy-face love songs might really be hate songs.[38] In that case, the objects of hatred—heartless women, Nashville, "they," "you"—fall into the familiar chain of similes from other hard country sagas. Rich's sudden death in a motorcycle accident in 1974 seemed to bring this cluster into a glaring limelight. When fiddler Rich joined Owens's band in 1959, Owens taught him to play guitar his way; when they sang together, the harmonies Rich provided were so tight that on many recordings the two voices were indistinguishable. Without him, though, Owens claimed, "I couldn't do it by myself. I missed Don so much every place I'd go"(Kienzle, 44). At this point, Owens began hitting the scandal sheets and talk shows with Hank Williams–like displays of loneliness and instability. The cover of his 1975 album *41st Street Lonely Hearts Club/Weekend Daddy* recounts Owens's troubles through a collage of (real) news clippings: "'Pore' Buck Still Seeking a Wife," screams one; "Buck Owens, co-star of TV's *Hee Haw*, is Rich, Famous and Miserably Lonely," proclaims another (although the four photos that are reproduced all feature Owens's familiar grinning face). The copy written expressly for the album boasts that as a result of this publicity, Owens received "50,000 inquiries. . . . It's become clear that there's more than one lonely girl in the world, in fact————it's almost created a BUCK OWENS' LONELY HEARTS CLUB."

Three years later, Owens was back in the tabloids after marrying his third wife (Buckaroo fiddler and *Hee Haw* cast member Jana Jae Grief) in Las Vegas and abandoning her the minute they returned to Bakersfield. He then took out a full-page newspaper advertisement begging her forgiveness and swore to reporters that he would do whatever it took to win her back. She, however, claimed that there were other women in his life. After a few more rounds of well-publicized reconciliation and abandonment, the marriage dissolved. Owens later explained to Dwight Yoakam that drinking caused the whole mess: "I never drank very much, but when I drank one time I drank a bottle and a half of wine . . . I got married. And when I sobered up, I got it annulled."[39] (In 1979, Owens married his current wife.) Sometime during this blitz, he also posed for *Playgirl* ("buck naked," in Randall Riese's words) although those pictures were never published.[40] Whether this real-life humiliation and "cheating heart attack" were temporary insanity or a calculated publicity extravaganza, they did nothing to spark Owens's recording career. Without Rich, Owens was living Nashville's clichés, getting drunk, cheating, and ending up lonely. Worse, he spent the late '70s recording lackluster country pop in Nashville—the very assembly-line music he had pledged to avoid.

At their peak, the Buckaroos as a unit seemed to say that hard country's hard times and hard feelings hardly mattered if they were set to music that was frantic enough. The exhilarating music vanquished the humiliating implications of the lyrics, somehow shifting the balance of power to where mainstream culture said it should be: with men. And these men, unlike Hank Williams and his ilk, managed somehow to keep their cool in spite of the pain they endured. More novel, though, was the way this music shifted the power of the new, youthful rock and roll into the hands of over-30 Okies who constantly sang about their domestic powerlessness and who hadn't had much power outside the home before. A liner note to a 1965 album, *Roll Out the Red Carpet for Buck Owens and the Buckaroos*, implicitly makes this contrast. The song it introduces, "I'm Gonna Roll Out the Red Carpet," is typically masochistic in looking forward to some wandering woman's homecoming, but the commentary shifts the accent to celebrating Owens himself (as does the album title): "Roll Out the Red Carpet for Buck Owens. Buck not only sings this sure-fire hit . . . he also composed it."[41] Likewise, the unattributed liner notes to *Buck Owens Live at the White House* (1968) stress Owens's masculine power, dubbing him "the big man from Bakersfield California who made country music grow up."

Ultimately, two songs that don't seem like country songs at all provide the key to Owens's hard country performance at the peak of his career: Chuck Berry's "Johnny B. Goode" (Chuck Berry) and "Big in Vegas," both released as singles in 1969. "Johnny B. Goode," recorded live at the London Palladium, opens with a tony British announcer introducing "the world's number one country artist," yet Don Rich's manically paced rock guitar work is the most prominent feature of the song "the number one country artist" chose to include in his show. "Big in Vegas" emphasizes pop techniques; it has both a languid string section and smooth backup vocals. According to Owens, "that's one of my most requested songs. I always used that song to close with. I'd end with 'Johnny B. Goode' and if I got an encore, I'd do 'Big in Vegas'" (Kienzle, 64). They belong together not only because they are examples of Owens's propensity to cross lines but also because they both seem to be *about* the performer's escape from domestic and rustic abjection to cosmopolitan masculine power. The country boy Johnny B. Goode, inspired by his mama's vision of seeing his name in lights, dreams of getting out of the backwoods. This subject, Owens insists, exemplifies country songs: "is there anything more country than mama and a guitar and a railroad train and . . . a boy sitting by it?"[42] In "Big in Vegas" (written with Terry Stafford), Mama begs her guitar-picking son to stay at home, but his dream is the same as Johnny's: he wants to see his name in lights. Every night, the tiger dragged her weak and unwilling mate to "where the bright lights are found"; as it turns out, he's happy to be there as long as he's in them.

By placing these two songs between the applause that elicits an encore and the applause that indicates the end of a successful show, Owens could realize the dreams they expressed: hard country stardom meant that the country boy was suddenly wildly desired where he had never been wanted before.[43] In other words, he was no longer a boy but a powerful man who could make country music grow up in his own image. No wonder, then, that Owens publicly refers to his success as "*Lady* Limelight."[44] In "Leaving Dirty Tracks" (and so many other songs), it is the woman who wanders off, leaving the man in quiet and seemingly permanent retreat. In these two closing songs, on the other hand, the man leaves home, following Lady Limelight into the city. That woman not only wanted him, she rejected many others.

That same urge to flaunt his desirability seems to have lured Owens on to *Hee Haw* the very year he recorded these songs. By 1980, Owens had disappeared from the radio and record stores; all that was left was *Hee Haw*. He claims to have known all along that the overfamiliarity created by a weekly television appearance would hurt his record sales, but he also says he would do it all over. After years of doing it the hard way, *Hee Haw* put him on easy street. Filming a year's worth of shows took only two weeks; "I'd leave and they'd hand me $200,000, and that was twenty-five years ago" (Dawidoff, 233). When Dwight Yoakam suggested to him that being invited to join the show also represented a new pinnacle of success, Owens agreed: "[Y]ou gotta remember that for many people that was a dream" *(Spin*, 46). Although Owens doesn't elaborate on the contrast with Rowan and Martin's *Laugh-In*, adapting that hip show to a country format must have appealed to Owens in the same way that putting electric guitar riffs in country songs did. Nevertheless, Owens recognizes that in some sense, this dream come true drowned out the country euphoria of his songs and revived the rustic stigma that he had hoped to erase with his Bakersfield-based "American music." Contrasting the show to his years of touring, he says,

> I couldn't tell you . . . of the times I had this said to me . . . "I didn't know country was this much fun" . . . They're thinkin'

about the guy with the corncob pipe sittin' on the porch with no shoes on and one tooth and it was green. See this wasn't the days when you have all these young good lookin' guys like country music today . . . So many people didn't know. It was before *Hee Haw*. And of course, all we did on *Hee Haw*, we just guaranteed it was true what they thought.

At some level, though, even this opprobrium can be seen as a hardship Owens shouldered in order to have some say about what it meant to be country, for he quickly reminded Yoakam that not only was a network television show a rarity for a country star,[45] it was also as ephemeral as the happy love affairs he sang about. "Of course, then they took it off. It was network for about a year and a half . . . maybe two years and a half."[46] Owens goes on to emphasize that the show's demise was tied to its countriness: "I remember what the guy said he was going to do to the network; he said he was going to 'deruralize' it" (*Spin*, 46). (The show immediately went into syndication, and over 600 episodes were produced through 1992; the Nashville Network still broadcasts reruns. Owens left the show in 1986.) Although Owens says that he thinks *Hee Haw* "was funny. It was a big put on,"[47] only a viewer steeped in hard country and sensitive to its shifting lines could perform that kind of interpretive feat.[48] Otherwise, in the prime-time mainstream, Owens was seen and heard only as a repellent cornball. Thus, on television, Owens glowed the hard way or no way, just as he did on records.[49]

In the late '80s, Dwight Yoakam refocused the picture. This Kentucky-born singer burst on the scene in early 1986 with a cover of Johnny Horton's 1956 "Honky-Tonk Man." Heading for California after being told he was "too country" for Nashville, ultimately making successful records with a fresh blend of rock and hard country sounds, and constantly professing his allegiance to Buck Owens in interviews, Yoakam reconnected Owens to his hard lines. The acknowledgments for his 1987 album *Hillbilly Deluxe* include "Very Special Thanks: to Buck Owens for all his records that still serve as an inspiration for the California honky-tonk sound." As Yoakam said in a 1985 interview, "I think that country lost its coolest side . . . after Buck Owens stopped recording in Los Angeles. Those records of his in the mid-sixties were incredible—the zenith of American hillbilly music."[50] One day in 1987, Yoakam showed up unannounced at Owens's office in Bakersfield and managed to talk his idol into singing with him at the county fair. The next summer they toured a bit together and recorded "The Streets of Bakersfield" (originally on Owens's 1973 album *Ain't It Amazing Gracie*). This duet resulted in

Yoakam's first number one single, and Owens's first charted song since 1981 and his first number one since 1972.

No matter how adolescent, Yoakam's constant insistence on "coolness" underscores the importance of California to this strain of hard country. As anyone who pays the slightest attention to popular culture knows, California is the capital of cool, and it has been since the movie industry cast the state in this trendsetting role early in the twentieth century.[51] (That's why fictional Jed Clampett and his family were told it was where they "oughta be"; they even looked like Okies as they drove into Beverly Hills with their overloaded jalopy.) For the Okies, migrating west in an era that had just been introduced to the notion of "white trash" by serious historians and sensational novelists like Erskine Caldwell, the imagery led to immediate culture clash. As historian James Gregory concludes, "these images compounded the sense of otherness and inferiority that California seemed in so many ways to impart."[52] Writer Gerald Haslam has referred to the Okie-settled San Joaquin Valley as "the other California."[53] Gregory sees California country music "from Gene Autry to Merle Haggard" as "the 'language' that communicated the essence of [Okie] subculture" (233).[54] In particular, he notes, it functions as "the clearest counterweight to California's critique of rural backwardness" (236);[55] in fact, it could be argued that by the '60s, when "California Dreamin'" seemed to have nothing to do with Okie hopes, country music in general counterbalanced California's embodiment of "cool." Such analysis, however, leaves little to say about Owens (Gregory simply notes that Haggard followed in his footsteps to stardom [241]). If anything, Owens and the grinning Buckaroos seemed blissfully ignorant of any "critique of rural backwardness" although Owens was well aware of it and simply flaunted his popularity to answer it. The giddiness of both the pledge to country music and the concept of "American music" was all about amplifying that answer.

In turn, this taut balance of disgrace and glory, of backwardness and hipness, allowed Owens to enter into hard country's abject dialogue with the outside world. Owens's emotional range addresses both sides of that dialogue. In fact, he sees this range as central to country stardom: "the ability to evoke emotion of one kind or another, sometimes happy, sometimes sad, but always evoke something. I think the people that get left by the wayside was the people that didn't make somebody glad or somebody mad."[56] Owens, of course, did both. Contributors to his *Fan Club Yearbook* provide remarkable testimony of his power to gladden them. "It matters not what life hands out. / Your music has put me on the right route. / It's easy now for my heart to sing, / For you touched it deep with a thousand strings," wrote Mr. and Mrs. James Hubbard in 1967. In that same issue, Marline Merigae Share called Buck and his band "the spirit of country music's salvation, / Embedded within from deep inspiration." In prose, Mrs. Betty Lou Page describes how discovering Buck Owens cured her homesickness after a move from Delaware to Idaho: "One day, as I was playing the radio, there you were, singing, and my heart was so full that I cried. . . . It wasn't long before everyone who knew me, knew how I felt. When I played your records, it was always so my neighbors without record players could hear too." Volume, pitch, electric guitars, and Owens's voice, then, seem to work some euphoric combination. The sound has power that the words, familiar to the point of cliché, don't; no wonder Owens compares it to a freight train. The chorus to Yoakam's "Turn It On, Turn It Up, Turn Me Loose" claims that louder is better, and the verses describe dancing to a Buck Owens song. That, the singer explains, is what makes his chosen honky-tonk so soothing to his lonely soul.[57] To explain how his music works, Owens refers to still more of Yoakam's testimony: "[I]f you look in the front of the Rhino book you'll see a thing there written by Dwight Yoakam and he says get that cassette and hit the road and turn it up loud and enjoy. And I think that'd be my first instruction."[58]

In Owens's mind, loud music serves not only to induce euphoria, but also to affront the sneering onlookers he once tried to win over with his "American music." He has recently opened a $7.5 million performing hall and museum in Bakersfield. You can drink and you can dance there, but it's not exactly a honky-tonk. Called Buck Owens's Crystal Palace, it has its inspiration in volume: "There were thirty years that I thought about that place, thirty years, and I'll tell you why. I would pull up to a stop sign, like here in Bakersfield. . . . They playing country music, they'd turn it down; I never did, I'd turn mine up. Let me hear it." To assert that pride more concretely, Owens says, he dreamed of "a place that was just as good if not better than the Philharmonic Orchestra." Owens is using his place to draw more lines between Bakersfield and Nashville, too. Owens was inducted into Nashville's Country Music Hall of Fame in 1996, but when he was asked to donate memorabilia, he thought "all of these things belong here."[59] Nevertheless, it's hard to imagine how a city of 360,000 people can support the facility; Owens himself admits that "if you're looking for dollars and sense, you go to Fresno, because it's twice as big as Bakersfield."[60] But once more, Owens set himself up to prove something back on the streets of Bakersfield where he started. Interestingly, local advertising for the Crystal Palace contrasts it favorably with a Bakersfield country club.

Down home, finally, is where denial breaks down and Owens's infection with the incurable unease begins to show. Although Bakersfield was reportedly often referred to as "Buckersfield" due to Owens's extensive business holdings in the area, Owens, at the peak of his career, never sang about his origins. It was Haggard who kept this city and its dust-bowl background in the public ear. His 1969 hit "Hungry Eyes" was set in a depression-era labor camp; later album cuts "Tulare Dust" and "They're Tearin' the Labor Camps Down" take the hardships of westward migration as their theme, and "Kern River" (Bakersfield and this river are in Kern County) reminds listeners that the south San Joaquin Valley is the home of many dust-bowl migrants (1985). Several songs focus more specifically on the music community of Bakersfield. His ribald 1974 single "Old Man from the Mountain" "is nothing short of a tribute to Fred [Maddox], complete with a bass fiddle track that replicates his slap sound and also mentions 'Friendly Henry' [Maddox]"—the band's mandolin player (Whiteside, 161).[61] Similarly, his "Bill Woods of Bakersfield" praises the bandleader who gave Owens and many other musicians their first professional jobs.[62] Haggard's 1981 hit "Leonard" acknowledges the support Tommy Collins (Leonard Sipes) gave him in those days. Leonard, he explains, not only taught him a lot about country songwriting, he also supplied occasional groceries in the days before "Okie from Muskogee" brought fame and plenty of money for food. His 1996 album cut "Beer Can Hill" celebrates "a place in Bakersfield . . . where Merle played his first all-night concerts to a crowd of four."[63] To reinforce the Bakersfield connection, guest vocalists Buck Owens, Dwight Yoakam, and boyhood friend Bob Teague take turns singing lines about the city. His 1991 album *All Night Long* opens with the Bob Wills title cut, which promises a musical party till dawn; the next cut, "Honky-Tonk Night-Time Man" also strikes this note,[64] but the album ends with "A Bar in Bakersfield," which tells the story of a musician who couldn't give up his family for stardom so instead supports them by playing every night in a local bar while his original bandmates hit the big time. The steady clanging of heavy machinery that accompanies this track stresses the connection between this grinding gig, hard labor, and honky-tonk party time. In the fade-out, this working man mentions playing in the Blackboard and the Lucky Spot, now-legendary honky-tonks where Owens, Haggard, and a host of unknowns got their start. (In Bakersfield or out, Haggard insists that being a hard country star is hard work; he told one reporter that he would "just as soon pick cotton for eight hours" [Grissim, 134] and another that "if you like your job you're not doing it right.")[65]

In 1989, "The Streets of Bakersfield" brought Owens back to the limelight with a song on a similar theme. The duet version, even more deceptively upbeat than Owens's 1973 album cut, added a rollicking Mexican-style accordion to the arrangement—quite appropriate given the city's current population mix. Nevertheless, what's most important about the song didn't change although it reached a larger audience due to its release as a single. The singers (fig. 4.1),

Fig. 4.1: Dwight Yoakam and Buck Owens, ca. 1988. Courtesy Country Music Foundation.

rather than being victimized by heartless women, are suffering from hard country's foundational conflict: the scorn and self-serving incomprehension of the well-heeled outside world. The verses tell the story of a man who has evidently given up on workaday success; in jail in San Francisco, he trades the symbols of middle class routine—his watch and his house key—for his drunken cellmate's money ($15), then hits the road for Bakersfield, where he hopes to find a better life. As the singer puts it, "I came here looking for something I couldn't find anywhere else." The chorus thus concludes by heaping scorn on the smug onlookers who already have made their start: "How many of you who sit and judge me ever walked the streets of Bakersfield?" it asks. Owens told me that walking the streets of Bakersfield "means . . . tryin' to find out where the starting line is." The chorus, though, indicates that even there, the "starting line" is closely guarded. "You don't know me but you don't like me," complains the frustrated singer as he walks the streets in the city of his country dreams.

In fact, when the songwriter, Homer Joy, wrote the lyrics, the "you" he had in mind was Buck Owens himself, who had repeatedly refused to listen to his songs (Roland, 533). But, as Kienzle notes, "Joy's persistence impressed Buck"; moreover, the irony of finding himself cast in the role of the "establishment" appealed to him so he agreed to record the song (67).[66] In other words, at that moment, Owens began to identify with Joy rather than with his own stardom. Moreover, the song bears traces of Owens's characteristically dogged hope. For example, it's difficult to ignore the sad, alliterative echo of Bobby Bare's 1966 "The Streets of Baltimore" in "The Streets of Bakersfield"; in Bare's song, a man sells his farm to fulfill his wife's dreams of urban excitement. Once settled in Baltimore, he takes a job in a factory while night life and alcohol alienate his wife's affections. He thus heads home while she stays behind "walking the streets of Baltimore."[67] On a 1970 album, Owens himself sang "No Milk and Honey in Baltimore," a similar tale about a disillusioned farmer who finds himself sweeping filthy streets in the city of his failed dreams. In contrast, the streets of Bakersfield still serve as a site for American dreaming; Joy got his break there, and in 1996, Chris Hillman and Herb Pedersen released an album called *Bakersfield Bound* with several Owens covers and an upbeat title track by Hillman and Steve Hill. This song, ostensibly about dust-bowl migration, also seems to be a hopeful comment on the Hillman/Pedersen partnership: they've found a new starting line, an event illustrated in the cover photo, which shows the two artists driving into Bakersfield in a classic convertible. Even Owens's 1973 "Songwriter's Lament" may be an oblique commentary on the advantages of starting in Bakersfield: in this unemotional ballad, a Tulsa boy, seeking his fortune in Nashville and later at Heaven's Gate is turned away at both points by exasperated gatekeepers: "Mister, we've got . . . a songwriter under every rock," moan both Nashville executives and Saint Peter. To avoid this particular stoning, the Tulsan probably should have headed West like his Okie predecessors. In fact, in Owens's mind, the starting line is now ensconced in the Crystal Palace. Referring to the two local bands that play there, Owens says "the opportunities are coming again; they've been gone for some time." Owens has thus taken his career from the spectacularly impotent expression of no hard feelings to the regally confident expenditure of $7.5 million in cold hard cash to build a hard country museum. The line, now, is right where he can oversee it.

Yoakam, though, may still be out there bending it. While much has been made of his filial relationship to Owens, neither his intensely nasal tenor nor his instrumental experimentation sounds that much like his idol, and except for "Playboy," a song that both Owens and Wynn Stewart recorded without much luck, and "The Streets of Bakersfield," he has never recorded an Owens song. (However, ex-Buckaroo Tom Brumley plays steel guitar on many of Yoakam's recordings.) Moreover, Yoakam's themes are far more abject; in fact, it often sounds as if he is deliberately darkening Owens's light approach to this state of mind. In early 1986, he introduced himself to the country audience as a compulsive "Honky-Tonk Man" who "can't seem to stop," alternately pursuing wild nightlife and begging some woman to let him come home.[68] The first album also introduces Yoakam's persistent interest in honky-tonk alcoholism, a theme Owens carefully avoided. The singer makes a boast worthy of George Jones when he announces that he'll fall from his bar stool then fall down in the street, but "It Won't Hurt," and the steel guitar and fiddle mimic this unsteady state. A woman's scorn, of course, drives this drinking, as it does on "This Drinking Will Kill Me" in 1987, "Since I Started Drinkin' Again" in 1990, and "Two Doors Down" in 1993.[69] In particular, Yoakam's vision of sexual relationships is more openly painful than those Owens portrayed. "Please, Please Baby" and "Little Ways" (both 1987) may be the most abject begging songs in hard country; by the end of the second verse of "Please, Please Baby," the singer collapses into a self-loathing confession of "Sweetheart, I plead guilty, darlin' / I'll take all the blame." Likewise, the singer of "Little Ways" foolishly reveals the very abjection he hopes to hide: "I'm too ashamed to let them know you make me cry," he tells the world. His 1993 album *This Time* explored this theme in several songs. The singer in "Fast as You" complains about the woman who controls him, makes him cry, and brings him to his knees. Another cut, "1000 Miles from Nowhere," picks up the familiar mirror motif, this time complaining that the face in the glass no longer is a man's. The title song ("This Time") confronts this theme most directly, stressing the repetitive injuries of the willing, almost boastful, victim: "this time is the last time" his evil woman will hurt him. On his live album (1995), he introduces it as a "psychobilly" number, implying "that this time is the last time" because of murderous rage.

In contrast to Owens's music, then, Yoakam's music evokes rather than suppresses the pain of being kicked around. Likewise, his voice, unlike Owens's tireless tenor, often sounds strained and distant. "This Time" is engineered to exaggerate that pinched sound: the backup vocals are recorded at almost the same level as the lead, and a slow barroom shuffle reinforces the sense of exhaustion. Although Owens's "You Ain't Gonna Have Ol' Buck to Kick Around No More" has similar lyrics, it postures instead of threatens when it says "last time was the last time" since Owens's typically zippy delivery suggests that no such dramatic emotional collapse will take place. What's worse, Yoakam's men never get the happy reunion that Owens favored. Instead, their freely displayed broken hearts and unrealized dreams turn them into fools.[70] "If There Was a Way," the title cut of Yoakam's fifth album (1990), places a lovelorn "fool" in his darkened home, wondering if a reunion is possible. The music, softer and more enervated than Owens ever used, says no. "The Heart That You Own" continues the theme, this time conflating the home with the heart: "I pay rent on a run-down place / There ain't no view but there's lots of space / In my heart / The heart that you own." "The Distance Between You and Me" and "Nothing's Changed Here," also on the 1990 album, express similar despair.[71] "Home for Sale" has the fool selling the house where Owens's men would wait with optimistic patience (1993). Yoakam also features many sad and angry songs in which men reject their wayward women's conciliatory invitations to get "together again." His answer to notes and phone calls from one particular temptress is that he "Ain't That Lonely Yet" (1993).[72] "You're the One" (1990) scornfully reminds her who initiated the breakup. On the other hand, his "King of Fools" (written with Kostas, 1993) reigns because he knows full well how temporary "together again" is but still falls for his fickle woman's charms. "The Same Fool" uses the word "fool" or its variants over 30 times to wryly suggest that the singer will at least be victimized in a new way; although he's the "Same Fool" he's now smart enough not to be fooled "the way that you fooled the last fool you fooled before."

From the beginning of his career, Yoakam staked his claim on more thematic territory than Owens ever explored, thereby linking himself to hard country singers outside of Bakersfield. In "I'll Be Gone" he casts himself as a familiar rambling man, announcing his imminent departure before a one-night stand even begins. His 1987 cover of Stonewall Jackson's 1959 single "Smoke Along the Track" reiterates this theme.[73] The relentless rambler in "Lonesome Roads" concludes with the extravagantly self-pitying lines: "I'm just a face out in the crowd that looks like trouble / Poor ol' worthless me is the only friend I ever made" (1993); the allusion to Elia Kazan's country-singing villain (Lonesome Rhodes in *A Face in the Crowd*), however, keeps the audience on their guard. "Twenty Years" names the prison sentence of a man framed by the woman he cheated on (1986). Other cover songs strike familiar notes, too, such as a version of Johnny Cash's "Ring of Fire" in 1986 and his "Home of the Blues" in 1988;[74] Ray Price's "Heartaches by the Number" is covered on the first album.[75] Elvis Presley's "Little Sister" was a hit single in 1987 as was Lefty Frizzell's "Always Late with Your Kisses" in 1988.[76] In the late '80s this sort of recycling actually sounded novel since, as Colin Escott points out, "Marie Osmond was number one on the week Yoakam broke through."[77] In fact, before Yoakam's first album was even released, the editor of the *Journal of Country Music* concluded his preface to a 1986 series of articles on hard country by asserting that Dwight Yoakam's "eventual success or failure may speak volumes about the prospects for new traditionalists in the years to come."[78]

Ten years later, Yoakam is still a star, and especially in the first years of his career, he did speak volumes about country music's traditions. His third album, *Buenas Noches from a Lonely Room* (1988), puts the elements of abjection together to tell the story of "a hillbilly wracked by an uncontrollable obsession and cast adrift in a vast melting pot of twenty million souls" (Escott, "Dwight Yoakam," 210). In Yoakam's words, "I get moody; I kill someone; then I get religion in the end" (cited in Roland, 544). Actually, the album opens with a sense of heartland stability; "I Got You" wryly evokes the familiar balance of hard times and domestic comfort. The singer complains about landlords and union bosses who don't understand the pressures placed on a hard-working family man. Yet the family, particularly the good woman at its center, makes all the struggle worthwhile. The tone quickly shifts in the next two songs, however. Both "One More Name" and "What I Don't Know" express a man's fears about a woman's infidelity. In the first, the woman's sleep-talking seems to implicate her; in the second, the man threatens that "Smith and Wesson juries hold a real mean, nasty court." Next, an old song, "Home of the Blues," both warns and invites the hellbent or hell bound to join the company of the miserable by following the road used by all losers. The title song reaches the end of that road: the singer's beloved leaves with a stranger, so he tracks them down and kills them on a neon-lit city street. The words of the title are never mentioned in the song itself, but as Yoakam told Escott, who admired it as "the quintessential California country song title," it serves as "a summary, a thesis of what that song was about" ("Dwight Yoakam," 210). The seventh and eighth cuts stress the anomie of California drifting and dreaming. In "I Sang Dixie," the singer recounts the death of an alcoholic southern migrant on the streets of Los Angeles. He sings "Dixie" as a sort of funeral prayer while no other passerby will even cast sympathetic eyes on the dying man. The more upbeat "Streets of Bakersfield" similarly articulates the despair of the nearly invisible outcast. In contrast, the ninth cut, "Floyd County," tells of the more satisfying funeral of a Kentucky coal miner whose work, "honest" and "simple," fed the family who now sincerely mourns him. The album closes with "Hold on to God" (which Yoakam dedicates to his mother), a traditional religious number advocating seclusion from worldly ways. As the image of the wretched southern exile shows, though, contemporary hard country stars can't fully claim such seclusion. To get his name in lights, the singer has to cross the Floyd County line, and, like the ghostly Hank Williams Sr., he must also haunt—but never cross—the line between this world and the next.

Yoakam thus makes a point of transgression. In addition to unearthing his country roots with cover songs, he also uses them to connect country with other genres. It is in this respect that he is most like Owens: his brand of country music is all about flaunting impurity. The honky-tonk revivals hit the country airwaves, but others draw and cross all sorts of lines: his version of Dave Alvin's "Long White Cadillac" recounts the death of Hank Williams (in first person) with acidulated rock guitar riffs and a radio-unfriendly jamming length.[79] His version of "Truckin'," on *Dedicated*, a 1991 Grateful Dead tribute compilation, connects Yoakam to the generation of California country rockers who followed Buck Owens, as does his duet version (with k. d. lang) of the Flying Burrito Brothers' "Sin City."[80] His 1991 European release, *La croix d'amour*, featured several British invasion revivals, including the Beatles' "Things We Said Today." (These songs reappeared with others on the 1997 American release, *Under the Covers*.) In 1990, he did an arena-pleasing version of Canned Heat's 1970 hit "Let's Work Together." *Dwight Live* (1995) crosses back to Yoakam's Appalachian heritage with an irreverent piano-charged, electric-guitar-picking, loud-drumming cover of Bill Monroe's "Rocky Road Blues," as well as a reverent version of "Suspicious Minds" that evokes Elvis in his lounge lizard mode down to the dizzying guitar riffs and eerie backup singing. When Yoakam isn't covering a predecessor's song, he's often layering one over another. "Dangerous Man" (1990) sounds like Johnny Rivers meeting the Marshall Tucker Band, while Rich Kienzle noted that "I Don't Need It Done" "conjures up early Fats Domino."[81]

Yoakam makes sure his listeners confront this miscegenation. Producer and lead guitarist Pete Anderson's commentary on the contents of the sixth album, *This Time* (1993), provides a genealogy for nearly every cut. He describes the opening song, "Pocket of a Clown," as the result of his taking "what could have been a country shuffle and add[ing] an Elvis Presley/Jordanaires background. Then, with the guitar solo, I took a western swing/jazz/Les Paul direction." He links "Home for Sale," with its "haunting organ" to Procol Harum, "Two Doors Down" to rhythm and blues, "Wild Ride" to the Rolling Stones, and "Lonesome Roads" to Luke the Drifter.[82] In interviews promoting his 1995 *Gone*, Yoakam willingly named his sources, agreeing with *New Country*'s Tom Lanham that "Sorry You Asked?" featured Herb Alpert–style trumpeting and telling him that "Don't Be Sad" was a "Ray Price shuffle."[83] Likewise, he agreed when *Country Music*'s Patrick Carr suggested that he heard the Yardbirds in "Never Hold You" and Stax Studio horns in "One More Night."[84] In that interview, in fact, he mentions a stew of influences:

> It's a melting pot . . . I don't think I'll ever be able to escape that. I think it'll become more and more that. . . . I come from that time when music just exploded on AM radio. You would hear Buck Owens come right behind The Beatles or The Stones and lead into them with Van Morrison and then go into maybe The Statler Brothers doing "Flowers on the Wall," Henson Cargill doing "Skip a Rope." All that stuff. King Curtis, of course, the "Soul Twist" stuff, and Booker T and the MG's, Otis Redding, The Box Tops; that Memphis thing exploded. Motown, too. (37)

By the time Carr interviewed Yoakam for his 1998 album, *A Long Way Home*, he emphasized that their conversations had assumed the air of ritual, and indeed, Yoakam's discussions of his musical echoes ranged from Waylon Jennings to the ancient Gauls.[85] The previous year, *Under the Covers* had already brought the melting pot to a boiling point with songs ranging from the Clash's "Train in Vain" (featuring background singing by bluegrass legend Ralph Stanley) to Sonny and Cher's "Baby Don't Go" (a duet with Sheryl Crow) to Jimmie Rodgers's "T for Texas." Although the album title announces that Yoakam is singing others' songs, the bedroom-themed photographs scattered throughout the liner notes suggest that a new generation of music is being created. To achieve that degree of creative license, Yoakam, like the Okies before him, had to head West. "I was drawn to Los Angeles by my earlobes . . . the country-rock sound, and the Bakersfield sound," he told Escott ("Dwight Yoakam," 206). Although he was signed to Warner-Reprise in 1985, he does his actual recording at Capitol Studios: "[T]hat's where Buck cut, where Merle cut. It was our connection to our predecessors in West Coast country music" (208).

No wonder, then, that Yoakam says "my music is hard country. . . . 'A friend told me, Your stuff is so hard, they're gonna think it's rock and roll.' And they did. You combine drummers and mountain people, and you've got hillbilly music" (Everett 113). To combine drummers and mountain people, though, you have to get the people out of the mountains. Then, once they're away from rural safety, mountain people experience country's hard feelings. The coal miner in "Miner's Prayer" (on the first album) doesn't have them, so he never thinks of bettering his lot. Instead, he begs God for another day of safety underground as he thanks Him for his children and few earthly possessions. Yoakam dedicated this gentle acoustic song "to the memory of Luther Tibbs. A Kentucky coal miner for forty years and my Grandpa." Yoakam's second single, though, "Guitars, Cadillacs," makes the hard feelings loud and clear.

It's "a lesson about a naive fool that came to Babylon" much like the farmer who came to Baltimore. Rather than returning to the country, though, Yoakam's disappointed dreamer finds urban solace in "guitars, Cadillacs, and hillbilly music." In other words, Yoakam doesn't bother to imagine any respite better than the "Honky-Tonk Blues" themselves. The music that accompanies this story provides a good example of that respite: twanging lead guitar, frantic, heavy-handed drumming, and a fiddle that the miracle of multichannel mixing makes louder and more insistent than the percussion. This onslaught of sound creates the same kind of emotional release that characterizes Owens's music. In this song, a vaguely sketched (and ultimately short-lived) love affair lured a man from his rural home, but in other songs migration follows a familiar socioeconomic impulse. In fact, Yoakam says that he called the album *Guitars, Cadillacs, Etc. Etc.* to offer "a real fond remembrance of my parents' desire to have an outward sign of their success, like owning a Cadillac. We couldn't afford one . . . but that's the world I'm talking about in my music . . . I see the beauty of my people's lives. . . . They're who gave me the spiritual fire that allowed me to recreate the images of that world in music."[86]

The next album, *Hillbilly Deluxe*, continues the family saga with "Readin' Rightin' Rt. 23," "written for and lovingly dedicated to my mother, Ruth Ann; to my Aunts Margaret, Mary Helen, Verdie Kay and Joy; and to my uncle, Guy Walton." "They," according to the lyrics, headed north from Kentucky to escape the hardships of the mines and to gain the material comforts of the city. In spite of this "rightin'," they discovered new forms of misery along the way. The title, with its odd pun on "writing," seems to make a political statement, and in his interviews, Yoakam extends that statement to his music in general:

> I'll have a fistfight with you about it . . . I'm tired of them peddling it, and soft-selling the categories. "Well, country can be anything." The hell you say. No you can't. . . . You know why? Because it's back to Dwight Yoakam doing this for Dwight and for a man named Luther Tibbs that mined coal . . . and had to get up off a chair and had to roll around on the floor to catch a breath because he had coal dust on his lungs. And I'll be damned if you're gonna tell me what country music is. (Everett, 13)[87]

Like Owens, Yoakam wants to draw the lines he crosses. Owens, though, draws it at the experience of failure. Unlike Owens, Yoakam insists that this possibility remain visible. The oxymoron of his second album's title—*Hillbilly Deluxe*—draws that line more specifically on the city streets where the Cadillacs cruise, where the music plays loud, where your name can be in lights, and where you can still feel an incurable unease.

The abject display is familiar from many other hard country songs although Yoakam celebrates it by eroticizing it. Indeed, Yoakam may be hard country's only sex symbol. He wears his jeans tight and torn, and, with his back to the audience, he wiggles suggestively during live performances. His early publicity even tried to construct him as an arbiter of taste. In 1989, Manuel Cuevas, his costume designer, launched a line of Yoakam-inspired western jackets, telling reporters that "Dwight is definitely a trendsetter. He has made country-Western hip again";[88] in another interview, Yoakam himself took credit for the jacket design.[89] He was also featured in *USA Weekend*'s fashion column as a male who makes a fashion statement with a hat.[90] He posed and pouted for photographers. *Country Music* editor Patrick Carr reported that the first pictures he saw made him "want to puke. Splatter stale Schlitz and half-digested chili and less mentionable hard-core country commodities all over the stuck-up little fashion plate's . . . Levi's" ("A Journey," 30). *Vanity Fair* devoted its August 1989 car column to Yoakam's musings on how the expensive Avanti compared to his pickup truck, vintage Cadillac, vintage convertible, and Jaguar. He thought his image might be enhanced by the four-seater Avanti: "I need a car that I can put four people in and not look like an old man driving around."[91]

In fact, so intent is Yoakam on controlling his image that he has been credited (or cocredited) with "art direction" for all of his album covers. His first records juxtaposed traditional hard country visuals with hip sex appeal. The front cover of *Guitars, Cadillacs, Etc., Etc.* features a tinted photograph of him captioned with '50s-style type; the back cover shows him (in living color) leaning against a black-and-white vintage Cadillac convertible parked on a bleak roadside. "I wanted it to look like those early albums I saw when I was a kid" he said (Escott, "Dwight Yoakam," 207). *Hillbilly Deluxe* similarly juxtaposed retro graphics with a hip glamour shot of Yoakam in torn jeans and a flashy jacket. The back cover balances tradition and contemporary sophistication even more explicitly: although it features an equally glamorous shot of an insouciantly slouching Yoakam, it is framed by a flurry of logos depicting cowboys lassoing spaceships and shooting laser guns. His later album art puts the emphasis almost entirely on the contemporary. *This Time* contains several Dali-esque images conflating time and mortality: a stopwatch with a cracked glass cover, calendar pages being carried off by the water from a running faucet, and so on. *Gone* offers many eerily tinted photographs of Yoakam navigating scenes of urban desolation, as well as a reproduction of a high-modern Hans Burkhardt painting titled simply "Abstraction" (1941). The only icon that unambiguously says "country" is the white cowboy hat that Yoakam wears in each scene of decay. While women of questionable virtue surround him, Yoakam guards his paradoxically hip innocence.

Although country stars have always flaunted their wealth, they have never before dared to flaunt their success as assuredly as Yoakam has. As a result, interviewers constantly raise the issue of Yoakam's authenticity. Like Owens, Yoakam claims that he doesn't drink, and, since he has never married, his knowledge of domestic turmoil is assumed to be abstract, even though his brief romance with Sharon Stone made tabloid headlines. (When they split up, she claimed she preferred "a dirt sandwich" to him.) "Personas or real-life? Yoakam will never tell. And he purposely blurs the two in his writing," laments Lanham (44). In the trendy *Details,* Anita Sarko provoked Yoakam by reporting that "it's been suggested that you're merely a talented opportunist playing dress-up." His response was neatly evasive about where he draws the line between style and substance: "[W]hat you saw at my show was not parody. It was real life, 1988" (141). Escott, marveling at Yoakam's vocabulary, wonders whether he isn't "too smart for a hillbilly singer" ("Dwight Yoakam," 210). Yoakam, however, insists that his background is the very stuff of country music: "[T]here was always a question about whether we would be able to maintain our level of existence. It's given me an uneasiness about security—and the world. You hear that in country music. The cultural ethnicity of country music is *Grapes of Wrath* culture" (206). It's also clear that he knows all about the incurable unease of having your feet on the street and your heart and head in the hard country. Like Owens, he has a lot of great clothes, but, metaphorically speaking, he's still not on the cover of the *Music City News.*

Likewise, Yoakam's frequent use of humor reassures his audience that he approaches them on their level. The drinking songs, in particular, get funnier with each album. "Sorry You Asked?" the first cut on his deathly serious *Gone,* hilariously portrays a drunken loser buttonholing the kind heart who has asked about the whereabouts of his estranged lover; "Baby Why Not" features an equally drunken fool begging a woman to waste her life with him. Similarly, his videos often balance defeat with hammy slapstick. "Always Late" features silly, prancing backup singers, and "Turn It On, Turn It Up, Turn Me Loose" shows Yoakam taking a pratfall in an otherwise bleak landscape. The questions about his authenticity arise, he suggests, because this is a condition we don't know how to separate from hard country itself. He complained to a reporter from *People* about the media's unreflective need to present the picture-imperfect hick: "[W]hen a performer shows up for an interview and doesn't go 'aw shucks' and kick the dirt and need to have coffee showered on him to get him out of a drunken stupor, something just doesn't sit right with the reporter."[92]

But the questions also arise because of Yoakam's increasingly original work; even those who should be familiar with hard country conventions have been taken by surprise as he evolves beyond overt statements about his roots. His drinking and urban angst compositions can easily be heard as homage, particularly when they are surrounded by covers of classics. However, the more ambitious (even pretentious) visual images, combined with the stranger musical blends and sparser lyrics of Yoakam's more recent discs, point somewhere else even as mainstream media hesitate to go there. For example, John Morthland's commentary on *This Time* strained to balance these aspects, noting "a sense of estrangement, of alienation, much deeper and stronger than on previous releases, a sense that is simultaneously smack in the country tradition from way back . . . and utterly contemporary." What Morthland still wants to know, though, is how this new sense of alienation relates to Yoakam's personal life; what Yoakam says is that his writing is a form of "role-playing" that allows him to reveal himself even though he says nothing about mama, trains, prison, or what was happening to him while he wrote his songs.[93] Similarly, Patrick Carr half-playfully attempts to bring Yoakam back to familiar territory by asking "here on *Gone* we have . . . eight songs written from the position of a man deserted, heartbroken, failed in love. Is your love life all messed up, Dwight?" (37). In response, Yoakam must belabor the obvious: "[M]aybe I'm expressing a lot of things that are very personal and very specific to things that have nothing to do with romantic love, but I'm doing so in that context. . . . It's something that throughout time, the prophets . . . have tried to explain to us. . . . Expel that pain and you'll be free from it, some day some way" (38).

Certainly, the songs on *Gone* implicitly raise hard questions about human connections and priorities that go beyond the familiar measures of success and failure. The twangy title song vaguely sketches a broken romance but the allegro chorus easily lends itself to a comment on mortality: "That'll be me you'll see / for not very long / 'cause that'll be me / you see / that'll be gone." In fact, according to Lanham, Yoakam chose this as the title song "because of all its latent mortal-coil implications" (40). The next song has an equally ominous title—"Nothing"—and offers an equally philosophical description of life after a broken romance: it's nothing but sadness, fear, and silence (written with Kostas). Muted guitars and a startling organ solo reinforce the contemplative tone of the lyrics. Likewise, the solemnly paced "This Much I Know" lists "how empty the world can be" among the lessons learned when love—or is it life here and now?—goes bad.

In other words, Yoakam's music is hard country even if it can't be taken as a literal transcription of his personal hard times. In fact, that's *why* it's hard country. It's about heartaches and hangovers but only because those things are metaphors for humiliation, now not only for the humiliation of the white male but also for the humiliation that accompanies the cultural hierarchies and practices that continue to isolate country music. That humiliation includes walking the line that Yoakam and Owens have refused to toe but have perhaps never completely crossed, either: the line around the field of stone, the elusive line that separates those whose speech is taken figuratively from those who are locked in the literal, those whose cultural and consumer choices reflect their cultural capital, and those whose cowboy boots and Crystal Palaces reflect their lack thereof. Yoakam's analysis of the situation, however, suggests that he's still hoping to break out before he's gone. His success hinges on escaping the same people that Owens fled: "[T]he people who market ethnic music in this country . . . perpetuate the myth that you can't be a really great country or blues artist unless you're illiterate and self-destructive. They're the ones who burn those artists up, use them, abuse them, then put them in coffins and collect the royalties on their estate" (Escott, "Dwight Yoakam," 210). For now, then, while Owens guards the starting line, Yoakam looks for a new finish line.

5

♪ying hard

**Hard country
at the
finish line?**

In the '70s, as Owens's career was fading, the much-heralded
Outlaw movement, led by Waylon Jennings and
Willie Nelson (but including a range of others),[1]
managed to buck the system in ways very similar
to Owens's. Like Owens, the Outlaws armed
themselves with Telecasters and a rock beat, and
then insisted on the right to produce their own
music. Like Owens, they preferred show venues
like Manhattan's hip Max's Kansas City or massive festivals and arenas to the staid and low-
paying *Opry*. "Who listens to the Opry nowa-
days? Ain't nobody out there listening any-
more," Jennings told Peter Guralnick in 1974
(208). According to Frye Gaillard, Roy Acuff denounced Nelson's rejection of the fold from the
Opry stage (146). However, this rebellion would
have been far less newsworthy if the rebels had
acknowledged their similarity to Owens. Instead,
one of Jennings's first appearances in the outlaw
mode introduces him as a pill-popping "psyche-
delic cowboy" and critic of Owens: "he does some
of the most ridiculous damn things I ever heard,"
Jennings complained (Grissim, 80).[2] Although
Jennings writes little of his own material, and in
that sense, is essentially a song stylist, he is as
country as Owens and shares Owens's rock leanings, perhaps even leaning more steeply. He
started in the music business as a member of
Buddy Holly's band; years later, while Nashville
was awash in bland countrypolitan, he took to
dressing in black leather and allied himself with a
trend-bucking studio known as "Hillbilly Cen-

tral." "If we called ourselves hillbillies, it was to put some people off guard, to put ourselves down and them on," he explains in his autobiography (221). This abject stance, however, rapidly evolved into a brief fling with superstarlike trend setting. According to Outlaw chronicler Michael Bane, Jennings's success "re-defined . . . the meaning of what it is to be a country star" (60).

Similarly, in 1971, after years as a successful songwriter (he wrote Patsy Cline's "Crazy") and clean-cut, middling singer in Nashville, Nelson head-quartered himself in Austin, Texas, grew his famous long red tresses, and be-came a star. His concept albums such as *Red Headed Stranger* (1975) and his autobiographical bent brought him serious attention; his "annual" Fourth of July picnic then became a country counterpart to Woodstock, drawing photo-genic flocks of hip young fans who reportedly partied peacefully with the rough-edged rednecks also in attendance (Bane, 108–110).[3] Public television launched *Austin City Limits*, its un-Nashville, un-*Opry* celebration of country hipness in 1976. For a short while, Waylon and Willie were stars of such mag-nitude that, like Cher and Elvis, they had no need for last names. Although they both gathered a vast audience, the differing fates of Waylon and Willie, the two biggest stars of the Outlaw movement, demonstrate once more the es-sential (yet metaphorical) rustication of hard country.

As Outlaws, they evoked something far more glamorous than the common criminals, public drunks, and big-time deadbeats who usually embodied hard country's legal problems. Although Michael Bane asserts that "'outlaw' meant resenting the way your record company hashed up your music, not that you'd knocked over a liquor store last Friday" (11), the Outlaws titillated the public with an aura of the Wild West. The cover of their 1976 *Wanted! The Outlaws* (with Jennings, Nelson, Tompall Glaser, and Jennings's wife, Jessi Colter) took the form of an old-fashioned wanted poster (fig. 5.1). Colter, née Miriam John-son, borrowed her stage name from her grandfather, a train robber (Bufwack and Oerman, 444). Nelson's 1975 *Red-Headed Stranger*, set in turn-of-the-century Montana, told the story of a cowboy who killed his adulterous wife and her lover. (In 1987, he starred in the film version of it.) Kris Kristofferson's precountry credentials as a Rhodes scholar and army pilot, as well as his post-country movie stardom, gave hillbilly singing the aura of a glamorous career option. While their battles with record companies lacked silver-screen drama, their success did seem to validate the American worship of wild and woolly en-trepreneurship. Like Frank Sinatra or William Randolph Hearst, the Outlaws made a lot of noise about doing it their way.

While their rocking anti-Nashville stance should have allied them with Owens, their pledges of allegiance to earlier hard country icons left them with few beams of Owens's California sunshine. Gaillard, in his perceptive report-

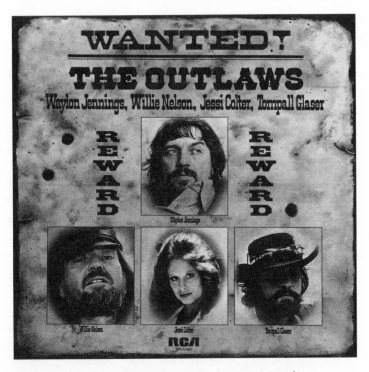

Fig. 5.1: The cover of *Wanted! The Outlaws*. Courtesy Country Music Foundation.

ing on country music in the '70s, called them "the tradition-minded rebels" who could save country music from pop dilution (22–33). Nevertheless, they were widely perceived as having eschewed the cheating and drinking laments so prevalent in country music. On his liner notes to *Wanted! The Outlaws*, for example, *Rolling Stone*'s Chet Flippo claimed that "their music didn't conform to the country norm of songs of divorce and alcohol and life's other little miseries."[4] (Yet "Whiskey River"—a desperate man's plea to keep the liquid flowing—has been one of Nelson's concert-opening tunes since 1978.)[5] In his history of the movement, journalist Jan Reid claims to have hated country music before discovering Willie Nelson. "Country music was worse than soap opera television,"[6] he asserted, until Willie and his cohorts "suggested an active disengagement, a quest for a freer way of life" (12). The Outlaws did sing about liberation and good times, but these pleasures were more often fueled by drugs and alcohol than optimism. In "Me and Bobby McGee," one of Kristofferson's most famous songs, freedom is a bleak condition equated with having nothing to lose. When Waylon, after his 1977 arrest for cocaine possession, sang about singing through his nose ("Don't You Think This Outlaw Bit's Done Got Out of Hand"), he alluded to more than a nasal twang. In 1978, he bragged that "I've Always Been Crazy," and publicly admitted that he recorded it while high on cocaine (Roland, 219). In many songs, his restless baritone and bass-heavy band mimicked such a rush while Nelson's loping, literally offbeat singing and soothing acoustic picking expressed a gentler type of intoxication. In "Me and Paul" (1971), he obliquely complained about a drug arrest, while in his autobiography he openly bragged about smoking marijuana on the roof of the Carter White House.[7]

Outlaw love affairs did slightly modify hard country's heartache and hangover themes. Bragging, for the most part, overtook complaining both in song and in the publicity of "real" life. Jennings's "Ladies Love Outlaws" named the movement (Bane, 4),[8] and "Good-Hearted Woman," his smash duet with Nelson, praised a woman who stood by her honky-tonk hedonist. "Amanda" (1979) similarly lauded a woman's devotion to a "country boy" who was never going to finish adolescence. He was 14 when he started playing guitar, the singer explains, and now that he's over 30, he still dresses and acts the same way.[9] While Jennings's rebel persona meshed with songs like "Never Could Toe the Mark" (1984), at other times he made an exception for attractive women: then he was "The Only Daddy That'll Walk the Line" (1968).[10] In their respective autobiographies, the queen of rock groupies, Pamela Des Barres, bragged and complained about her flings with Jennings (her one foray into country),[11] while Jennings crowed about all the women who offered themselves to him (154). Two of Nelson's movies, *Honeysuckle Rose* (1980) and *Songwriter* (1984), portray him as a thinly fictionalized Lothario and troubadour who still manages to keep the love of a good woman at home. Kissing and telling reached almost repellent heights in "To All the Girls I've Loved Before,"[12] Nelson's 1984 duet with Latin crooner Julio Iglesias. Likewise, "Put Another Log on the Fire,"[13] Tompall Glaser's notorious contribution to *Wanted! The Outlaws*, mocked good-ol'-boy chauvinism by quoting a grotesque husband issuing a chain of absurd commands to a beleaguered wife. Such songs allowed these supposedly tough loners to stand by their female fans without becoming emotionally solid and economically sound breadwinners.

It is this affiliative ability (with every one but Owens) that made the Outlaw movement so successful. While commentators now almost ritually explain the movement as little more than a marketing ploy,[14] it marketed to the mainstream what had never been marketed before or since: hard country.[15] *Wanted! The Outlaws* made country music history when it became the first country album to be awarded for reaching platinum-level sales.[16] According to Flippo, this milestone created a large market for country albums—a province of rock and roll until then—in a field heretofore dominated by less profitable single sales.[17] (The achievement is particularly remarkable given that the album was a compilation of previously released material.) In fact, it was the rock market that boosted the Outlaws' sales—just as it would for Garth Brooks in the early '90s. Earlier attempts to name the movement, such as "progressive country" or "redneck rock," already hinted at this appeal; in his autobiography, Jennings credits Flippo, whose *Rolling Stone* masthead gave him hip credibility, with spreading the word to a huge new fan base (241).

Many of their songs (perhaps unintentionally) played to the rock crowd's prejudice against country music. Jennings's "Are You Sure Hank Done It This Way," a country chart-topper in 1975, criticized Nashville's rhinestone and Cadillac aesthetic and demanded change. Nelson's album cut "Write Your Own Song" was even more belligerent, accusing a controlling music executive of performing obscene and physically impossible gestures in order to avoid the powerful emotions conveyed by a Willie Nelson song. They also borrowed well-known rock material; in 1969, Jennings released Chuck Berry's "Brown-Eyed Handsome Man" as a single; in 1976 he covered Neil Young's "Are You Ready for the Country?" In 1980, Nelson covered the Allman Brothers' "Midnight Rider."[18] *Wanted! The Outlaws* featured Waylon's and Jessi Colter's duet version of Elvis's "Suspicious Minds."[19] No wonder David Allan Coe's genealogical "Willie, Waylon, 'n Me" (1976) mentioned only rock stars (as diverse as the Beatles and the Flying Burrito Brothers) as the predecessors of the Outlaws.[20]

In spite of his rock covers, Jennings claimed that he "couldn't go pop with a firecracker in [his] mouth,"[21] and he and Nelson frequently flashed their hard country credentials. Nelson's tributes to his country predecessors took the form of cover songs; in 1975 he covered Roy Acuff's "Blue Eyes Crying in the Rain" and in 1976 he borrowed Lefty Frizzell's "If You've Got the Money I've Got the Time." Jennings paid tribute by singing about his ancestors; in 1975, he had a double-sided hit when he backed "Are You Sure Hank Done It This Way" with "Bob Wills Is Still the King." Williams, hard country's biggest star, had a special place in the Outlaw pantheon. Jennings claims to have kept an empty bunk in his hearselike tour bus (named Black Maria) for the ghost of Williams, and he wrote the name "Hank" on the bathroom door (Guralnick 211). In songs like the Jennings/Hank Williams Jr. duet "The Conversation," Hank Sr.'s drug and alcohol use was emulated (right on the record) by the singers who proclaimed Williams the most wanted outlaw of all.[22] Kristofferson, too, wrote an inane tribute to Williams ("If You Don't Like Hank Williams [You Can Kiss My Ass]"). In songs like "Honky-Tonk Heroes" (1976) and "Luckenbach, Texas" (1977), Nelson and Jennings ostensibly refused to revel in stardom, presenting themselves instead as hard drinking men who rejected the trappings of bourgeois success in favor of the usual symbols of country music: small towns and guitars.[23] Their 1978 hit "Mammas Don't Let Your Babies Grow Up to Be Cowboys" warned that the life of a [Telecaster] cowboy precluded the pleasures of middle-class stability and advised women to make their children be "doctors and lawyers."[24] In fact, neither managed to hold on to the millions of dollars they made in the '70s. In 1981, Jennings found himself $2.5 million in debt, and in 1990, Nelson's $16 million tax bill forced him to liquidate nearly everything but his battered guitar.

Although they have outlived Williams, their hard country stardom has not. As early as 1978, Jennings was asking "Don't You Think This Outlaw Bit's Done Got Out of Hand"? and in 1992, he diagnosed and abjured the "Hank Williams Syndrome" as a drugging compulsion that nearly killed him. Nelson, though, didn't stick around to complain about it. In 1978, he released *Stardust*, a collection of pop standards. Shortly thereafter, he signed several Hollywood motion picture deals. As a result, his star continued to gain magnitude while the death knells for the Outlaw movement rang. In her 1982 introduction to country music, Martha Hume (Chet Flippo's wife) declared that the label outlaw "should be dropped because there is no longer an Outlaw movement in country music" (11). Bane, describing an interminable wait for an interview outside Nelson's bunkerlike house in Austin, concludes that success itself, always so inimicable to hard country, defeated outlawhood. Instead of living the hard way, the Outlaws got "caught up in the maelstrom of hype, hangers-on and just plain nonsense that defines the star-maker machinery behind the popular song" (152; Bane does not credit Joni Mitchell for this line).

Yet espousing a very ordinary life has done little for Jennings's career. In 1981, Hank Williams Jr. had a number one hit as he complained that "All My Rowdy Friends Have Settled Down," counting his mentor Waylon among this domesticated, iced-tea–sipping crowd. Jennings, in fact, seems doomed to finish his career as a "country graybeard" practically banished from the airwaves and alternately lamenting and rejecting the good old days.[25] In 1985, he recorded a duet with *Sesame Street*'s Big Bird; at the same time, he joined forces with Nelson, Johnny Cash, and Kris Kristofferson as "The Highwaymen." With them, he smugly referred to his past as a series of "Songs That Made a Difference"[26] sung by an "Endangered Species."[27] Nelson, on the other hand, has tangled famously with the IRS, does Taco Bell commercials, and is still being cast in big budget movies such as *Wag the Dog*. He is, in Flippo's words, "the godfather of crossover."[28]

A new Waylon and Willie duet recorded for the 20th anniversary version of *Wanted! The Outlaws* provides an interesting commentary on the fate of these two artists who brought hard country its greatest audience. They chose

"Nowhere Road," written by Steve Earle, a '90s version of an outlaw: ex-convict, recovered heroin addict, and struggling singer/songwriter stuck somewhere between rock and roll and mainstream country. The song epitomizes the fate of the hard country star. It tells of a road in Oklahoma that is reputed to lead to the "big highway" but in fact doesn't. As a result, it's taught plenty of "country boys" the hard way, sings Waylon in one of his verses. In fact, Waylon has wandered down just such a hard road. Stranded in the country, he's standing in the field of stone where his machismo can almost automatically be questioned. Bruce Feiler, who was present at the taping of this song, reports that "the scene seemed straight out of *Grumpy Old Men*" even though Waylon threatened to kill him for asking stupid questions and later stormed out of the studio when Steve Earle, who was also producing, refused to grant Waylon's request to record a twelfth version of the harmony (164). Willie, on the other hand, sang his part and hit the road—and for him, the road *is* a highway. He has found his way to the fast track that takes him right out of hard country.[29]

The fate of George Jones, the reigning king of hard country, provides a final perspective on hard country's dialogue with both country music and the outside world. Jones has had a remarkably long career, with hits on the chart in every decade since the 1950s. References to him abound in country songs, and he has lent his voice to many singers by joining them for a line or two in their songs, or by recording duets with them. On other occasions, performers make a point of singing *about* Jones or imitating him. These affiliative gestures are not nearly so prominent in other forms of popular music, and even within country, Jones has surely been imitated more often and been alluded to more often than other stars. He has also recorded numerous duets with numerous partners. The purpose of these practices is not difficult to recognize: they create or amplify the sense of tradition and shared outlook so important to hard country music. Importantly, Jones occupies a pivotal position in the transmission of the hard way, allying himself with Hank Williams and anointing members of the new generation who ally themselves with him. His duet with Mark Chestnutt, "Talking to Hank,"[30] enacts just such a bond as the two singers giddily discuss the perils of ornery women and alcohol with a preternaturally aged 29-year-old whom they conclude is Hank Williams Sr. Although the purpose of these collaborative and allusive practices may be clear, they create varied meanings, and in the rest of this chapter, I will trace the evolution of Jones's persona and the use of that persona by other country artists. While Jones's persona bemoans his fate and until recently seemed to be talking about the life of the real George Jones, other singers now seek to play possum or to define themselves as both keeping up with Jones and keeping away from him. For them, taking the hard road now seems more difficult than ever.

Jones's songs are archetypically hard country, un-middle-American in their themes and out of step with the ethos of their time. While Jones's followers can use his image to claim their place in country music, Jones almost invariably casts himself as an outcast. Whereas country-music-loving presidents advocate frugality, hard work, and moderation, Jones—at least until recently—stands for bankruptcy, extravagance, and addiction. Likewise, Jones was sad in the midst of the '50s happy days, square (although far from straight) in the age of Aquarius, and sinking on the charts during country music's peak of popularity in the early '90s. He's always been "Country When Country Wasn't Cool."[31] Suffering and indignity are the essence of his performing style; in his marriage to Tammy Wynette, he seems to have lived all the heartbreaks implied in the Hank and Audrey Williams story, and during his cocaine and alcohol addictions, he suffered as much as the Outlaws enjoyed. The tabloids have made this personal turmoil public, and thus his songs of woe sound like chapters in his autobiography. *I Am What I Am*, the title of a 1980 album, typifies his autobiographical gambit; the record doesn't even have a song with that title. If there is a record to set straight, Jones certainly hasn't been eager to do it. "I don't care what people think," he has said, "if it will help sell albums" (332).[32] His success is thus based on failure of the most abject kind. As an article from *Possum Tracks*, his fan club newsletter, puts it, "the most admirable thing about him is that he went through a few years of hell, only to resurface in better shape than ever. He suffered through failed marriages, alcoholism, . . . and near bankruptcy."[33] Nevertheless, when he falls, he doesn't take it like a man; he usually finds himself reduced to tears. In the early stages of his career, he released songs with titles like "World's Worst Loser" and "Big Fool of the Year."[34] Yet another song announced that a "Drunk Can't Be a Man" and in those days, Jones was a notorious drunk. His disgrace didn't keep him from going around mirrors, but he did have to confess that his image had "Aged Twenty Years in Five" thanks to alcohol.[35] More recently, he admits that he sleeps like a baby and acts like one too, since he wakes up crying every hour.[36] In short, Jones's hard-core techniques resonate because he links them to hard drinking, hard luck, and hard times.

Ever the lonesome loser, never the rugged individualist, Jones expresses most clearly his commitment to the hard way in his frequent songs about dream houses decaying into nightmares. In his early "Ragged but Right" and "Small-Time Laboring Man" (written with Earl Montgomery), he evinced a rather trite pride in poverty as well as a naive eagerness to win women's hearts through lavish spending; in "Tall, Tall Trees" (written with Roger Miller), for example, he promises to buy the object of his affections a mansion and a limousine. His 1966 "Four-0-Thirty-Three" (with Earl Montgomery) gives the address of a happy home. Beginning in the mid '60s, however, the characters he sings about have more wistfully adopted mainstream ways of measuring success. As sociologist Stephanie Coontz points out in her discussion of postwar culture, "acceptance of domesticity was the mark of middle-class status and upward mobility."[37] Jones's characters start their ascent by acquiring a suburban dream house, a fixture of the American dream since the postwar years, and then go on to lose it in great detail.

When Jones sings these tales of woe, they seem to be the story of his life, and when he tells us the story of his life, he insists on his attachment to this particular aspect of the modern American dream. Although he often pleads lost memory and lost documents to explain vast gaps in his autobiography, *I Lived to Tell It All*, he can remember a great deal about his real estate transactions. During the height of his cocaine addiction he recalls buying seven houses in Florence, Alabama. In the early days of his marriage to Tammy Wynette, the couple was dubbed "Mr. and Mrs. Country Music" but Jones claims "Mr. and Mrs. Suburbanite" would have been more accurate, and he doesn't intend this revision as an insult.[38] He remembers fondly their move from Nashville to Lakeland, Florida, and the dabbling in real estate they did there. "I loved being concerned about the things that never concerned me before, such as how to rid the lawn of weeds or whether it was time to clean the shutters" (149), he explains. He thus particularly resents (and denies) Wynette's accusation that he destroyed their house during a drinking spree. Although he admits to hurting many of the people closest to him, he finds it unfathomable that he would have destroyed what he himself repeatedly describes as his Florida "dream house" (150, 158).

> A lot of folks would be surprised to learn that I enjoy interior decorating. I can walk into a shell with a roof and tell you what it would look like after six months of work. Then I can walk through a furniture store and tell you just what would go with what and in what room. That's the kind of personal interest, or passion, that I took in Tammy's and my Lakeland home. (151)

Now, supposedly in recovery from alcohol and drug addiction, he counts compulsive lawn mowing among his greatest satisfactions (333). The back cover of *I Lived to Tell It All* (1996), the compact disc named after his autobiography, even shows him wearing jeans, tennis shoes, and a big smile as he perches on top of a John Deere riding mower.[39]

Given this publicly professed belief in the dream house, when Jones sings about broken homes, the emotions he evokes are both banal and convincingly intense, and he rarely paints a character who willfully does the breaking. In comparison to Hank Williams's vaguely evoked lost dreams, Jones's songs vividly describe domestic settings. Yet unlike Williams, he rarely offers religious solace; although Jones has recorded a few religious songs and a gospel album, none of his signature songs has religious themes. As far as his characters are concerned, there couldn't possibly be "a better home awaitin' in the sky."[40] Instead, they are intensely attached to, and inexplicably excluded from, a secular dream house. Jones's 1965 hit "Things Have Gone to Pieces" evokes suburban distress with a typical strain of passivity. The abandoned singer's home crumbles around him while he presents himself as blamelessly overwhelmed. The song opens with an unprioritized list of complaints about dripping faucets, burnt-out light bulbs, and lost jobs while the chorus mixes masculine pain with feminine perfidy. He's hanging on to what's left of his dream although there's no indication he can put the pieces back together.[41] The song itself is addressed to an impersonal audience rather than to the capricious woman; it's a display of self-pity, not an attempt to reconcile.

Ten years later, "These Days I Barely Get By" (cowritten with Wynette) repeats this scenario with one crucial difference: this song explicitly connects the shame the singer feels to the plight of his listeners. Again, the singer casts himself as a blameless victim, waking up in pain, going to work in spite of it, then walking home in the rain only to find that his wife has left him without giving an explanation. In the next verse, he imagines bankruptcy and unemployment will follow since he lost his last two dollars at the horse races and his boss is threatening to lay him off. After a crying spell, he concludes the swelling third verse by threatening suicide; he says he feels like giving up and dying. The final refrain, little more than the title, builds to a crescendo on the word "by" and then Jones elongates a reprise, changing "I barely get by," to "one barely gets by," which allows him to construct a whole neighborhood in decay, a neighborhood where misery loves Jones's company. Similarly, in "The Grand Tour," the singer invites you to inspect his lonely house where once again, the mistress has left for no apparent reason. In the beginning of another song, he casts himself as a real estate agent promising his listeners the perfect three-bedroom house with hardwood floors. The chorus quickly uncovers the ruse (and announces the song's title) since it directs us to the house "Where the Tall Grass Grows."[42] We won't be accompanied by the singer since he explains that he can't bear to confront the memories the house contains (let alone mow the lawn). But once we visit those houses, we're all in on the secret misery that lurks behind the suburban dream.

Jones claims one of his first songs in this genre, 1960's "Window Up

Above," as his favorite record, and the song also marked a milestone in his career, placing Jones as a master of the wrenchingly sad ballad.[43] The emotional
intensity of the song may best be demonstrated by the illogic of the lyrics. The
singer claims he watched his wife's adulterous liaison from the window up
above, which suggests that the wife and her lover must have been in the yard
or the street, but in that case, it's hard to understand his next statement—that
he can hear his wife whisper to her lover. Instead, the song makes sense
through the reiteration of familiar elements: the singer is foolishly happy with
domestic life until he can see—this time through spying and eavesdropping—
his home breaking. Then, he cries as his illusions crumble. The logistical confusion may even amplify the way this song, like all of Jones's dream-house
songs, strips the euphemism "broken home" of its anesthetic intent and instead makes the expression painfully metaphoric. The home, the private space
where identity is nurtured, and the house, which makes a public statement
about who we are, sings of failure. To further embody such failure, Jones commissioned a Nudie suit decorated with tear-stained faces peeking through windows.[44] The most striking thing about the song, though, is the way Jones's
nasal singing and hard-core diction reinforce the theme.[45] In the song's first
line—in which the singer says he loves the "new way" he's been living—Jones
bends the word "new" into a hyperbolically nasal and nonstandard pronunciation that immediately suggests how easily a woman gulled this rustic with a
dream of domesticity and how violently unrestrained his emotions could be in
response. "New," he implies, isn't really the word that describes the way he
was living. Nearly every line that follows has at least one surprisingly stressed
and mangled word that echoes the singer's descent into gloom.

In "Two-Story House," a duet with Wynette, even a house at the height of
the social scale harbors failure. "What splendor" Jones moans in the chorus as
Wynette describes the mansion's features such as chandeliers and marble
floors. But the title tells of the couple's defeat. In this house, both the woman
and the man have a story, but neither one has a happy ending.[46] "A Good Year
for the Roses" describes a house in full suburban glory, but the song gains its
pathos from the singer's knowledge that decay will come quickly. His wife has
just left him—her half-drunk cup of coffee and half-smoked cigarette are still
in plain sight, the roses that she planted are still in bloom—but now that she's
gone, he lacks the will to stave off the encroaching grass and weeds. Most grue-
some, though, is the singer's view of himself. The most worthless objects that
surround him have more value than he does. The roses, after all, had a good
year, and he even wishes he were the lipstick-stained cigarette and coffee cup
that his wife at least touched. He sees *himself* as the about-to-be-broken-down
house, which explains why the only comment he can make as his wife walks

out the door is "it's been a good year for the roses."[47] In "The King Is Gone," the house falls apart as the singer speaks: he pulls up a chair to begin his narrative of abandonment, and a piece of floor comes up with it. He, too, disintegrates before our eyes as he drunkenly hallucinates a conversation with Fred Flintstone and Elvis. Another song, "If My Heart Had Windows," makes the comparison between broken homes and personal failure more direct,[48] and the comparison stretches into absurd solipsism in "The Door" when the singer shamelessly complains that the hollow sound of a departing woman's slam caused more pain than wars and earthquakes.[49]

In some songs, it is the man who leaves his home, but unlike the woman, he returns. The variation, however, works only to intensify the singer's humiliation since by the time he crawls back, the house has been abandoned. In "You Couldn't Get the Picture," the singer takes us on yet another grand tour; this time we're shown a house covered with post-it notes from an aggrieved and vanished wife. Typically, the song lists the many objects adorned with yellow paper: the refrigerator, the microwave, the pillow on the couple's bed. The sum total of these notes hopes that even though this poor fool couldn't get the picture he might be able to "read the writing on the wall."[50] Two years earlier, Jones recorded a similar song entitled just that—"The Writing on the Wall." In place of yellow post-its are purple crayon messages left by bewildered and long-gone children, futilely proclaiming their love for their father. The realization of what he has lost leads to yet another burst of tears.[51] In both these songs, then, the writing on the wall is exactly what the cliché holds it to be: a message of doom. The singer suddenly sees years of lonely decay ahead for him and his house. "There's the Door" and "Hell Stays Open All Night Long" slightly vary this notion by quoting hard-hearted women who refuse their mate's apologetic attempts to return.[52] Thus, even when the songs cast men as the wanderers, Jones retains the dual role of victim and bearer of bad news about our visions of hard work rewarded by domestic bliss. In turn, he seeks both comfort and complicity with his audience. No wonder his "He Stopped Loving Her Today," in which he narrates the story of a similarly pathetic character, revived his career in 1980.

Of course, not all of these songs are completely straight-faced. As I argued in chapter 2, both "The Grand Tour" and "The King Is Gone" invite our laughter along with our sympathy. Such a response, though, only confirms the humiliation of the characters that Jones creates, and it doesn't alter our sense that we're hearing the emotional truth of hard experience no matter how comically embellished the details may be. Being in on the joke adds to our complicity. This is precisely the relationship with an audience that Jones's newest followers seek to avoid even as they hope to hitch themselves to his star. Older duets, like David Allan Coe's and Jones's alcoholic "This Bottle in My Hand" or Jones's and Johnny Paycheck's "When You're Ugly Like Us" (both from 1980), deal with shared humiliations and hardships. On the other hand, "Just Playing Possum," an Alan Jackson album cut from 1991, exemplifies a far softer dynamic. The song's chorus begins with the singer telling us that he's "playin' possum," which means at least three things: first, that the singer is listening to George Jones—supposedly to ease the pain of a broken romance. Secondly, he's deliberately "playing" with the kind of behavior expected from someone who sings hard country: he's "layin' low." Finally, although he mentions suffering, his "laying low" may result from other motives—in fact, the song's brisk tempo and manic punning suggest optimism, and in another line of the chorus, the singer asserts that he's right where he wants to be. In other words, he's playing possum in the original sense of that phrase: to gain some advantage. While Jones bemoans his fate, Jackson is seeking his destiny. As if to confirm the effectiveness of this strategy, on the recording Jones himself sings the last line of the song (a slight alteration of the first line of the chorus): "*he's* playin' possum, *he's* layin' low."[53] In the end, then, the song isn't about pain and sorrow at all; it's about Jackson's stardom, which Jones's presence validates.

Jackson's more famous "Don't Rock the Jukebox" makes a similar move: he tells us he's a hillbilly with a broken heart hoping to listen to George Jones,[54] but the dramatically mundane scenes that Jones draws in his dream-house songs are missing; the real purpose of "Don't Rock the Jukebox" is to allow Jackson to affirm his loyalty to country music by opposing it to rock and roll. He may have learned the hard way from listening to Jones, and he claims that he's always tried to sound like Jones,[55] but he doesn't play the role of the hard-living abject male. Whatever the autobiographical aura may be (and in albums like *Who I Am* Jackson gestures toward creating it) and however traditional he sounds, the glamorous Jackson relates to his audience as a superstar rather than as an inhabitant of hard country. In *I Lived to Tell It All*, Jones expresses his dismay over the fact that their 1994 duet version of "A Good Year for the Roses" failed to crack the Top 40 even though Jackson was riding a wave of number ones. While Jones attributes this failure to radio programmers' lack of interest in him (330), it is just as likely that the song didn't connect with Alan Jackson's fans. Even in his saddest songs—"(Who Says) You Can't Have It All,"[56] for example—Jackson avoids gory details like comparing himself to a lipstick-stained cigarette butt.[57]

The new generation of singers has had some success covering Jones's upbeat and novelty numbers. Jackson, himself, recently did well with his version of "Tall, Tall Trees"; George Strait had good luck with "The Love Bug," and Sawyer Brown did a rollicking "Race Is On."[58] When they sing about Jones, though, their themes are seldom wholeheartedly hard. The Judds' 1985 "Have Mercy" provides an early example. Although fairly upbeat, the song describes a woman's suffering at the hands of a two-timing spendthrift. Part of her plea for mercy suggests that he not listen to Haggard and Jones since she believes they aid and abet his mischief.[59] Doug Stone's 1992 "Warning Labels" states a similar theme: the singer complains about the pain of losing his wife, but in the last line, he claims that nothing hurts his heart more than Haggard and Jones.[60] So he's not advocating that marriage licenses come with warning labels; instead he says that it's hard country records that need them. Even "A Few Ole Country Boys," a 1990 mutual admiration duet with Randy Travis, celebrates stardom; it stands out only because it presents country boys as an endangered species rather than home-wrecking record collectors.[61]

Of course, Jones does more with duets than lend credibility to lesser stars. More recently, he also needed to reach the audience that those stars had built for themselves. Thus, since 1979, he has released four duet albums including a reunion album with Tammy Wynette, although, as his experience with "A Good Year for the Roses" indicates, these attempts have not been completely successful. *My Very Special Guests* (1979) paired Jones with James Taylor and Elvis Costello. *The Bradley Barn Sessions* (1994) included the Rolling Stones' Keith Richards. (With no scandal or joke to "be in on," these duet teams hold little interest; for example, the 1995 reunion with Wynette, when both were happily married to others, didn't come close to their '70s duets in airplay and sales.) Likewise, "I Don't Need Your Rockin' Chair," a single with backup singing provided by a host of hot young artists (including Garth Brooks), barely made the Top 40.[62] "The song was my attitude set to music," says Jones (327).

As it turns out, after all his mourning for lost dream houses, he's not ready to enjoy life on the front porch. What hard country star could admit to having laurels (or a front porch) to rest on? By refusing the rocking chair, then, Jones occupies what must by now be the alienated "comfort zone" he sang about in "Wrong's What I Do Best": out of the mainstream, deep in the country. Thus, he is openly critical of today's stars: "they're not country, they're clones," he says (325). His "Billy B. Bad," a 1996 album cut, sarcastically tells the story of just such a clone, a Texas suburbanite who lacks Johnny B. Goode's drive and talent. Billy's best skill is filling out a cowboy suit. Before his singing debut, his management force-feeds him Strait and Jones.[63] The lesson doesn't take, though, since after a short hot streak, Billy's records hit the oldies bins. Jones's most lasting words on learning the hard way, then, may have been sung more than a decade ago: the dirgelike roll call that imagines the disappearance of hard country's greatest stars, "Who's Gonna Fill Their Shoes?" (1985).[64] The question is still waiting for an answer. Richard Petersen has convincingly predicted that country music will continue to fabricate its authenticity with a dialectic between pop-oriented soft country and hard-core sounds, but Jones's question, and mine, is: what's left to learn from the hard way? With the whole world gone country, what special connection can a hard country artist make with his audience? If Jones's fate is any indication, hard country artists may find themselves losing not only the American dream but also their own fertile fields of stone.

Alan Jackson's 1995 hit "Gone Country" hints at just such iconoclasm.[65] While the lyrics alone provide a cynical look at the early '90s boom in country music sales, Jackson's delivery is also bland enough to profit from the boom.[66] His voice conveys no sarcasm or cynicism; he told at least one interviewer that it was "just a fun song . . . celebrating how country music has become more widespread and accepted by all types of people" (Leamer, 282), and it seems that many people were able to hear it that way. Bruce Feiler, for example, uses some of the most sarcastic lines in the song—"I hear down there it's changed you see; they're not as backward as they used to be"—as a straightforward epigraph for his otherwise excellent book about Nashville in the early '90s. The three verses describe how an aging Long Island–born Las Vegas lounge singer, a righteous Greenwich Village folk singer, and a "serious" Hollywood-based composer don cowboy boots and head to Nashville in hopes of finding an easy route to the big time. Country, in this song, remains a refuge for losers, and although country gives these losers hope, it also turns them into opportunists: they don't see themselves as permanent residents of the territory.

Some of them, though, may turn out to be. Jackson himself may never become the superstar he plays. His hard country sound may lead him to hard country's fields of stone. In the meantime, the hardest new voices now lurk in what is known as "alternative country." There the unease is still epidemic, and it still springs from a dual conflict with the institutions of country music and the realities of American dreaming. Dale Watson begs for Haggard's help as he moans about "breaking out in a Nashville Rash." Chris Gaffney calls his band the "Cold Hard Facts" and his album *Loser's Paradise*. Robbie Fulks lives in "Rock Bottom, Population 1."[67] If these voices grow as loud as Buck's, or the Hag's, or the Possum's once were, they may actually draw another battle line between the scandalized onlookers and ardent fans that Hank Williams Sr. brought to hard country. Those used shoes that Jones worries about will find some new owners.

Notes

Introduction

1. Susan Sontag may have provided the first for-
mulation of this model although she called it a
"new sensibility" rather than postmodernism.
Susan Sontag, "One Culture and the New Sensibility," in *Against Interpretation and Other
Essays* (New York: Farrar, Straus, & Giroux,
1966), 293–304. Among postmodern theorists,
see Jim Collins, *Uncommon Cultures: Popular
Culture and Post-Modernism* (New York: Routledge, 1989); Andreas Huyssen, *After the Great
Divide: Modernism, Mass Culture, Postmodernism* (Bloomington: Indiana University Press,
1986); and Fredric Jameson, *Postmodernism, or,
The Cultural Logic of Late Capitalism* (Durham: Duke University Press, 1991).

2. Waylon Jennings with Lenny Kaye, *Waylon:
An Autobiography* (New York: Warner Books,
1996), 130. Loretta Lynn explains her songwriting procedure similarly: "I'd think up a title
first, then write some words, then pick out a
tune on my little old rhythm guitar." Loretta
Lynn, with George Vecsey, *Coal Miner's
Daughter* (New York: Warner Books, 1976), 109.

3. Peter Guralnick, *Lost Highway: Journeys and
Arrivals of American Musicians* (Boston: Godine, 1979), 24.

4. Simon Frith, *Performing Rites: On the Value of
Popular Music* (Cambridge: Harvard University
Press, 1996), 160.

5. Although she doesn't distinguish between mainstream and hard country music, Cecelia Tichi
makes this claim one of the key arguments of her

book *High Lonesome: The American Culture of Country Music* (Chapel Hill: University of North Carolina Press, 1994). Frederick E. Danker calls hard country music "an American version of pastoral" in "Country Music," *Yale Review* 63 (1974): 400.

6. "An Interview with Porter Wagoner," *Country Song Roundup*, February 1969, 15.

7. See Nolan Porterfield, "Country Music Discography: Esoteric Art and Humanistic Craft," *Southern Quarterly* 22, no. 3 (1984): 15–29, for a discussion of the difficulties of country music discography.

8. Cited in Frye Gaillard, *Watermelon Wine: The Spirit of Country Music* (New York: St. Martin's Press, 1978), 96.

9. George Bush, "My Country and Western 'tis of Thee," in *Forbes*, May 9, 1994, S81.

10. Richard A. Peterson, *Creating Country Music: Fabricating Authenticity* (Chicago: University of Chicago Press, 1997), 150–56.

1. "Country 'til I die"

1. For an excellent account of this development, see Joli Jensen, *The Nashville Sound: Authenticity, Commercialization, and Country Music* (Nashville: Country Music Foundation and Vanderbilt University Press, 1998).

2. Ronnie Pugh, "Country Music: An Etymological Journey," *Journal of Country Music* 19, no. 1 (1997): 37. Also see Archie Green, "Hillbilly Music: Source and Symbol," *Journal of American Folklore* 78 (1965): 204–228.

3. "Folk Music Fireball Elvis Presley," *Country Song Roundup* (September 1955), 14.

4. Larry Arnett, "Joan Baez in Nashville," *Country Song Roundup* (May 1969), 30.

5. "Glen Campbell—A Conversation," *Country Song Roundup* (September 1969), 10.

6. "Can Ricky Nelson Sing? What Do You Think?" *Country Song Roundup* (January 1960), 16.

7. "Is He or Isn't He a Hillbilly?" *Country Song Roundup* (September 1960), 5–8.

8. Owen Bradley, "An Interview with Owen Bradley," *Country Song Roundup* (January 1969), 45.

9. Ray Price, "An Interview with Ray Price," *Country Song Roundup* (October 1969), 9.

10. Porter Wagoner, "An Interview with Porter Wagoner," *Country Song Roundup* (May 1970), 11; and Curly Putman, "Curly Putman: An Exclusive CSR Interview," *Country Song Roundup* (April 1970), 34.

11. S. D. Shafer, "Soft Lights and Hard Country Music."

12. Jerry Cupit, Janice Honeycutt, and Ken Mellons, "Jukebox Junkie."

13. Bill Malone, *Country Music USA*, rev. ed. (Austin: University of Texas Press, 1985), 285.

14. John Grissim, *Country Music: White Man's Blues* (New York: Paperback Library, 1970), 113.

15. Paul Hemphill, *The Nashville Sound: Bright Lights and Country Music* (New York: Simon and Schuster, 1970), 49–50.

16. Ken Tucker, "Why Ricky, Reba, and George Are Hard at It," *Journal of Country Music* 11, no. 1 (1986): 4.

17. Christopher Wren, "Country Music," *Look* (13 July 1971), 13.

18. See James Clifford, *The Predicament of Culture: Twentieth-Century Ethnography, Literature, and Art* (Cambridge: Harvard University Press, 1988), 8–9, for a more general discussion of this tendency.

19. Martha Hume, *You're So Cold I'm Turning Blue: Martha Hume's Guide to the Greatest in Country Music* (New York, Viking Press: 1982), 9.

20. Elsewhere, Hume contrasts "hard country" to "easy listening," noting that "hard country music, like hard rock, has gained its identity precisely because it is objectionable to some people." "Easy Listening, Hard Times," *Chicago Sun Times* (21 August 1977).

21. Michael Crawford, "Country Music Awards," *New Yorker* (27 May 1996), 111.

22. *New Yorker*, Special Music Issue (26 August and 2 September 1996).

23. Nicholas Dawidoff, *In the Country of Country: People and Places in American Music* (New York: Pantheon, 1997), 13.

24. Cited in Linnell Gentry, *A History and Encyclopedia of Country, Western, and Gospel Music* (St. Clair Shores, MI: Scholars Press, 1972), 53.

25. Florence King, "Red Necks, White Socks, and Blue Ribbon Fear: The Nashville Sound of Discontent," *Harper's* (July 1974), 30.

26. Karen Levine, *Keeping Life Simple* (Pownal, VT: Storey Books, 1996), 30.

27. Peter Applebome, "Hank Williams. Garth Brooks. BR-549?" *New York Times Sunday Magazine* (27 October 1996), 41.

28. Laurence Leamer, *Three Chords and the Truth: Hope, Heartbreak, and Changing Fortunes in Nashville* (New York: Harper Collins, 1997).

29. Bruce Feiler, *Dreaming Out Loud: Garth Brooks, Wynonna Judd, Wade Hayes, and the Changing Face of Nashville* (New York: Avon, 1998), 7.

30. John Fiske, *Understanding Popular Culture* (New York: Routledge, 1991), 166.

31. Simon Frith, "The Cultural Study of Popular Music," in *Cultural Studies*, ed. Lawrence Grossberg, Cary Nelson, and Paula A. Treichler (New York: Routledge, 1992), 180.

32. Bill Anderson, "The Cold Hard Facts of Life."

33. Ernest Tubb, "Ernest Tubb: A Conversation," *Country Song Roundup* (March 1969), 34.

34. Felice and Boudleaux Bryant, "Country Boy."

35. See D. K. Wilgus, "Country Western Music and the Urban Hillbilly," *Journal of American Folklore* 83 (1970): 157–184, for a more general discussion of this issue.

36. Homer Joy, "The Streets of Bakersfield."

37. John Schweers and Byron Hill, "Born Country."

38. John Anderson, Troy Seals, and Eddie Setser, "Country 'til I Die."

39. Pierre Bourdieu, *Distinction: A Social Critique of the Judgment of Taste*, trans. Richard Nice (Cambridge: Harvard University Press, 1984). I have discussed the application of Bourdieu's sociology of culture to country music in "Acting Naturally: Cultural Distinction and Critiques of Pure Country," *Arizona Quarterly* 49.3 (1993): 107–125. For yet another discussion, see Tex Sample, *White Soul: Country Music, the Church, and Working Americans* (Nashville: Abingdon Press, 1996), especially part one.

40. The term "omnivore" is Richard A. Peterson's. See his "Understanding Audience Segmentation: From Elite and Mass to Omnivore and Univore," *Poetics* 21 (1992). He defines it by noting that because currently, "status is gained by knowing about, and participating in (that is to say, by consuming) many, if not all forms [of cultural and leisure activities], the term 'omnivore' seems appropriate for those at the top of the emerging status hierarchy." Thus, the elite attend the symphony and buy Garth Brooks records while those at the bottom of the hierarchy (univores) feel confident about participating in only one activity (252). See also Richard A. Peterson and Roger M. Kern, "Changing Highbrow Taste: From Snob to Omnivore," *American Sociological Review* 61 (October 1996), 900–907.

41. A journal title provides the handiest example: *The Journal of Urban and Cultural Studies*, founded in 1992.

42. Peter Stallybrass and Allon White, *The Politics and Poetics of Transgression* (Ithaca: Cornell University Press, 1986), 5.

43. Andrew Ross, *No Respect: Intellectuals and Popular Culture* (New York: Routledge, 1989), 227.

44. The term comes from Stallybrass and White, 3.

45. Brown and R. Avis, "Semi-Crazy."

46. Lawrence Levine, *Highbrow/Lowbrow: The Emergence of Cultural Hierarchy in America* (Cambridge: Harvard University Press, 1988) provides a historical perspective on this phenomenon in the United States, while Barbara Ehrenreich's discussion of the nervous search for class distinction in the contemporary United States confirms that Bourdieu's analysis is still operative here. See *Fear of Falling: The Inner Life of the Middle Class* (New York: Pantheon, 1989). More recently, Juliet B. Schor, *The Overspent American: Upscaling, Downshifting, and the New Consumer* (New York: Basic Books, 1998), makes specific reference to Bourdieu's relevance to the contemporary United States.

47. It should be noted that after complaints from Oklahomans, Freixenet stopped using the advertisement.

48. Williams never released this song although he did make a demonstration version of it, an indication that he was planning to record it.

49. George Vaughn, "Hillbilly Fever."

50. "The Top 100 Country Songs of All Time," *Country America* (October 1992), 26–52.

51. Tony Arata, "The Dance."

52. Garth Brooks, "The Dance," on *Garth Brooks*, prod. Martin Fischer, dir. Bud Schaetzle, 30 min., Liberty Home Video, 1991, videocassette.

53. Tony Arata, *The Dance* (New York: Hyperion, 1993).

54. Bobby Braddock and Curly Putman, "He Stopped Loving Her Today."

55. My analysis of this song owes much to Katie Stewart's essay on it, "Engendering Narratives of Lament in Country Music," in *All That Glitters: Country Music in America*, ed. George H. Lewis (Bowling Green: Bowling Green State University Popular Press, 1993), 221–225.

56. Tom Roland, *The Billboard Book of Number One Country Hits* (New York: Billboard, 1991), 261.

57. Stewart is not referring to any critique in particular but rather to the mainstream tendency to complain about "whiny excess" in country songs.

58. Green discusses at length the pejoratives that lurk in the term "country." See also Ching, 108–110, and Gerald Creed and Barbara Ching, "Recognizing Rusticity," in *Knowing Your Place: Rural Identity and Cultural Hierarchy*, ed. Ching and Creed (New York: Routledge, 1997), 1–38.

59. Aaron A. Fox, "'Ain't It Funny How Time Slips Away': Talk, Trash, and Technology in a Texas 'Redneck' Bar," in *Knowing Your Place: Rural Identity and Cultural Hierarchy*, ed. Ching and Creed (New York: Routledge, 1997), 105–130, demonstrates how elaborately and elegantly "musical discourse is embedded" in the defensively "rustic" lives of his subjects (126). And they're not talking about "that top 40 crap" (123).

60. Tom T. Hall, "Country Is."

61. Arlie Carter and William Warren, "The Wild Side of Life."

62. J. D. Miller, "It Wasn't God Who Made Honky-Tonk Angels."

2. The Possum, the Hag, and the Rhinestone Cowboy

1. Although in his 1971 song with that title, he righteously claims that his outfit signifies his mourning for the world's downtrodden.

2. Daniel Cooper, "Johnny Paycheck: Up from Low Places," *Journal of Country Music* 15, no. 1 (1992): 38.

3. See Hume, *You're So Cold*, 44–49, and Catherine Rambeau, "Pick the Nickname," *Country Weekly* (30 April 1996), 48, for more examples of stage names and nicknames.

4. The names do make an impact on the fans; this excerpt, from an undated, mimeographed newsletter put out by Johnny Paycheck's fan club (*The Paycheck Press: Publication of the Johnny Paycheck International Fan Club*), merits quotation at some length as an example:

> PAYCHECK . . . What's in a name??????
>
> Sounds like a very improbable name, doesn't it?
>
> Improbable . . . Except in the event that it happens to be JOHNNY PAYCHECK and you are as rabid a fan of his, as I am.
>
> In THAT case; it becomes a totally appropriate and thoroughly fitting NAME.
>
> CONSIDER THE FOLLOWING:
>
> There is hardly anything most of us look forward to more, than our paycheck. Most also wish our paycheck came more often.
>
> Now I ask you what could be truer for Johnny's fans, than the above?

The letter goes on to fill a sheet of typing paper comparing the singer to the positive qualities of paychecks.

5. D. Goodman and R. Schulman, "When You're Ugly Like Us."

6. Jennings and Basil McDay, "Too Dumb for New York City and Too Ugly for L.A."

7. But on abjection alone, see Julia Kristeva, *Powers of Horror: An Essay on Abjection*, trans. Leon S. Roudiez (New York: Columbia University Press, 1982). See especially Michael André Bernstein, *Bitter Carnival: Ressentiment and the Abject Hero* (Princeton: Princeton University Press, 1992), for a discussion of the cultural manifestations of abjection.

8. See John Jump, *Burlesque* (London: Methuen, 1972), and Gérard Genette, *Palimpsestes: La littérature au second degré* (Paris: Seuil, 1982), for general discussions of the burlesque. According to Robert C. Allen, in *Horrible Prettiness: Burlesque and American Culture* (Chapel Hill: University of North Carolina Press, 1991), American burlesque is "inextricably tied to . . . troubling questions about how . . . femininity should and could be represented" (21). To the extent that burlesque implies a skin show, that's true. Allen's book is excellent, but in this case, he is generalizing from a rather limited field.

9. See, however, my 1994 article, and Don Cusic, "Comedy and Humor in Country Music," *Journal of American Culture* 16, no. 2 (1993): 45–50, for a general discussion of humor in country music.

10. Aaron A. Fox, "The Jukebox of History: Narratives of Loss and Desire in the Discourse of Country Music," *Popular Music* 11, no. 1 (1992): 69. See also his

"Split Subjectivity in Country Music and Honky-Tonk Discourse," in *All That Glitters: Country Music in America*, ed. George H. Lewis (Bowling Green: Bowling Green State University Popular Press, 1993): 131–139.

11. Buck Owens, Charles Stewart, Jerry Abbott, "Play 'Together Again' Again."

12. Peter Stearns, *American Cool: Constructing a Twentieth-Century Emotional Style* (New York: New York University Press, 1994), 1.

13. Loren Baritz, *The Good Life: The Meaning of Success for the American Middle Class* (New York: Knopf, 1988), 225.

14. Daniel D. Darst and Robert Altman, "Black Sheep."

15. For a general overview, see the issue of the *Journal of Country Music* devoted to "Black Artists in Country Music" (14.2). Guralnick stresses the common roots of country music and the blues. The Country Music Foundation has also compiled a compact disc set—*From Where I Stand: The Black Experience in Country Music* (Warner Brothers 1998; B000002NBV)—documenting black artists' contributions to country music. Nick Tosches, *Country: Living Legends and Dying Metaphors in America's Biggest Music*, rev. ed. (New York: Scribner's, 1985), devotes a chapter to the topic (162–217) as does Gaillard (82–100). The subject has fascinated scholars; see Pete Daniel, "Rhythm of the Land," *Agricultural History* 68, no. 4 (1994): 1–22, and Rebecca Thomas, "There's a Whole Lot o' Color in the 'White Man's Blues': Country Music's Selective Memory and the Challenge of Identity," *Midwest Quarterly* 38 (1996): 73–89. Denise Noe, "Parallel Worlds: The Surprising Similarities (and Differences) of Country-Western and Rap," *Humanist* 55, no. 4 (1995): 20–22, discusses common attitudes toward sex and crime in the two genres.

16. Jeff Woods, "Color Me Country: Tales from the Frontlines," *Journal of Country Music* 14, no. 2 (1992): 11.

17. Ben Peters, "Kiss an Angel Good Morning."

18. Ann Malone, too, notes that Pride's "choice of happy, ebullient themes reflects his optimistic state of mind." See "Charley Pride," in *Stars of Country Music: Uncle Dave Macon to Johnny Rodriguez*, ed. Bill C. Malone and Judith McCulloh (Urbana: University of Illinois Press, 1975), 352.

19. Charley Pride with Jim Henderson, *Pride: The Charley Pride Story* (New York: Morrow, 1994), 193.

20. Bill Malone's analysis of Pride's style underscores his mass appeal: "[H]is singing contained almost none of the vocal inflections identified with black singers. . . . He was a handsome man but with little of the overt sexuality projected by many of the younger black singers, and he avoided any references to civil rights or political topics. He was therefore basically unthreatening to white masculinity, civil order, or the identity of country music" (*Country Music USA*, 314).

21. Chip Taylor, "Blackbird." See Guralnick for a discussion of this song in the context of Edwards's career (264–275).

22. D. Frazier and A. L. Owens, "Hank and Lefty Raised My Country Soul."

23. Abner Knowles, Obie McClinton, and Steven McCorvey, "(Country Music Is) American Soul."

24. Tammy Wynette and Billy Sherrill, "Stand By Your Man."

25. Mary A. Bufwack and Robert K. Oermann, *Finding Her Voice: The Saga of Women in Country Music* (New York: Crown, 1993), provide a thorough historical overview of women in country music.

26. "Answer songs," a country phenomenon of the '50s and '60s, generally rewrote the lyrics to a hit tune to express the opposite sex's point of view on a given theme. In practice, women nearly always responded to men rather than the other way around. See Colin Escott, Liner notes for . . . *And the Answer Is!* Bear Family, BCD 15-791 AH and BCD 15-793 AH, 1994.

27. Written by J. D. Miller.

28. Loretta Lynn, O. V. Lynn Jr., T. D. Bayless, and Don McHan, "The Pill."

29. Becky Hobbs, Don Goodman, and Mack Vickery, "Jones on the Jukebox."

30. Flores and Leroy Preston, "Girl Haggard."

31. Donnie Fritts, "My Life Would Make a Damn Good Country Song."

32. Walter Breeland, Paul Buskirk, and Willie Nelson, "Night Life."

33. Daniel Cooper, *Lefty Frizzell: The Honky-Tonk Life of Country Music's Greatest Singer* (Boston: Little, Brown, 1995), 253.

34. J. Johnson and P. Frizzell, "Just Can't Live That Fast Any More."

35. Becky Hobbs's "Mama Was a Working Man" makes note of the fact that women work, too (1988).

36. This theme occurs throughout Haggard's career: hear also "Uncle Lem" (written by Tommy Collins, 1990), about an ex-slave who offends the ladylike sensibilities of the garden club with his ill-kept shack, and "Irma Jackson," about an interracial romance (ca. 1970). Speaking more generally, Gaillard notes that "songs about the shared wisdom of blacks and whites in the rural South" became a "genre in country music" in the '70s (95).

37. Steven Brett Beavers, James Barry Poole, and James Matthew Beavers, "The First Redneck on the Internet."

38. Byron Hill and Zack Turner, "High-Tech Redneck."

39. Hear also Randy Travis's 1991 "Better Class of Loser" (written with Alan Jackson), in which the singer is preparing to abandon a snooty female and her technologically sophisticated crowd in favor of those who don't use computers to pay their bills.

40. Tony Scherman, "Country," *American Heritage* (November 1994), 46.

41. See Malone for a discussion of the origins of the honky-tonk (*Country Music USA*, 153–155). Also see Tosches, *Country*, 26–27.

42. Joe Diffie's "Honky-Tonk Attitude" (1993, written with Lee Bogan), for example, exults that the honky-tonk is "where everybody goes" to chase away their blues.

43. Oddly enough, Charley Pride's unself-conscious cover version of this song was a number one hit in 1980. For the sake of authenticity, Pride went so far as to hire some of Williams's band members to play on the record (Roland, 254).

44. George McCorkle and Rick Williamson, "William and Mary," as sung by Davis Daniel in 1994.

45. Glenn Sutton, "What's Made Milwaukee Famous (Has Made a Loser Out of Me)."

46. Written with Russ Hull and Mary Jean Shurtz, 1953. See Malone for a discussion of the controversy provoked by this song (*Country Music USA*, 234).

47. Bob Merrill and Terry Shand, "You Don't Have to Be a Baby to Cry."

48. J. Chambers, L. Jenkins, and B. Sherrill, "I Sleep Just Like a Baby."

49. Larry Lee, "The Real Mr. Heartache."

50. John Moffatt and Michael Heeney, "Still Doin' Time."

51. See Jensen for further discussion of the meaning of the "honky-tonk" in country songs (24–37).

52. B. Harden, "Hell Stays Open All Night Long."

53. Pat Alger, Larry B. Bastain, and Garth Brooks, "Unanswered Prayers."

54. David Allan Coe, "Take This Job and Shove It."

55. Charles Conrad, "Work Songs, Hegemony, and Illusions of Self," *Critical Studies in Mass Communication* 5 (1988), asserts that such stasis is typical of country music work songs (189).

56. Lester Blackwell, "I'm Gonna Burn Your Playhouse Down." Hear also Jones singing Wayne Kemp's "Burn the Honky-Tonk Down."

57. Roger Ferris, "The King Is Gone."

58. Dickey Lee, Mike Campbell, and Freddy Weller, "Wrong's What I Do Best." Hear also Jones's version of L. Reynolds's "The World's Worst Loser."

59. Gilbert Brim, *Ambition: How We Manage Success and Failure Throughout Our Lives* (New York: Basic Books, 1992), 102–104.

60. Richard Sennett and Jonathan Cobb, *The Hidden Injuries of Class* (New York: Random House, 1972), 264.

61. George Richey, one of the writers of this song, used this phrase to describe the speaker of the first line (Roland, 120).

62. Norro Wilson, Carmol Taylor, and George Richey, "The Grand Tour."

63. Richard Beresford and Harlan Saunders, "If Drinkin' Don't Kill Me."

64. Billy Sherrill, liner notes to *George Jones Anniversary: Ten Years of Hits* (Epic ECK38323, 1982), unpaginated.

65. Bob Allen, *George Jones: The Life and Times of a Honky Tonk Legend* (New York: Birch Lane Press, 1994), explains the nickname as resulting from the possumlike cast of Jones's close-set eyes (81). However, he catalogs many incidents of Jones's "possumlike" stupors (156, 176–177, 180, 201). Jones seems perfectly content with his nickname; he dubs his current backup singers "The Possumettes."

66. Lefty Frizzell and Sanger D. Shafer, "I Never Go Around Mirrors." Aaron Fox also discusses this song in "Split Subjectivity," 135.

67. While Jones generally leans toward a more comic approach than Haggard, his biographer, Bob Allen, notes that the 1976 George Jones/Earl Montgomery composition "A Drunk Can't Be a Man" provides an unusually "precise . . . autobiographical confession" on Jones's part. The lyrics note that the drunk causes himself misery at the same time that he embarrasses his family. The conclusion turns the title into a paradox that sums up the dialogue of abjection: a man can occasionally get drunk but "a drunk can't be a man."

68. See Patricia Averill's "Esoteric-Exoteric Expectations of Redneck Behavior and Country Music," *Journal of Country Music* 14, no. 2 (1973):35.

69. Dorothy Horstman, *Sing Your Heart Out, Country Boy: Classic Country Songs and Their Inside Stories by the Men and Women Who Wrote Them*, 3rd ed. (Nashville: Country Music Foundation Press and Vanderbilt University Press, 1996), 251.

70. Melton A. McLaurin, "Songs of the South: The Changing Image of the South in Country Music," in *You Wrote My Life: Lyrical Themes in Country Music*, ed. Melton A. McLaurin and Richard A. Peterson (Philadelphia: Gordon and Breach, 1992), also argues that the positive statements such as this one are "the key lines" (25).

71. Sam's Town River Palace Arena, Tunica, Mississippi, 1 October 1994.

72. Quoted in Paul Hemphill, "Merle Haggard," in *Stars of Country Music: Uncle Dave Macon to Johnny Rodriguez*, ed. Bill Malone and Judith McCulloh (Urbana: University of Illinois Press, 1975), 331.

73. Bryan Di Salvatore cites "the alleged Merle quote" in "Ornery," *New Yorker* (12 February 1990), 56. Haggard relates some of his marijuana-induced antics in his autobiography. See Merle Haggard, with Peggy Russell, *Sing Me Back Home: My Story* (New York: Simon and Schuster, 1981).

74. The very mention of the drink echoes George Jones's first number one hit, "White Lightning" (J. P. Richardson). In another skillful drunken-sounding performance, Jones stresses the lawlessness of the brew that the singer's father supposedly perfected, noting that a host of government agents were searching

for the smoking still. The last verse describes how an arrogant "city slicker" passed out after taking one sip.

75. Jimmie N. Rogers, *The Country Music Message: Revisited* (Fayetteville: University of Arkansas Press, 1989), 173.

76. Ray Wylie Hubbard, "Up Against the Wall, Redneck." Hear, for contrast, Haggard's "Mama Tried" (1968). In this song, the singer, who "turned 21 in prison doing life without parole," accepts full responsibility: "I have only me to blame 'cause Mama tried."

77. Written with C. Chavin.

78. Charlie Daniels's 1989 "What This World Needs (Is a Few More Rednecks)" hints at the issue by limiting the definition of "redneck" to a working man (written with J. Gavin, C. Hayward, and T. DiGregorio).

79. Likewise, he objected to sitting on a bale of hay for an appearance on *Hee Haw* (Grissim, 139). On the other hand, he told Di Salvatore that his disagreement with the Sullivan show was not about singing Rodgers and Hammerstein but rather about the effeminate dance number he was expected to do while he sang (66).

80. J. McClinton, "Obie from Senatobie."

81. Coe claims that he murdered a fellow convict who tried to rape him; researchers have never been able to confirm this tale although it is true that Coe spent most of his first 30 years in institutions ranging from a reform school to the Ohio State Penitentiary. Larry King provides a sympathetic explanation for the muddle: "I get the notion that whether or not Coe is a killer, he believes he is . . . it represents something vital and deep in his craw—something he would *like* to have done—a necessary purge, striking back at all those buckled and badged bastards who've caged him and shoved him and crowded him for almost as long as he can remember" ("David Allan Coe's Greatest Hits," *Esquire* [July 1976], 144). Several years later, Coe told Alanna Nash that "I always want to be thought of . . . as David Allan Coe, ex-convict, because that's what I am" (*Behind Closed Doors: Talking with the Legends of Country Music* [New York: Knopf, 1988], 90).

82. Charlie Daniels's "Long Haired Country Boy" makes a similar distinction between country boys and hippies. The first verse mixes hippie and honky-tonk hedonism; in spite of public disapproval, the long-haired country boy devotes his mornings to getting stoned and his afternoons to drinking. The menacing chorus, however, stresses the country boy's withdrawal from society. Accompanied by a growling bass and Daniels's deadpan drawl, this chorus actually seems to deliver an angry ultimatum as it concludes a typical dialogue of abjection. If the interlocutors don't like the way the singer lives, they should "leave this long haired country boy alone."

83. David Allan Coe and Jimmy Rabbit, "Longhaired Redneck."

84. Michael Bane, *The Outlaws: Revolution in Country Music* (New York: Doubleday, 1978), 132.

85. As Hume points out, it doesn't say anything about cheating or cowboys (*You're So Cold*, 81).

86. Steve Goodman, "You Never Even Called Me by My Name."

87. New fans are carefully taught that such songs are "insider" jokes rather than examples of ineptitude. See, for example, Gerry Wood, "Mama, Those Cliché Songs Are Driving Me to Drink," *Country Weekly* (30 April 1996), 80–81, in a special issue titled "What Every Country Fan Should Know." This article includes a brief interview with Coe and lists of songs covering the mama, drinking, truck, prison, and train themes.

3. The hard act to follow

1. Charles Hirshberg and Robert Sullivan, "The 100 Most Important People in the History of Country," *Life* (1 September 1994), 20.

2. In an attempt to demythify Williams, his most recent biographer adopts a studiedly neutral title: Colin Escott with George Merritt and William MacEwen, *Hank Williams: The Biography* (Boston: Little, Brown, 1994).

3. Don Cusic, ed., *Hank Williams: The Complete Lyrics* (New York: St. Martin's Press, 1993), xviii.

4. Richard Leppert and George Lipsitz, "Age, the Body, and Experience in the Music of Hank Williams," in *All That Glitters: Country Music in America*, ed. George H. Lewis (Bowling Green: Bowling Green State University Popular Press, 1993), 22–37. See also Kent Blaser, "'Pictures from Life's Other Side': Hank Williams, Country Music, and Popular Culture in America," *South Atlantic Quarterly* 84, no. 1 (Winter 1985): 12–24, who notes that "Williams's music . . . was hardly a paean to American optimism, innocence, and the good life" (23).

5. For example, Roger M. Williams, in *Sing a Sad Song: The Life of Hank Williams*, 2nd ed. (Urbana: University of Illinois Press, 1981), claims that "without Audrey and the problems he felt she caused him, many of Hank's best songs would not have been written. Few people doubt that his greatest laments . . . were composed with his marriage uppermost in his mind" (166–167).

6. Leppert and Lipsitz claim that Williams's voice, with its limited range and tendency to waver, "registers uncertainty, vulnerability and . . . the sorts of failure that only age can produce" (27).

7. See Roger M. Williams for a good discussion of the song's chord progression (81).

8. Lycrecia Williams and Dale Vinicur, *Still in Love with You: The Story of Hank and Audrey Williams* (Nashville: Rutledge Hill Press, 1989), 48.

9. Leppert and Lipsitz remark that "Williams was a chronologically young man long past youth, indeed, a man who seemingly never experienced youth as was borne out by his physical appearance" (24). See Escott for a discussion of "Hank" as a country-star name *(Hank Williams: The Biography,* 18–19).

10. Peterson, too, notes that "what is remarkable for an artist whose performance model was Roy Acuff, the 'king of the hillbillies,' is that he never looked the part of a hillbilly on stage" *(Creating,* 175–176).

11. Cited by Lycrecia Williams, 66.

12. Escott, however, says that as early as 1947, the *Montgomery Advertiser* was referring to Williams by that name, "suggesting that Hank himself may have had some role in perpetuating it" *(Hank Williams: The Biography,* 111).

13. Rufus Jarman, "Country Music Goes to Town," *Nation's Business* (February 1953). Cited in Gentry, 123–124.

14. David Brackett gives a similar analysis of the economic and gender roles in Williams's "Hey Good Lookin'," *Interpreting Popular Music* (Cambridge: Cambridge University Press, 1995), 78–84. Lefty Frizzell's 1950 breakthrough hit "If You've Got the Money, I've Got the Time" (written with J. Beck) reiterates a gigolo's invitation to honky-tonking.

15. Cusic prints the full lyric *(Hank Williams,* 27), and Williams sings this verse in his demonstration version of the song.

16. Billy Rose, Mort Dixon, and Ray Henderson, "Too Many Parties and Too Many Pals."

17. Bonnie Dodd, "Be Careful of the Stones That You Throw."

18. Roger M. Williams's biography gives an extended discussion of the Rose/Williams collaboration (116–131).

19. Chet Flippo, *Your Cheatin' Heart: A Biography of Hank Williams* (New York: St. Martin's, 1981), 78.

20. "Transition," *Newsweek* (12 January 1953), 52.

21. As Bill Malone concludes, "even in death, it seems, Hank Williams was still too rural to present in unvarnished form to city listeners" ("Hank Williams: Voice of Tradition in a Period of Change," in *Hank Williams: The Legend,* ed. Thurston Moore [Denver: Heather Enterprises, 1972], 4).

22. Because Williams emphasizes the word "cry" rather than "die," Tichi interprets this song as demonstrating "the pact in American culture—an implicit agreement not to say outright just how profound is the feeling of loneliness in the experience of this nation and its people" (101).

23. Before Dickens got a chance to release the record, Williams rewrote it as "Please Make Up Your Mind" and released it as a Luke the Drifter recitation (and as the flip side of another tune originally recorded by Dickens—"Be Careful of the Stones That You Throw") (Escott, *Hank Williams: The Biography,* 203).

24. In *Hank Williams: A Bio-bibliography* (Westport CT: Greenwood Press), 1983, George William Koon also remarks on the frequency of this image although he doesn't comment on its abjectness (79).

25. The last song was written by Curley Williams.

26. According to Escott, Williams's original version was "I Lose Again"; it was Fred Rose who urged him to shift the emphasis (*Hank Williams: The Biography*, 202).

27. Ellison gives statistics, claiming that 20 percent rely on sardonic humor. "Yet even here," he adds, "the overwhelming preoccupation is with romantic relationships; 75 percent of these songs evoke laughter at a man's treatment by a woman" (76).

28. Slim Sweet and Curley Kinsey, "I've Just Told Mama Goodbye." "I Dreamed About Mom Last Night" was written by Fred Rose and recorded by Luke the Drifter. Luke, of course, dreamed about "mama" rather than "mom."

29. The liner notes by Colin Escott and Hank Davis to *Hank Williams: The Collectors' Edition*, Polygram 314 527 419-2, 1985, outline the fate of the songs discussed in this chapter.

30. Minnie Pearl with Joan Dew, *Minnie Pearl: An Autobiography* (New York: Simon and Schuster, 1980), 215.

31. Reprinted in Moore, 45.

32. Christopher Metress, "Sing Me a Song About Ramblin' Man: Visions and Revisions of Hank Williams in Country Music," *South Atlantic Quarterly* 94, no. 1 (Winter 1995): 22–25. Tichi's more limited discussion of songs about Williams also focuses on him as a restless ghost (65–69).

33. J. B. Detterline Jr. and Gary Gentry, "The Ride."

34. Jay Caress, *Hank Williams: Country Music's Tragic King* (New York: Stein and Day, 1979), 143.

35. Country music scholar Nolan Porterfield provides excellent testimony as he recalls how learning of Williams's death was "at once comforting and disturbing" (176). In retrospect, he sees himself as suffering from "hypertoxic cultural dysfunction," loving Williams's music but longing to escape "my country roots, get as far as I could from all the . . . hard-scrabble hickness that seemed to plague me everywhere I turned" (178). The outpouring of grief precipitated by Williams's death made him see that he was not suffering this unease alone. "The Day Hank Williams Died: Cultural Collisions in Country Music," in *America's Musical Pulse*, ed. Kenneth J. Bindas (Westport, CT: Praeger, 1992).

36. Hank Williams Jr. with Michael Bane. *Living Proof: An Autobiography* (New York: Putnam, 1979), 12.

37. It appears that Hank Sr. never intended to record this although both Hank Jr. and Audrey did.

38. Colin Escott, liner notes to *Hank Williams, Jr. Living Proof: The MGM Recordings, 1963–1975*, Mercury Polygram 314-517 320-2: 1992, 7.

39. Cited in Hank Williams Jr.'s fan club magazine, *Bocephus News* (Spring/Summer 1987), 12.

40. This is the explanation offered on "The Official Hank Williams Jr." web site.

41. It's worth noting, however, that other Williams imitators, such as the now-forgotten "Hank the Drifter" had little success in comparison to Hank Jr. See "The Inside Story on 'Hank the Drifter,'" *Country Song Roundup* (November 1961):30.

42. Metress provides an interesting analysis of Hank Jr.'s (and others') history of reinterpreting Hank Sr.'s legacy.

43. Likewise, in early 1975, he sang about "a devil in the bottle" that wouldn't rest until he was dead. Bobby David, "There's a Devil in the Bottle."

44. His account of his life is quite different from those analyzed by Pamela Fox; where her female autobiographers (Tammy Wynette, Loretta Lynn, and others) insist on a continuity, Hank Jr. insists on a rift. Pamela Fox, "Recycled 'Trash': Gender and Authenticity in Country Music Autobiography," *American Quarterly* 50 (1998): 240.

45. In his autobiography, Hank Jr. reproduces a letter that Audrey wrote for the Hank Williams fan club although she addressed it to "Dear Hank" (at that point, he had been dead two years): "Little Bocephus is a prince of a little guy and every day in every way he looks more like you. . . . Oh and what a voice he has. One of these days before too long he'll be singing for you" (74).

46. Although there is an imitator—David Street—currently advertising his tribute show on the internet.

47. Danny Mayo and Bob Regan, "It's a Start."

48. Dickey Betts and Bonnie Bramlett, "Hank Williams Junior-Junior."

49. Donny Lowery and Mac McAnally, "Tennessee."

50. Vic McAlpin, "How's My Ex Treating You."

51. Robert Cantwell, *Bluegrass Breakdown: The Making of the Old Southern Sound* (New York: DaCapo, 1992), 35.

52. Stephen T. Young, "Long Way to Hollywood."

53. The version of this song on 1992's *Maverick* is slightly different.

54. Jimmy Guterman, liner notes to *The Bocephus Box: The Hank Williams Jr. Collection, 1979–1992* (Warner Brothers 9 45104-2, 1992), unpaginated.

55. B. Maddox and D. Moore, "If Heaven Ain't a Lot Like Dixie."

56. Hank Jr. did campaign for Wallace in 1968. "I didn't think the other candidates amounted to a nickel's worth of beans, certainly not when they talked about anything that had to do with the South," he explains in his autobiography (129).

57. The South's Gonna Rattle Again" (Jodie Emerson, Vince Emerson, and William Emerson, 1982) nearly equates the South with country music and white southern rock.

58. Evidently, this claim is accurate. *Bocephus News*, the glossy publication of the Hank Williams Jr. fan club, features photos of Bocephus look-alikes from Vermont to California—often posed in front of a Confederate flag.

59. "I've Been Down"(B. Keel, T. Stampley, and H. Williams Jr., 1982) also critiques Reaganomics.

60. This song was never released until it was included in the Bocephus Box.

61. Porter Grainger, Robert G. Prince, Clarence Williams, and James Witherspoon, "Ain't Nobody's Business."

62. Billy Sherrill and Glenn Sutton, "Almost Persuaded."

63. Ronnie Van Zant and Gary Rossington, "Simple Man."

64. Jerry Crutchfield and E. Humphrey, "(I've Got My) Future on Ice."

65. Freddie Hart and Eddie Dean, "Hank Williams's Guitar."

66. Hart's song begins as he *walked* into the Country Hall of Fame; it goes on to imagine a conversation with the guitar. Bocephus's opening changes "walked" to "went."

67. Bob Millard, "The Three Hanks." *Country Music* (January/February 1997), 46.

68. Hank Williams Sr. and Mel Foree, "'Neath a Cold Gray Tomb of Stone." This song was recorded by Charlie Monroe (brother of Bill Monroe).

4. Drawing hard lines

1. See Mark Fenster, "Under His Spell: How Buck Owens Took Care of Business," *Journal of Country Music* 12, no. 3 (1989): 24–25, and "Buck Owens, Country Music, and the Struggle for Discursive Control," *Popular Music* 9, no. 3 (1990): 275–290.

2. Rich Kienzle, liner notes to *The Buck Owens Collection*, (Rhino Records R2 71016, 1992): 24.

3. "No Grand Ole Opry for Buck?" *Country Song Roundup 1966 Yearbook*, 55.

4. Buck Owens, "A View of Country Music," *All-American* 1, no. 5 (October 1969): unpaginated.

5. Robert Price, "King of His Own Country," *Bakersfield Californian*, 13 July 1997, sec. F, p. 11.

6. Robert Price, "The Bakersfield Sound," *Bakersfield Californian*, 22 June 1997, sec. A, p. 6.

7. Buck Owens, interview by author, tape recording, Bakersfield, CA, 20 May 1997.

8. Buck Owens, interview by author.

9. Fenster concludes his analysis of the pledge and its placement by noting that "the implications of . . . [Owens's] rhetoric are clear: Owens's is pure, authentic music, and it is his music that is more appealing to true country fans than music produced in Nashville" ("Under," 25).

10. Shel Silverstein, Owens, and Jim Shaw, "The Cover of *The Music City News*."

11. Buck Owens, interview by author.

12. J. R. Pleakins, "Buck Owens Drops a Bombshell," *Country Song Roundup*, June 1966, 8. Ellipses in original.

13. Buck Owens, "A View of Country Music." Ellipses in original.

14. Buck Owens, liner notes to *Bridge Over Troubled Water* (Capitol Records 685, 1970).

15. Buck Owens, interview on *Bakersfield Country*, 1991, KCET/PBS, Los Angeles.

16. R. J. Jones, "California Oakie." In contrast, Bakersfield-raised Dallas Frazier's "California Cotton Fields" (sung by Haggard) tells how "Daddy" left his heavily mortgaged Oklahoma farm only to spend the rest of his life picking California cotton instead of fulfilling his California dreams.

17. J. Shaw and Rocky Topp, "Country Singer's Prayer."

18. Owens's letter inside his 1967 *Fan Club Yearbook* says "I wrote and recorded a song based on my motto, 'It Takes People Like You to Make People Like Me.' I hope each and everyone [sic] of you will take this as a personal thank you from me."

19. Yet Owens told Kienzle that "we played there twice and some guy shot his gun off through the ceiling. And the next time we played there, somebody tried to drive their car through the front door" (61).

20. Buck Owens, interview by author.

21. At this point, tiger songs were everywhere. Humorist Jim Nesbitt released "Tiger in My Tank" a week after Owens's tiger made her debut; in May, Tex Williams complained about the prevalence of tigers in "Too Many Tigers" (L. Lee and T. South): in gas tanks, at the breakfast table, and on the record about the man who has "one by the tail." Nevertheless, in June, Claude King had a top 10 record about an irresistible "Tiger Woman" (Claude King and Merle Kilgore) who repeatedly put her "good man down."

22. Jonny Whiteside, *Ramblin' Rose: The Life and Career of Rose Maddox* (Nashville: Country Music Foundation and Vanderbilt University Press, 1997), 95.

23. The onstage clowning captured on *Buck Owens and the Buckaroos Live at Carnegie Hall* (Country Music Foundation Records CMF-012-D, 1988) indicates that burlesque cutups were part of Owens's live act before *Hee Haw* ever hit the airwaves. The record was originally released by Capitol Records in 1966.

24. Dale Vinicur, liner notes to *Tommy Collins Leonard* (Bear Family Records BCD 15577 EI, 1992), 12.

25. McMichen and Puckett, "Sally Let Your Bangs Hang Down."

26. Kienzle assumes the original is "You're for Me," a very different song, credited to Tommy Collins and Buck Owens, which was the flip side of Collins's "Whatcha Gonna Do Now?"

27. Joe Maphis, Rosa Lee Maphis, and Max Fidler, "Dim Lights, Thick Smoke (and Loud, Loud, Music)."

28. Buck Owens and Harlan Howard, "Foolin' Around."

29. Dusty Rhodes and Rollie Weber, "Fool Me Again."

30. Harlan Howard and Fuzzy Owen, "The One You Slip Around With"; Harlan Howard, "The Key's in the Mailbox." Jan Howard (then Harlan Howard's wife) released a single of "The One You Slip Around With" in 1960; Freddie Hart charted "The Key's in the Mailbox" that same year.

31. John Russell and Voni Morrison, "Act Naturally."

32. Red Simpson, "Close Up the Honky-Tonks." The Flying Burrito Brothers recorded this in 1970.

33. Buck Owens, Don Rich, and Nat Stuckey, "Waitin' in Your Welfare Line."

34. Bill Carlisle, "Too Old to Cut the Mustard." This song was originally recorded in 1952 by both the Carlisles and a duo comprised of Ernest Tubb and Red Foley. A few other songs with this theme have surfaced on the country charts; in 1968, Nat Stuckey sang "My Can Do Can't Keep Up with My Want To," and in 1969, Cal Smith confessed that "It Takes All Night Long (to Do What I Used to Do All Night)."

35. Eddie McDuff and Orville Couch, "Hello Trouble." Orville Couch had a number-five hit with this song in 1962; Owens recorded it for the 1964 album *Together Again/My Heart Skips a Beat*; it also appears on the 1975 album *41st Street Lonely Hearts Club*. Chris Hillman's and Herb Pederson's neo-Bakersfield Desert Rose Band recorded it in 1988.

36. Dick Flood, "Trouble's Back in Town."

37. Interview with author.

38. Although Owens, speaking of his "younger days," said "I met a lot of women . . . I loved women" (Dawidoff, 237).

39. Buck Owens, interview by Dwight Yoakam, "A Couple of Cowboys Sittin' Around Talkin'," in *Spin*, December 1988, 47.

40. Randall Riese, *Nashville Babylon: The Uncensored Truth and Private Lives of Country Music's Greatest Stars* (New York: Congdon and Weed, 1988), 127–130.

41. Chuck Owen, liner notes to *Roll Out the Red Carpet for Buck Owens and the Buckaroos* (Capitol Records T-2443).

42. Interview with author.

43. The unattributed liner notes to *The Buck Owens Show: Big in Vegas* (1969)

vaunt the success of Owens's "two jam-packed weeks at Las Vegas' Bonanza Hotel," concluding that "Buck Owens is big in Vegas and everywhere else, too" (Capitol Records ST 322).

44. Interview with author.

45. According to Malone, *Hee Haw* was one of three country shows the networks originated in 1969; the others were *Glen Campbell's Goodtime Hour*, also on CBS, and *The Johnny Cash Show* (ABC) (*Country Music USA*, 272).

46. *Hee Haw* began on CBS as a summer replacement for *The Smothers Brothers Show* in 1969. It was so popular that CBS renewed it for prime time; nevertheless, the show was cancelled in 1971.

47. Interview with author.

48. The retro band BR-549, for example, got their name from one of the show's popular skits featuring a used car lot with this phone number.

49. It's interesting to note the way he presented the syndicated television show he produced: several issues of the *Fan Club Yearbook* repeat the statement that "viewers would be surprised to see that the Buck Owens TV Ranch Show . . . featured . . . some of the most tastefully appointed sets on television today." The show was produced between 1966 and 1973.

50. Todd Everett, "Dwight Yoakam: Not Just Another Hat," *Journal of Country Music* 15, no. 3 (1993): 13.

51. Kevin Starr, *Material Dreams: Southern California Through the 1920's* (Oxford: Oxford University Press, 1990).

52. James N. Gregory, *American Exodus: The Dust Bowl Migration and Okie Culture in California* (New York: Oxford University Press, 1989), 111.

53. Gerald Haslam, *The Other California: The Great Central Valley in Life and Letters* (Santa Barbara, CA: Capra Press, 1990).

54. See also James D. Houston, "How Playing Country Music Taught Me to Love My Dad," *The Men in My Life: And Other More or Less True Recollections of Kinship* (Berkeley, CA: Creative Arts, 1987). Houston recounts his youthful rejection of his heritage: "It was worse than Hicksville. It was Okie music. And I was anything but an Okie" (34). Thus, while his father played country music, Houston pursued classical guitar. "Those days now stand for what pushed me farthest from him," he mourns. "Call it my own yearning for sophistication" (35). Admitting that he loved country music, and beginning to play it, allowed Houston, long after his father's death, to "embrace what [he] had resisted for so long" (37).

55. The self-consciously Californian Victor Davis Hanson belabors a similar critique in his bitter account of his family's San Joaquin fruit farm: "[T]he ugly agrarian alone is the now increasingly rare voice that says no to popular tastes, no to the culture of the suburb, no to the gated estate." *Fields Without Dreams: Defending the Agrarian Idea* (New York: Free Press, 1996), 122.

56. Interview with author.

57. Kostas and Wayland Patton, "Turn It Up, Turn It On, Turn Me Loose."

58. Interview with author.

59. Mike Stepanovich and Donna Corum, "Buck!" *Destination Bakersfield* (1998), 11.

60. Interview with author.

61. He included "Philadelphia Lawyer" on his *Fightin' Side* album (1970).

62. Red Simpson, a lesser-known Bakersfield artist, also recorded this song.

63. Theresa Lane Haggard, liner notes to *Merle Haggard, 1996* (Curb Records D2-77796, 1996), unpaginated.

64. First recorded for his 1974 album, *Merle Haggard Presents His 30th Album*.

65. Christopher Wren, "Merle Haggard," *Look* (July 13, 1971), 38.

66. Interview with author: "'You don't know me, but you don't like me.' Who's you?" Owens: "It's the establishment."

67. Tompall Glaser and Harlan Howard, "The Streets of Baltimore."

68. J. Horton, T. Franks, and H. Hausey, "Honky-Tonk Man."

69. Yoakam and Kostas, "Two Doors Down."

70. See Fox, "Split Subjectivity," 134 ff., for a discussion of the "fool" in country music discourse.

71. Yoakam and Kostas, "Nothing's Changed Here."

72. Kostas and James House, "Ain't That Lonely Yet."

73. Alan Rose and Don Helms, "Smoke Along the Track."

74. June Carter and Merle Kilgore, "Ring of Fire." J. Cash, Glenn Douglas, and Lillie McAlpine, "Home of the Blues."

75. Harlan Howard, "Heartaches by the Number."

76. Doc Pomus and Mort Shuman, "Little Sister." Lefty Frizzell and Blackie Crawford, "Always Late with Your Kisses."

77. Colin Escott, "Dwight Yoakam: Hillbilly Deluxe," in *Tattooed on Their Tongues: A Journey Through the Backrooms of American Music* (New York: Schirmer Books, 1996), 209.

78. Paul Kingsbury, "The Old Sound of New Country," *The Journal of Country Music* 11, no. 1 (1986): 3.

79. Dave Alvin, "Long White Cadillac."

80. Gram Parsons and Chris Hillman, "Sin City."

81. Review of *If There Was a Way*, in *Country Music*, January/February 1991, 54.

82. Peter Anderson, "This Time," *Journal of Country Music* 15, no. 3 (1993): 15.

83. Tom Lanham, "A Thousand Miles from Nowhere," *New Country*, November 1995, 40; 43.

84. Patrick Carr, "Dwight Yoakam: Semantics and Style," *Country Music*, November/December 1995, 37.

85. Patrick Carr, "A Journey with Dwight Yoakam," *Country Music*, July/August 1998, 30–34. In fact, Carr quotes the introduction to his 1985 interview, which states that his interviews with Yoakam have "an aspect of ritual."

86. Patrick Carr, "Dwight Yoakam Remembers the Hillbilly Cats," *Country Music*, May/June 1988, 32.

87. Although this interview appears as a sidebar to Everett's article, it is prefaced by the note that "we" interviewed Yoakam in October 1985. In fact, the comments are drawn from Paul Kingsbury, "Dwight Yoakam: Honky-Tonk as Cutting Edge," *Journal of Country Music* 11, no. 1 (1986): 12–14.

88. Michael Quintanilla, "Jacket Sets Standard for Cowboy Cool," *Norfolk Virginian Pilot*, 30 November 1989.

89. Anita Sarko, "Dwight Lights Big City," *Details*, December/January 1989, 142.

90. Cecelia Reed, "Mad About Hats," *USA Weekend*, 17–19 March, 1989, 20.

91. Mark Ginsburg, "Grand Ole Avanti," *Vanity Fair*, August 1989, 142.

92. Tim Allis, "Chatter," *People*, November 28, 1988, 190.

93. John Morthland, "Dwight Yoakam: Ramblin' Man," *Country Music*, May/June 1993, 41.

5. Dying hard

1. Michael Bane in *The Outlaws* covers Cowboy Jack Clement, David Allan Coe, Jessi Colter, Tompall Glaser, and Kris Kristofferson in addition to Nelson and Jennings. Dave Hickey, "In Defense of the Telecaster Cowboy Outlaws," *Country Music*, January 1974, 90, lists "Waylon and Willie and Roger [Schutt] and Red and Kris [Kristofferson] and Billy Joe [Shaver] and Tompall [Glaser] and Kinky [Friedman] and Lee and Mickey [Newberry] and Troy [Seals] and Townes [Van Zant]." Stephen R. Tucker, "Progressive Country Music, 1972–1976: Its Impact and Creative Highlights," *Southern Quarterly* 22, no. 3 (1984): 93–109, mentions Asleep at the Wheel, Guy Clark, Kinky Friedman, Steven Fromholz, Michael Murphey, Willis Alan Ramsey, Dough Sahm, Billy Joe Shaver, and Jerry Jeff Walker.

2. Grissim, writing in the late '60s from an avowedly Haight-Asbury point of view, could not even recognize Jennings as a country star, claiming he was "not a country boy but a pop singer" (69).

3. At least one firsthand account, however, claims the mixing was highly exaggerated. "There were some [rednecks] there, all right. About six. The other 25,000 were freaks or freak-ish, all under 25." William C. Martin, "Growing Old at Willie Nelson's Picnic," *Texas Monthly*, October 1974, 94.

4. Chet Flippo, liner notes to *Wanted! The Outlaws* (New York, RCA 17863-66841-2, 1976), unpaginated.

5. John Bush Shinn III, "Whiskey River."

6. Jan Reid, *The Improbable Rise of Redneck Rock* (Austin TX: Heidelberg Publishers, 1974), xvii.

7. Willie Nelson, with Bud Shrake, *Willie: An Autobiography* (New York: Simon and Schuster, 1988), 195–196.

8. Lee Clayton, "Ladies Love Outlaws."

9. Bob McDill, "Amanda." Don Williams had a Top 40 country single with this song in 1973.

10. Ivy J. Bryant, "Only Daddy That'll Walk the Line."

11. Pamela Des Barres, *I'm with the Band: Confessions of a Groupie* (New York: Beech Tree, 1987), 185–186; 263–264.

12. Hal David, Albert Louis Hammond, and David Casa, "To All the Girls I've Loved Before."

13. Shel Silverstein, "Put Another Log on the Fire."

14. Malone, for example, says that the Outlaws "lived only in the fertile minds of publicists and press agents, and in the fantasies of many listeners" (398). Sometime in the late '70s, Jennings himself told Bane, "I resent it. Hey, my name is Waylon, and it's Waylon's music. It's Willie's music *he* plays. It's not 'Outlaw' or 'contemporary' or 'folk-country' or 'country'—hey, man, that's *merchandising*"(68).

15. Ken Tucker, "9 to 5: How Willie Nelson and Dolly Parton Qualified for 'Lifestyles of the Rich and Famous,'" in *Country: The Music and the Musicians*, ed. Paul Kingsbury and Alex Axelrod (New York: Abbeville Press, 1988), 398.

16. The recording industry didn't give platinum-level awards until 1976.

17. Chet Flippo, "From the Bump-Bump Room to the Barricades: Waylon, Tompall, and the Outlaw Revolution," in *Country: The Music and the Musicians*, ed. Paul Kingsbury and Alex Axelrod (New York: Abbeville Press, 1988), 470–471.

18. Gregory Allman, "Midnight Rider."

19. Mark James, "Suspicious Minds."

20. Stephen Tucker, writing several years after Coe, covers similar ancestors (94).

21. Cited in Hume, *You're So Cold*, 196.

22. Richard D. Albright, Waylon Jennings, and Hank Williams Jr., "The Conversation."

23. Billy Joe Shaver, "Honky-Tonk Heroes"; Bobby Gene Emmons and Chips Moman, "Luckenbach, Texas (Back to the Basics of Love)."

24. Ed and Patsy Bruce, "Mammas Don't Let Your Babies Grow Up to Be

Cowboys." In contrast, Michael Dunne has argued that Nelson and Jennings preyed upon their audience's "sympathetic disposition" toward the cowboy in order to engage in "pathetic whining" about the rigors of stardom ("Romantic Narcissism in 'Outlaw' Cowboy Music," in *All That Glitters: Country Music in America*, ed. George Lewis [Bowling Green: Bowling Green State University Popular Press, 1993], 228).

25. On country radio programming and older stars, see Peter Applebome, "Country Graybeards Get the Boot," *New York Times*, 21 August 1994, sec. H, p. 1; p. 28, and Rick Haydan and Catharine S. Rambeau, "Legends Turned Off by Radio—But They Won't Be Silenced," *Country Weekly*, 28 October 1997, 18–25.

26. John R. Cash, "Songs That Made a Difference."

27. Waylon Jennings and Tony Joe White, "Endangered Species."

28. Chet Flippo, "Crossing Over: A Two-Way Street." *Rolling Stone*, 29 November 1979, 28.

29. Interestingly enough, Nelson seems to think that someone should always be following the less lucrative outlaw road, which he defines as "wanting to do your music the way you want it to sound and not be influenced and pressured by executives or accountants or lawyers who tell you that this is the way to do it. I think as long as there is a music business there should be music outlaws trying to do music the way they hear it." Cited in Joseph Laredo, liner notes to *Willie Nelson: The Early Years: The Complete Liberty Recordings Plus More* (Nashville: Liberty Records C2 7243-8-28077-2-8, 1994), unpaginated.

30. Bobby Harden, "Talking to Hank."

31. Kye Fleming and Dennis Morgan, "Country When Country Wasn't Cool."

32. When Alanna Nash asked him if he "consciously pick[ed] songs that reflect what's going on in [his] life," he responded "not really" (228).

33. Susan Casey, "Meet Your Hero," *Possum Tracks*, June 1981, 3. According to a note at the bottom of the page, this article originally appeared in the *Chicago Sun Times* although no date is given.

34. Justin Tubb, "Big Fool of the Year."

35. B. Parrish and C. Gordon, "I've Aged Twenty Years in Five."

36. Joe Chambers, Larry Jenkins, and Billy Sherrill, "I Sleep Just Like a Baby."

37. Stephanie Coontz, *The Way We Never Were: American Families and the Nostalgia Trap* (New York: Basic Books, 1992), 28.

38. George Jones with Tom Carter, *I Lived to Tell It All* (New York: Villard, 1996), 147.

39. The lawn mower, however, is not only a symbol of male domesticity; it's also a reminder of one of Jones's most famous drunken stunts. When his second wife

tried to keep him from drinking by taking away his car keys, he drove a riding mower to the liquor store. In "Now I Think I Know How George Feels," Hank Williams Jr. steals a mower from the Country Music Hall of Fame's lawn crew so he can escape from his record company's demand that he produce another album. In "One More Last Chance" (written with Gary Nicholson), Vince Gill portrays a drunken husband who promises to reform even as he gets to the liquor store the same way Jones did. Jones, probably because he still sees himself as a hard country singer, can't quite cut this aspect of his legend down. In fact, his "Honky-Tonk Song" (Frank J. Meyers and Billy Yates) on the *I Lived to Tell It All* disc perpetuates it: the singer so urgently needs to get to a bar (to hear Hank Williams songs) that he drives a mower there.

40. In his interview with Alanna Nash, Jones seems reluctant to admit to being religious in spite of the fact that he writes and sings gospel songs: "I'm not a fanatic, and I don't guess I could even say I was saved" (232). For an opposing view, see Ellison's attempt to put Jones in the evangelical tradition (138–142).

41. Leon Payne, "Things Have Gone to Pieces." In contrast, Tammy Wynette describes writing a triumphant song that also details the contents of a house in order to demonstrate that the memories (of Jones) attached to them no longer distress her. "I featured [it] in my show for a long time, always telling the audience that every line in it actually happened." Tammy Wynette with Joan Dew, *Stand By Your Man* (New York: Simon and Schuster, 1979), 235.

42. John Boudreaux, Kerry Phillips, and Andrew Spooner, "Where the Tall Grass Grows."

43. Dawidoff, 204; Jones told Alanna Nash that when he wrote the song, he had "no reason for it—no problems at home, or nothin'" (231).

44. Nick Tosches, "George Jones: The Grand Tour," *Journal of Country Music* 16, no. 3 (1994): 27

45. As Rich Kienzle notes, Jones's "tense, emotional delivery not only created a memorable recording, it was the first real demonstration of his increasingly powerful phrasing as he twisted and wrenched every drop of emotion out of the simple lyrics." Liner notes, *The Essential George Jones: The Spirit of Country,* Sony Music Entertainment B0000028LN, 1994.

46. David Lindsey, Glenn Tubb, and Tammy Wynette, "Two-Story House."

47. Jerry Chesnut, "A Good Year for the Roses."

48. Dallas Frazier, "If My Heart Had Windows."

49. Billy Sherrill and Norris Wilson, "The Door."

50. Chuck Harter, "You Couldn't Get the Picture."

51. Robert Warren and Frederick Weller, "The Writing on the Wall."

52. Gene Nelson and Paul Nelson, "There's the Door."

53. Alan Jackson, Jim McBride, and Gary Overton, "Just Playing Possum."

54. Alan Jackson, Roger Murrah, and Keith Stegall, "Don't Rock the Jukebox."

55. Michael McCall, "Alan Jackson: Who He Is," *Journal of Country Music* 17, no. 3 (1995): 19.

56. Alan Jackson and Jim McBride "(Who Says) You Can't Have It All."

57. Likewise, Jackson allies himself with Hank Williams even as his songs like "Midnight in Montgomery" (written with Don Sampson) separate Jackson from Williams's desperate demise. Jackson visits Williams's grave and senses a whiskey-reeking ghost in Montgomery, but he escapes simply by boarding his starmobile (a Silver Eagle) and heading back to Nashville.

58. Wayne Kemp and Wayne Curtis, "The Love Bug"; Don Rollins, "The Race Is On."

59. Paul Kennerly, "Have Mercy."

60. Kim Williams and Oscar Turman, "Warning Labels."

61. Troy Seals and Mentor Williams, "A Few Ole Country Boys."

62. Marion Dycus, William Yates, and Kerry Phillips, "I Don't Need Your Rockin' Chair."

63. Bobby Braddock, "Billy B. Bad."

64. Max Barnes and Troy Seals, "Who's Gonna Fill Their Shoes."

65. Bob McDill, "Gone Country."

66. According to Leamer, McDill deliberately constructed the song so that the "catchy chorus" would soften the bite of the verses (281–282).

67. Robbie Fulks and Dallas Wayne. "Rock Bottom, Pop. 1."

Works Cited

Allen, Bob. *George Jones: The Life and Times of a Honky Tonk Legend.* New York: Birch Lane Press, 1994.

Allen, Robert C. *Horrible Prettiness: Burlesque and American Culture.* Chapel Hill: University of North Carolina Press, 1991.

Allis, Tim. "Chatter." *People,* November 28, 1988, 190.

Anderson, Peter. "This Time." *Journal of Country Music* 15.3 (1993): 15.

Applebome, Peter. "Country Graybeards Get the Boot." *New York Times,* 21 August 1994, sec. H, p. 1, 28.

———. "Hank Williams. Garth Brooks. BR-549?" *New York Times Sunday Magazine,* 27 October 1996, 38–43.

Arata, Tony. *The Dance.* New York: Hyperion, 1993.

Arnett, Larry. "Joan Baez in Nashville." *Country Song Roundup,* May 1969, 29–30.

Averill, Patricia. "Esoteric-Exoteric Expectations of Redneck Behavior and Country Music." *Journal of Country Music* 4, no. 2 (1973): 34–38.

Bane, Michael. *The Outlaws: Revolution in Country Music.* New York: Doubleday, 1978.

Baritz, Loren. *The Good Life: The Meaning of Success for the American Middle Class.* New York: Knopf, 1988.

Bernstein, Michael André. *Bitter Carnival: Ressentiment and the Abject Hero.* Princeton: Princeton University Press, 1992.

Blaser, Kent. "'Pictures from Life's Other Side': Hank Williams, Country Music, and Popular Culture in America." *South Atlantic Quarterly* 84, no. 1 (1985): 12–24.

Bocephus News, Spring/Summer 1987.

Bourdieu, Pierre. *Distinction: A Social Critique of the Judgement of Taste*. Translated by Richard Nice. Cambridge: Harvard University Press, 1984.

Brackett, David. *Interpreting Popular Music*. Cambridge: Cambridge University Press, 1995.

Bradley, Owen. "An Interview with Owen Bradley." *Country Song Roundup*, January 1969, 44–45.

Brim, Gilbert. *Ambition: How We Manage Success and Failure Throughout Our Lives*. New York: Basic Books, 1992.

Brooks, Garth. "The Dance," on *Garth Brooks*. Produced by Martin Fischer. Directed by Bud Schaetzle. 30 min. Liberty Home Video, 1991. Videocassette.

Bufwack, Mary A., and Robert K. Oermann. *Finding Her Voice: The Saga of Women in Country Music*. New York: Crown, 1993.

Bush, George. "My Country and Western 'tis of Thee." *Forbes*, 9 May 1994, supplement, 80–87.

"Can Ricky Nelson Sing? What Do You Think?" *Country Song Roundup*, January 1960, 16.

Cantwell, Robert. *Bluegrass Breakdown: The Making of the Old Southern Sound*. New York: Da Capo, 1992. Reprint, Urbana: University of Illinois Press, 1984.

Caress, Jay. *Hank Williams: Country Music's Tragic King*. New York: Stein and Day, 1979.

Carr, Patrick. "Dwight Yoakam Remembers the Hillbilly Cats." *Country Music*, May/June 1988, 28–33.

———. "Dwight Yoakam: Semantics and Style." *Country Music*, November/December 1995, 34–38.

———. "A Journey with Dwight Yoakam." *Country Music*, July/August 1998, 30–34.

Casey, Susan. "Meet Your Hero." *Possum Tracks*, June 1981, 3.

Ching, Barbara. "Acting Naturally: Cultural Distinction and Critiques of Pure Country." *Arizona Quarterly* 49, no. 3 (1993): 107–125.

Clifford, James. *The Predicament of Culture: Twentieth-Century Ethnography, Literature, and Art*. Cambridge: Harvard University Press, 1988.

Collins, Jim. *Uncommon Cultures: Popular Culture and Post-Modernism*. New York: Routledge, 1989.

Conrad, Charles. "Work Songs, Hegemony, and Illusions of Self." *Critical Studies in Mass Communication* 5 (1988): 181–201.

Coontz, Stephanie. *The Way We Never Were: American Families and the Nostalgia Trap*. New York: Basic Books, 1992.

Cooper, Daniel. "Johnny Paycheck: Up from Low Places." *Journal of Country Music* 15, no. 1 (1992): 36-47.

———. *Lefty Frizzell: The Honky-Tonk Life of Country Music's Greatest Singer*. Boston: Little, Brown, 1995.

Crawford, Michael. "Country Music Awards." *New Yorker*, 27 May 1996, 110–111.

Creed, Gerald W., and Barbara Ching. "Recognizing Rusticity: Identity and the

Power of Place." In *Knowing Your Place: Rural Identity and Cultural Hierarchy*, edited by Barbara Ching and Gerald Creed, 1–38. New York: Routledge, 1997.

Cusic, Don. "Comedy and Humor in Country Music." *Journal of American Culture* 16, no. 2 (1993): 45–50.

Cusic, Don, ed. *Hank Williams: The Complete Lyrics*. New York: St. Martin's Press, 1993.

Daniel, Pete. "Rhythm of the Land." *Agricultural History* 68.4 (1994): 1–22.

Danker, Frederick E. "Country Music." *Yale Review* 63 (1974): 392–404.

Dawidoff, Nicholas. *In the Country of Country: People and Places in American Music*. New York: Pantheon, 1997.

Des Barres, Pamela. *I'm with the Band: Confessions of a Groupie*. New York: Beech Tree, 1987.

Di Salvatore, Bryan. "Ornery," *New Yorker*, 12 February 1990, 39–77.

Dunne, Michael. "Romantic Narcissism in 'Outlaw' Cowboy Music." In *All That Glitters: Country Music in America*, edited by George Lewis, 226–238. Bowling Green: Bowling Green State University Popular Press, 1993.

Ehrenreich, Barbara. *Fear of Falling: The Inner Life of the Middle Class*. New York: Pantheon, 1989.

Ellison, Curtis W. *Country Music Culture: From Hard Times to Heaven*. Jackson: University of Mississippi Press, 1995.

"Ernest Tubb: A Conversation." *Country Song Roundup*, March 1969, 33–35.

Escott, Colin. "Dwight Yoakam: Hillbilly Deluxe." In *Tattooed on Their Tongues: A Journey Through the Backrooms of American Music*, 204–211. New York: Schirmer Books, 1996.

———. Liner notes to . . . *And the Answer Is!* Bear Family BCD 15-791 AH and BCD 15-793 AH, 1994.

———. Liner notes to *Hank Williams, Jr. Living Proof: The MGM Recordings, 1963–1975*. Mercury Polygram 314–517 320–2, 1992.

Escott, Colin, and Hank Davis. Liner notes to *Hank Williams: The Collectors' Edition*, Polygram 314 527 419-2, 1985.

Escott, Colin, with George Merritt and William MacEwen. *Hank Williams: The Biography*. Boston: Little, Brown, 1994.

Everett, Todd. "Dwight Yoakam: Not Just Another Hat." *Journal of Country Music* 15, no. 3 (1993): 11–15.

Feiler, Bruce. *Dreaming Out Loud: Garth Brooks, Wynonna Judd, Wade Hayes, and the Changing Face of Nashville*. New York: Avon, 1998.

Fenster, Mark. "Buck Owens, Country Music, and the Struggle for Discursive Control." *Popular Music* 9, no. 3 (1990): 275–290.

———. "Under His Spell: How Buck Owens Took Care of Business." *Journal of Country Music* 12, no. 3 (1989): 18–27.

Fiske, John. *Understanding Popular Culture*. New York: Routledge, 1991.

Flippo, Chet. "Crossing Over: A Two-Way Street." *Rolling Stone*, 29 November 1979, 27–28.

164 ·

Works Cited

————. "From the Bump-Bump Room to the Barricades: Waylon, Tompall, and the Outlaw Revolution." In *Country: The Music and the Musicians*, edited by Paul Kingsbury and Alex Axelrod, 453–475. New York: Abbeville Press, 1988.

————. Liner notes to *Wanted! The Outlaws*. New York, RCA 17863-66841-2, 1976.

————. *Your Cheatin' Heart: A Biography of Hank Williams*. New York: St. Martin's Press, 1981.

"Folk Music Fireball Elvis Presley." *Country Song Roundup*, September 1955, 14.

Fox, Aaron A. "'Ain't It Funny How Time Slips Away': Talk, Trash, and Technology in a Texas 'Redneck' Bar." In *Knowing Your Place: Rural Identity and Cultural Hierarchy*, edited by Barbara Ching and Gerald Creed, 105–130. New York: Routledge, 1997.

————. "The Jukebox of History: Narratives of Loss and Desire in the Discourse of Country Music." *Popular Music* 11, no. 1 (1992): 53–72.

————. "Split Subjectivity in Country Music and Honky-Tonk Discourse." In *All That Glitters: Country Music in America*, edited by George H. Lewis, 131–139. Bowling Green: Bowling Green State University Popular Press, 1993.

Fox, Pamela. "Recycled 'Trash': Gender and Authenticity in Country Music Autobiography." *American Quarterly* 50 (1998): 234–266.

Frith, Simon. "The Cultural Study of Popular Music." In *Cultural Studies*, edited by Lawrence Grossberg, Cary Nelson, and Paula A. Treichler, 174–186. New York: Routledge, 1992.

————. *Performing Rites: On the Value of Popular Music*. Cambridge: Harvard University Press, 1996.

From Where I Stand: The Black Experience in Country Music. Warner Brothers B000002NBV, 1998; Compact Disc.

Gaillard, Frye. *Watermelon Wine: The Spirit of Country Music*. New York: St. Martin's Press, 1978.

Genette, Gérard. *Palimpsestes: La littérature au second degré*. Paris, Seuil: 1982.

Gentry, Linnell. *A History and Encyclopedia of Country, Western, and Gospel Music*. St. Clair Shores, MI: Scholarly Press, 1972.

Ginsburg, Mark. "Grand Ole Avanti." *Vanity Fair*, August 1989, 142–144.

"Glen Campbell—A Conversation." *Country Song Roundup*, September 1969, 8–11.

Green, Archie. "Hillbilly Music: Source and Symbol." *Journal of American Folklore* 78 (1965): 204–228.

Gregory, James N. *American Exodus: The Dust Bowl Migration and Okie Culture in California*. New York: Oxford University Press, 1989.

Grissim, John. *Country Music: White Man's Blues*. New York: Paperback Library, 1970.

Guralnick, Peter. *Lost Highway: Journeys and Arrivals of American Musicians*. Boston: Godine, 1979.

· 165

Works Cited

Guterman, Jimmy. Liner notes to *The Bocephus Box: The Hank Williams Jr. Collection, 1979–1992*. Warner Brothers 9 45104-2, 1992.

Haggard, Merle, with Peggy Russell. *Sing Me Back Home: My Story*. New York: Simon and Schuster, 1981.

Haggard, Theresa Lane. Liner notes to *Merle Haggard 1996*. Curb Records D2-77796, 1996.

Hanson, Victor Davis. *Fields Without Dreams: Defending the Agrarian Idea*. New York: Free Press, 1996.

Haslam, Gerald. *The Other California: The Great Central Valley in Life and Letters*. Santa Barbara, CA: Capra Press, 1990.

Haydan, Rick, and Catharine S. Rambeau. "Legends Turned Off by Radio—But They Won't Be Silenced." *Country Weekly*, 28 October 1997, 18–25.

Hemphill, Paul. "Merle Haggard." In *Stars of Country Music: Uncle Dave Macon to Johnny Rodriguez*, edited by Bill Malone and Judith McCulloh, 326–339. Urbana: University of Illinois Press, 1975.

———. *The Nashville Sound: Bright Lights and Country Music*. New York: Simon and Schuster, 1970.

Hickey, Dave. "In Defense of the Telecaster Cowboy Outlaws." *Country Music*, January 1974, 90–95.

Hirshberg, Charles, and Robert Sullivan. "The 100 Most Important People in the History of Country." *Life*, 1 September 1994, 18–39.

Horstman, Dorothy. *Sing Your Heart Out, Country Boy: Classic Country Songs and Their Inside Stories by the Men and Women Who Wrote Them*. 3rd ed. Nashville: Country Music Foundation and Vanderbilt University Press, 1996.

Houston, James D. "How Playing Country Music Taught Me to Love My Dad." In *The Men in My Life: And Other More or Less True Recollections of Kinship*, 31–38. Berkeley, CA: Creative Arts, 1987.

Hume, Martha. "Easy Listening, Hard Times." *Chicago Sun Times*, 21 August 1977.

———. *You're So Cold I'm Turnin' Blue: Martha Hume's Guide to the Greatest in Country Music*. New York: Viking, 1982.

Huyssen, Andreas. *After the Great Divide: Modernism, Mass Culture, Postmodernism*. Bloomington: Indiana University Press, 1986.

"The Inside Story on 'Hank the Drifter.'" *Country Song Roundup*, November 1961, 30.

"Is He or Isn't He a Hillbilly?" *Country Song Roundup*, September 1960, 5–8.

Jameson, Fredric. *Postmodernism, or, The Cultural Logic of Late Capitalism*. Durham, NC: Duke University Press, 1991.

Jennings, Waylon, with Lenny Kaye. *Waylon: An Autobiography*. New York: Warner Books, 1996.

Jensen, Joli. *The Nashville Sound: Authenticity, Commercialization, and Country Music*. Nashville: Country Music Foundation and Vanderbilt University Press, 1998.

Johnny Paycheck Fan Club. *The Paycheck Press: Publication of the Johnny Pay-check International Fan Club*. Undated.

Jones, George, with Tom Carter. *I Lived to Tell It All*. New York: Villard, 1996.

Jump, John. *Burlesque*. London: Methuen, 1972.

Kienzle, Rich. Liner notes to *The Buck Owens Collection*. Rhino Records R2 71016, 1992.

———. Liner notes to *The Essential George Jones: The Spirit of Country*. Sony Music Entertainment B0000028LN, 1994.

King, Florence. "Red Necks, White Socks, and Blue Ribbon Fear: The Nashville Sound of Discontent." *Harper's*, July 1974, 30–34.

King, Larry L. "David Allan Coe's Greatest Hits." *Esquire*, July 1976, 71–73, 142–144.

Kingsbury, Paul, ed. *Black Artists in Country Music*. Spec. issue of the *Journal of Country Music* 14, no. 2 (1992): 8–42.

———. "Dwight Yoakam: Honky-Tonk as Cutting Edge." *Journal of Country Music* 11, no. 1 (1986): 12–14.

———. "The Old Sound of New Country," *Journal of Country Music* 11, no.1 (1986): 2–24.

Koon, George William. *Hank Williams: A Bio-bibliography*. Westport, CT: Green-wood Press, 1983.

Kristeva, Julia. *Powers of Horror: An Essay on Abjection*. Translated by Leon S. Roudiez. New York: Columbia University Press, 1982.

Lanham, Tom. "A Thousand Miles from Nowhere." *New Country*, November 1995, 38–45.

Laredo, Joseph. Liner notes to *Willie Nelson: The Early Years: The Complete Liberty Recordings Plus More*. Nashville: Liberty Records C2 7243-8-28077-2-8, 1994.

Leamer, Laurence. *Three Chords and the Truth: Hope, Heartbreak, and Changing Fortunes in Nashville*. New York: Harper Collins, 1997.

Leppert, Richard, and George Lipsitz. "Age, the Body and Experience in the Music of Hank Williams." In *All That Glitters: Country Music in America*, edited by George H. Lewis, 22–37. Bowling Green, OH: Bowling Green State University Popular Press, 1993.

Levine, Karen. *Keeping Life Simple*. Pownal, VT: Storey Books, 1996.

Levine, Lawrence. *Highbrow/Lowbrow: The Emergence of Cultural Hierarchy in America*. Cambridge: Harvard University Press, 1988.

Lynn, Loretta, with George Vecsey. *Coal Miner's Daughter*. New York: Warner Books, 1976.

Malone, Ann. "Charley Pride." In *Stars of Country Music: Uncle Dave Macon to Johnny Rodriguez*, edited by Bill C. Malone and Judith McCulloh, 340–356. Urbana: University of Illinois Press, 1975.

Malone, Bill. *Country Music USA*. Rev. ed. Austin: University of Texas Press, 1985.

———. "Hank Williams: Voice of Tradition in a Period of Change." In *Hank Williams: The Legend,* edited by Thurston Moore, 2–4. Denver: Heather Enterprises, 1972.

Martin, William C. "Growing Old at Willie Nelson's Picnic." *Texas Monthly,* October 1974, 94–98, 116–124.

McCall, Michael. "Alan Jackson: Who He Is." *Journal of Country Music* 17, no. 3 (1995): 18–23.

McLaurin, Melton A. "Songs of the South: The Changing Image of the South in Country Music." In *You Wrote My Life: Lyrical Themes in Country Music,* edited by Melton A. McLaurin and Richard A. Peterson, 15–33. Philadelphia: Gordon and Breach, 1992.

Metress, Christopher. "Sing Me a Song About Ramblin' Man: Visions and Revisions of Hank Williams in Country Music." *South Atlantic Quarterly* 94, no. 1 (Winter 1995): 7–27.

Millard, Bob. "The Three Hanks." *Country Music,* January/February 1997, 46–47.

Moore, Thurston, ed. *Hank Williams: The Legend.* Denver: Heather Enterprises, 1972.

Morthland, John. "Dwight Yoakam: Ramblin' Man." *Country Music,* May/June 1993, 38–42.

Nash, Alanna. *Behind Closed Doors: Talking with the Legends of Country Music.* New York: Knopf, 1988.

Nelson, Willie, with Bud Shrake. *Willie: An Autobiography.* New York: Simon and Schuster, 1988.

New Yorker, Special Music Issue, 26 August and 2 September, 1996.

Noe, Denise. "Parallel Worlds: The Surprising Similarities (and Differences) of Country-Western and Rap." *Humanist* 55, no. 4 (1995): 20–22.

"No Grand Ole Opry for Buck?" *Country Song Roundup 1966 Yearbook,* 54–55.

Owen, Chuck. Liner notes to *Roll Out the Red Carpet for Buck Owens and the Buckaroos.* Capitol Records T-2443, 1965.

Owens, Buck. *Buck Owens and the Buckaroos Live at Carnegie Hall.* Country Music Foundation Records CMF-012-D, 1988. The record was originally released by Capitol Records in 1966.

———. *The Buck Owens Show: Big in Vegas.* Capitol Records ST 322, 1969.

———. Interview by author, tape recording, Bakersfield, CA, 20 May 1997.

———. Interview by Dwight Yoakam, "A Couple of Cowboys Sittin' Around Talkin'." *Spin,* December 1988, 45–47.

———. Interview on *Bakersfield Country,* 1991, KCET/PBS, Los Angeles.

———. Letter in [Buck Owens's] *1967 Fan Club Yearbook,* inside cover.

———. Liner notes to *Bridge Over Troubled Water.* Capitol Records 685, 1970.

———. *Live at the White House.* Capitol Records ST-11105, 1968.

———. "A View of Country Music." *All-American* 1, no. 5 (October 1969): unpaginated.

Pearl, Minnie, with Joan Dew. *Minnie Pearl: An Autobiography.* New York: Simon and Schuster, 1980.

Peterson, Richard A. *Creating Country Music: Fabricating Authenticity*. Chicago: University of Chicago Press, 1997.

———. "Understanding Audience Segmentation: From Elite and Mass to Omnivore and Univore." *Poetics* 21 (1992): 243–258.

Peterson, Richard A., and Roger M. Kern. "Changing Highbrow Taste: From Snob to Omnivore." *American Sociological Review* 61 (October 1996): 900–907.

Porterfield, Nolan. "Country Music Discography: Esoteric Art and Humanistic Craft." *Southern Quarterly* 22, no. 3 (1984): 15–29.

———. "The Day Hank Williams Died: Cultural Collisions in Country Music." In *America's Musical Pulse: Popular Music in Twentieth-Century Society*, edited by Kenneth J. Bindas, 175–183. Westport, CT: Praeger, 1992.

Pleakins, J. R. "Buck Owens Drops a Bombshell." *Country Song Roundup*, June 1966, 8–9.

Price, Ray. "An Interview with Ray Price." *Country Song Roundup*, October 1969, 8–11.

Price, Robert. "The Bakersfield Sound." *Bakersfield Californian*, 22 June 1997, sec. A, p. 1; 6.

———. "King of His Own Country." *Bakersfield Californian*, 13 July 1997, sec. F, p. 1; 11.

Pride, Charley, with Jim Henderson. *Pride: The Charley Pride Story*. New York: Morrow, 1994.

Pugh, Ronnie. "Country Music: An Etymological Journey." *Journal of Country Music* 19, no. 1 (1997): 32–38.

Putman, Curly. "Curly Putman: An Exclusive CSR Interview." *Country Song Roundup*, April 1970, 34-35.

Quintanilla, Michael. "Jacket Sets Standard for Cowboy Cool." *Norfolk Virginian Pilot*, 30 November 1989.

Rambeau, Catharine. "Pick the Nickname." *Country Weekly*, 30 April 1996, 48.

Reed, Cecelia. "Mad About Hats." *USA Weekend*, 17–19 March 1989, 20.

Reid, Jan. *The Improbable Rise of Redneck Rock*. Austin, TX: Heidelberg Publishers, 1974.

Review of *If There Was a Way*, in *Country Music*, Jan/Feb 1991, 54.

Riese, Randall. *Nashville Babylon: The Uncensored Truth and Private Lives of Country Music's Greatest Stars*. New York: Congdon and Weed, 1988.

Rogers, Jimmie N. *The Country Music Message: Revisited*. Fayetteville: University of Arkansas Press, 1989.

Roland, Tom. *The Billboard Book of Number One Country Hits*. New York: Billboard, 1991.

Ross, Andrew. *No Respect: Intellectuals and Popular Culture*. New York: Routledge, 1989.

Sample, Tex. *White Soul: Country Music, the Church, and Working Americans*. Nashville: Abingdon Press, 1996.

Sarko, Anita. "Dwight Lights Big City." *Details*, December/January 1989, 139–142.

Scherman, Tony. "Country." *American Heritage,* November 1994, 38–57.

Schor, Juliet B. *The Overspent American: Upscaling, Downshifting, and the New Consumer.* New York: Basic Books, 1998.

Sennett, Richard, and Jonathan Cobb. *The Hidden Injuries of Class.* New York: Random House, 1972.

Sherrill, Billy. Liner notes to *George Jones Anniversary: Ten Years of Hits.* Epic ECK38323, 1982.

Sontag, Susan. "One Culture and the New Sensibility." *Against Interpretation and Other Essays,* 293–304. New York: Farrar, Straus, & Giroux, 1966.

Stallybrass, Peter, and Allon White. *The Politics and Poetics of Transgression.* Ithaca: Cornell University Press, 1986.

Starr, Kevin. *Material Dreams: Southern California Through the 1920's.* Oxford: Oxford University Press, 1990.

Stearns, Peter. *American Cool: Constructing a Twentieth-Century Emotional Style.* New York: New York University Press, 1994.

Stepanovich, Mike, and Donna Corum, "Buck!" In *Destination Bakersfield: The 1998 Greater Bakersfield Convention and Visitors Bureau Guide,* 9–11, 44–45.

Stewart, Katie. "Engendering Narratives of Lament in Country Music." In *All That Glitters: Country Music in America,* edited by George H. Lewis, 221–225. Bowling Green: Bowling Green State University Popular Press, 1993.

Thomas, Rebecca. "There's a Whole Lot o' Color in the 'White Man's Blues': Country Music's Selective Memory and the Challenge of Identity." *Midwest Quarterly* 38 (1996): 73–89.

Tichi, Cecelia. *High Lonesome: The American Culture of Country Music.* Chapel Hill: University of North Carolina Press, 1994.

"The Top 100 Country Songs of All Time." *Country America,* October 1992, 26–52.

Tosches, Nick. *Country: Living Legends and Dying Metaphors in America's Biggest Music.* Rev. ed. New York: Scribner's, 1985.

————. "George Jones: The Grand Tour." *Journal of Country Music* 16, no. 3 (1994): 15–34.

"Transition." *Newsweek,* 12 January 1953, 52.

Tucker, Ken. "9 to 5: How Willie Nelson and Dolly Parton Qualified for 'Lifestyles of the Rich and Famous.'" In *Country: The Music and the Musicians,* edited by Paul Kingsbury and Alex Axelrod, 374–405. New York: Abbeville Press, 1988.

————. "Why Ricky, Reba, and George Are Hard at It." *Journal of Country Music* 11, no. 1 (1986): 4–11.

Tucker, Stephen R. "Progressive Country Music, 1972–1976: Its Impact and Creative Highlights." *Southern Quarterly* 22, no. 3 (1984): 93–109.

Vinicur, Dale. Liner notes to *Tommy Collins Leonard.* Bear Family Records BCD 15577 EI, 1992.

Wagoner, Porter. "An Interview with Porter Wagoner." *Country Song Roundup,* February 1969, 15–16.

Works Cited

———. "An Interview with Porter Wagoner." *Country Song Roundup*, May 1970, 8–11.

Whiteside, Jonny. *Ramblin' Rose: The Life and Career of Rose Maddox*. Nashville: Country Music Foundation and Vanderbilt University Press, 1997.

Wilgus, D. K. "Country Western Music and the Urban Hillbilly." *Journal of American Folklore* 83 (1970): 157–184.

Williams, Hank Jr., with Michael Bane. *Living Proof: An Autobiography*. New York: Putnam, 1979.

Williams, Lycrecia, and Dale Vinicur. *Still in Love with You: The Story of Hank and Audrey Williams*. Nashville: Rutledge Hill Press, 1989.

Williams, Roger M. *Sing a Sad Song: The Life of Hank Williams*. 2nd ed. Urbana: University of Illinois Press, 1981.

Wood, Gerry. "Mama, Those Cliché Songs Are Driving Me to Drink." *Country Weekly*, 30 April 1996, 80–81.

Woods, Jeff. "Color Me Country: Tales from the Frontlines." *Journal of Country Music* 14, no. 2 (1992): 9–12.

Wren, Christopher. "Country Music." *Look*, 13 July 1971, 11–13.

———. "Merle Haggard." *Look*, 13 July 1971, 36–41.

Wynette, Tammy, with Joan Dew. *Stand By Your Man: An Autobiography*. New York: Simon and Schuster, 1979.

Index

Songwriters, when not the performer of a listed song, are named in the endnotes.